RESIDEnTIAL APARTheID:

THE AMERICAN LEGACY

CAAS Urban Policy Series
Volume 2

RESIDENTIAL APARTHEID:
THE AMERICAN LEGACY

edited by

Robert D. Bullard

J. Eugene Grigsby, III

Charles Lee

with essays by

Joe R. Feagin

Nancy A. Denton

Joe T. Darden

Franklin J. James

J. Eugene Grigsby, III

Gary A. Dymski & John Veitch

Robert D. Bullard

Nestor Rodriguez

Veronica M. Reed

Gregory Squires

Shanna L. Smith

FIRST PRINTING

Published by
CAAS Publications
Center for Afro-American Studies
University of California, Los Angeles
160 Haines Hall, 405 Hilgard Avenue
Los Angeles, CA 90024-1545

Cover design by
The WestWork Group, Culver City, CA

Cover art by
Roberto Gutierrez

PRINTED IN THE UNITED STATES OF AMERICA

Library of Congress Cataloging-in-Publication Data

Residential Apartheid : the American Legacy / edited by Robert D. Bullard, J. Eugene
Grigsby III, Charles Lee ; with essays by Joe R. Feagin . . . [et al.].
    p.   cm. -- (CAAS urban policy series ; v. 2)
    Includes bibliographical references and index.
    ISBN 0-934934-43-6 (pbk.) : $18.95
    1. Discrimination in housing--United States. 2. Afro-Americans--Housing.
3. Race discrimination--United States. 4. United States--Race Relations. I. Bullard,
Robert D. (Robert Doyle), 1946-   . II. Grigsby, J. Eugene. III. Lee, Charles. IV.
Feagin, Joe R. V. Series.
HD7288.76 U5R47   1994   94-33754
363.5'1--dc20   CIP

TABLE OF CONTENTS

LIST OF ILLUSTRATIONS

LIST OF TABLES

FOREWORD

Thirty years ago, I first went to Washington, D.C., as a twenty-one-year-old student, to begin a historic journey called a Freedom Ride. When we traveled across the South, from Washington into Virginia, through North Carolina, South Carolina, Georgia, Alabama. and Mississippi, I saw signs that read: WHITE MEN, COLORED MEN; WHITE WOMEN, COLORED WOMEN; WHITE WAITING, COLORED WAITING.

Today, those signs are gone, and they will never return. But in every major city in America, we still have invisible signs that say, "you cannot live here and you cannot live there." The fact is that almost thirty years after the 1964 Civil Rights Act, the 1965 Voting Rights Act, and the 1968 Fair Housing Act, the scars and stains of racism are still deeply embedded in every corner of American society.

I have said on occasion during the past three decades that we have witnessed a nonviolent revolution, a revolution of values and ideas. In a sense, we have come a great distance—but, in another sense, we are still a society divided by race and by class. Even in a city like Atlanta, Georgia, the capital of the New South, with its new buildings and changing skyline, thousands of people have been left out and left behind because of racial discrimination. Atlanta, like most other major American cities, is still two cities: one black and one white. And in urban America, residential apartheid keeps racial and ethnic groups separate and apart.

The majority of the thirty million African Americans are as segregated now as they were at the height of the Civil Rights Movement in the 1960s. Housing discrimination is the major culprit in maintaining residential segregation. Real estate brokers, lending institutions, and insurance companies all engage in practices that severely limit home ownership opportunities for African Americans and other people of color.

We must find ways to dismantle these barriers and to bring down those invisible signs. We need to use the same discipline, the same sense of moral commitment, and the same sense of righteous indignation that we used during the 1960s to say no to segregation in public accommodations and public transportation.

I expect to see greater efforts on the part of private fair housing organizations, the legal community, community groups, and those of us of goodwill in Congress to press for an end to housing discrimination. There may be setbacks, delays, and interruptions, but we all must stay in the fight. In the same way that we fought for the right to vote, we need to put the issue of ending discrimination in housing at the top of the American agenda.

Congressman John Lewis

PREFACE

The idea for this book originated at a symposium entitled Race and Housing in the United States: Challenges for the 21st Century, which was held in Atlanta on December 6 and 7, 1991. It was my pleasure to preside over the symposium in the capacity of Executive Director of the Commission for Racial Justice of the United Church of Christ, which sponsored the event.

There were several assumptions behind the symposium and presentations. First, the Commission believed that in light of mounting evidence on the lack of progress and worsening trends in equal opportunity in housing for people of color, we needed to revisit fair housing as a basic civil rights issue. Second, besides intrinsically being an important determinant of the quality of life, housing discrimination and residential segregation negatively affect many other areas of our society, such as education, employment, access to municipal services, and political representation. Third, the federal commitment to housing the nation's low and moderate income families appeared to have reached an all-time low; at the same time, hopelessness was increasing.

Persisting residential segregation of African Americans and heightened segregation of Latino Americans and Asian Americans may signal a new urban crisis. In hindsight, these words uttered at the fair housing symposium seem most prophetic, for no more than six months after the symposium, South Central Los Angeles erupted in the greatest outbreak of urban violence in the history of this country.

The Los Angeles uprising came in the wake of the acquittal of four Los Angeles police officers accused of the brutal beating of Rodney King. The events in Los Angeles became a metaphor for urban crisis in the 1990s. But it should not be forgotten that many social justice leaders warned public officials that it was a only matter of time before our urban centers—where many residents are isolated from the economic mainstream—would erupt as Los Angeles did in the spring of 1992.

The United States is a divided land. Residents of central cities are segregated from those who live in the suburbs. Strong race and class divisions separate neighborhoods from one another. Racial apartheid operates to keep people of color separate from whites. Especially for most

African Americans at all class levels, the word *apartheid* is a most fitting description of their residential pattern. American apartheid created separate and unequal life chances for African Americans and whites in a wide range of areas, including education, employment, health care, and the political arena.

Government has been slow to erase the vestiges of slavery and Jim Crow. Despite the laws, executive orders, and mandates, African Americans still face extreme barriers in housing and residential options. Institutional racism exacts a heavy economic and psychological toll on people of color. Social change has been slow to recognize the damage caused by discrimination—mainly because most of the victims of discrimination are people of color. Historically, discrimination has been easy to practice because the price of discrimination was cheap. It took more than two decades for Congress to strengthen the 1968 federal Fair Housing Act.

The Fair Housing Amendment went into effect in 1989. This new and improved law offers some challenging opportunities to make the individuals who discriminate pay for their crime with penalties that hurt: large monetary damage awards. Housing activists, advocates, and scholars were able to move fair housing issues, despite opposition from a hostile administration during the 1980s.

While large monetary awards will not likely repair the hurt caused by discrimination, they do signal that the federal government is beginning to treat discriminatory acts as a crime and perpetrators as lawbreakers.

If housing discrimination is to be eliminated, coordinated efforts must be undertaken among state and private enforcement agencies and the private housing industry. In addition, efforts must be undertaken to provide affordable housing. These efforts must be extended as the links between race, housing affordability, and disinvestment become more apparent. This involves improved expertise in community reinvestment, economic development, nondiscriminatory mortgage lending, and creative partnerships with community development organizations and government.

This book, which includes the symposium papers and several other essays, represents the commitment of the Commission for Racial Justice to eliminate all forms of discrimination in American society. We must make equal opportunity a reality. If we do not, today's tragic but quiet riots will become a deafening roar.

Benjamin F. Chavis, Jr.

ACKNOWLEDGMENTS

We wish to thank the Commission for Racial Justice of the United Church of Christ for sponsoring the fair housing symposium and making this book possible. Special thanks must be given to Robin Whittington for her assistance in proofing early drafts of the manuscript. We are especially grateful to managing editor Toyomi Igus and copyeditor Jacqueline Tasch at the Center for Afro-American Studies for their patience and dedication in getting this book out in a timely manner.

INTRODUCTION

Racism and American Apartheid

by Robert D. Bullard & Charles Lee

America's large urban centers, where the majority of people of color are concentrated, have become forgotten places. They seem to get attention rarely—only when conditions reach crisis status or when human frustration spills over into major urban riots and uprisings. But day to day and year to year, too many of our cities and their inhabitants are at risk from poor housing, poverty, economic abandonment, and infrastructure decline.

Much of the nation's urban infrastructure is fraying at the seams. The physical infrastructure includes such things as roads and bridges, housing stock, schools, job centers, public buildings, parks and recreational facilities, public transit, water supply, waste-water treatment, and waste disposal systems. Taken as a whole, this infrastructure decline has a negative impact on the well-being and quality of urban life (Bullard 1992). The poor infrastructure conditions in urban areas are a result of a host of factors, including the distribution of wealth, patterns of racial and economic discrimination, redlining, housing and real estate practices, location decisions of industry, and differential enforcement of land use regulations.

RESIDENTIAL APARTHEID

All communities are not created equal. Apartheid-type housing and development policies have resulted in limited mobility, reduced neighborhood options, decreased residential choices, and diminished job opportunities for millions of Americans. American cities continue to be racially separate and unequal. Residential apartheid is the dominant housing pattern for most African Americans—the most racially segregated group in America. Nowhere is this separate-society contrast more apparent than in the nation's large metropolitan areas. Urban America typifies this costly legacy of slavery, Jim

Crow, and institutionalized discrimination (Kushner 1980; Feagin and Feagin 1986; Bullard and Feagin 1991).

Residential apartheid did not result from some impersonal superstructural process. Historically, racism has been and continues to be a "conspicuous part of the American sociopolitical system, and as a result, black people in particular, and ethnic and racial minority groups of color, find themselves at a disadvantage in contemporary society" (Jones 1981, 47). Racial patterns of cities were "caused" by an array of actors—white slaveholders, merchants, and shippers of the early period; the white business elite, politicians, and workers in the periods since slavery.

Institutionalized racism is part of the national heritage. Racism created this nation's "dark ghettos." Nearly three decades ago, noted psychologist Kenneth Clark (1965) observed:

> The dark ghetto's invisible walls have been erected by white society who have power both to confine those who have *no* power and to perpetuate their powerlessness. The dark ghettos are social, political, educational, and—above all—economic colonies. Their inhabitants are subject people, victims of the greed, cruelty, insensitivity, guilt and fear of their masters. (11)

White racism serves the interests of the group endorsing it (Doob 1993, 6). Some two and a half decades ago, the National Advisory Commission on Civil Disorders implicated white racism in creating and maintaining the black ghetto and the drift toward two "separate and unequal societies" (National Advisory Commission on Civil Disorders 1968). These same conditions exist today (Willie 1989; Hacker 1992). The black ghetto, for example, is kept isolated and contained from the larger white society through well-defined institutional practices, private actions, and government policies (Massey and Denton 1993).

The legacy of institutional racism lowers the nation's gross national product by almost 2 percent a year, or roughly $104 billion in 1989 (Updegrade 1989). A large share of this loss is a result of housing discrimination. The "roots of discrimination are deep" and have been difficult to eliminate (James, McCummings, and Tynan 1984, 138). White real estate agents, brokers, and lenders cater to the racism of their white clients—and in effect determine the racial composition of communities and neighborhoods. Few whites are willing to accept even a minimal black presence—the 12 or 13 percent that would reflect the overall national proportion (Hacker 1992). Law professor Derrick

Bell (1992) summarized the "racial schizophrenia" exhibited by whites who discriminate against African Americans:

> When whites perceive that it will be profitable or at least cost-free to serve, hire, admit, or otherwise deal with blacks on a nondiscriminatory basis, they do so. When they fear—accurately or not—that they may be at a loss, inconvenience, or upset to themselves or other whites, discriminatory conduct usually follows. (7)

White prejudice is reinforced by direct discrimination. Many whites see nothing wrong with these practices, and most deny their existence. Moreover, most U.S. whites do not believe that housing discrimination exists. The results from a 1990 national survey revealed that 75 percent of whites felt that blacks had as good a chance as whites to obtain housing they could afford. Only 47 percent of blacks in the survey felt this way (Gallup and Hugick 1990). Contrary to popular belief, housing discrimination and many other manifestations of institutionalized racism were not eradicated with the enactment of civil rights legislation in the 1960s.

Housing discrimination denies a substantial segment of the African American community a basic form of wealth accumulation and investment through home ownership. The number of African American home owners would probably be higher in the absence of discrimination by lending institutions (Bullard 1987; Darden 1989). Only about 59 percent of the nation's middle-class African Americans own their homes, compared with 74 percent of whites.

Studies over the past twenty-five years have clearly documented the relationship between redlining and disinvestment decisions and neighborhood decline (Feins and Bratt 1983). Redlining accelerates the flight of full-service banks, food stores, restaurants, and other shopping centers in inner-city neighborhoods. In their place, inner-city neighborhoods are left with check-cashing stations, pawn shops, storefront grocery stores, liquor stores, and fast-food operations—all well buttoned up with wire mesh and bulletproof glass.

From Boston to Los Angeles, people of color still do not have the same access to lending by banks and saving institutions as their white counterparts. A 1991 report by the Federal Reserve Board found that African Americans were rejected for home loans more than twice as often as Anglos (Rosenblatt and Bates 1991). After studying lending practices at 9,300 U.S. financial institutions and more than 6.4 million loan applications, the federal study reported that the rejection rates for conventional home mortgages were 33.9 percent for

African Americans, 21.4 percent for Latinos, 22.4 percent for American Indians, 14.4 percent for Anglos, and 12.9 percent for Asians.

Housing discrimination is a crime. Yet, federal regulators continue to ignore discrimination in lending. Despite these alarming loan-rejection statistics, some government and industry officials remain in doubt as to whether the culprit is a function of discrimination or neutral "market forces." Discriminatory lending practices subsidize the physical destruction of communities of color.

Many inner-city neighborhoods have been strangled by the lack of long-term financing as a direct result of redlining practices by banks, savings and loans, mortgage firms, and insurance companies. The federal government recognized this problem when it passed the Community Reinvestment Act (CRA), a 1977 law designed to combat discriminatory practices in poor and minority neighborhoods. The CRA requires banks and thrifts to lend within the areas where their depositors live. The CRA has been used in conjunction with the Home Mortgage Disclosure Act, a law that requires banks and thrifts to disclose their mortgage lending by census tracts (Foust 1987; Yang, Oneal, and Anderson 1988; Glastris and Minerbrook 1989). It is ironic that many of the same banks and thrifts that are now in default actively redlined neighborhoods populated by people of color. These same redlined communities must now share in paying, through their tax dollars, the hundreds of billions of dollars to rescue the failed savings and loan institutions (Bullard and Feagin 1991).

The nation's housing and residential areas continue to be segregated along racial lines. For example, eight out of every ten African Americans live in neighborhoods where they are in the majority. Residential segregation decreases for most racial and ethnic groups with additional education, income, and occupational status (Tobin 1987; Denton and Massey 1988). However, this scenario does not hold true for African Americans. African Americans, no matter what their educational or occupational achievement or income level, are exposed to higher crime rates, less effective educational systems, higher mortality risks, more dilapidated surroundings, and greater health threats (i.e., lead in housing) because of their race.

THE ROLE OF GOVERNMENT

The development of spatially differentiated metropolitan areas where people of color are segregated from whites have resulted from governmental policies and marketing practices of the housing industry and lending institutions.

Segregation isolates economically depressed central-city neighborhoods—significant segments of society—from the expanding suburban job centers.

Residential options that are available to most Americans were shaped largely by: (1) federal housing policies, (2) individual and institutional discrimination in housing markets, (3) geographic changes that have taken place in the nation's metropolitan areas, and (4) limited incomes because of historical job discrimination. Decades of federal government policies have played a key role in the development of spatially differentiated metropolitan areas where blacks and other visible minorities are segregated from whites and the poor are segregated from more affluent citizens. This has been especially so since World War II (Momeni 1986; Goering 1986).

Federal mortgage subsidies facilitated white movement out of the cities, at the same time that federal restrictions made lending difficult to African Americans desiring to move to the suburbs. Such policies fueled the white exodus to the suburbs and accelerated the abandonment of central cities. Federal tax dollars funded the construction of freeway and interstate highway systems.

Many of the freeway construction projects cut paths through neighborhoods where people of color predominated, physically isolated residents from their institutions, and disrupted once-stable communities. African Americans and Latino Americans are regularly displaced for highways, convention centers, sports arenas, and a host of downtown development projects (Bullard 1987). They are forced into other segregated areas with little input into the removal process. The nation's apartheid-type policies have meant community displacement, gentrification, limited mobility, reduced housing options and residential packages, decreased environmental choices, and diminished job opportunities for those who live in cities, while good jobs often move to the suburbs (Massey and Eggers 1990).

Over five decades of federal housing policies, programs, and legislation have not eliminated the institutional barriers to free choice. Title VI of the Civil Rights Act of 1964 and Title VIII of the Civil Rights Act of 1968 (Fair Housing Act) are two major pieces of federal legislation designed to remove the barriers to free choice in the housing market. The 1968 Fair Housing Act was a paper tiger. The federal Fair Housing Act was amended and strengthened in 1988 because of the persisting problem of discrimination. The new fair housing law went into effect in 1989.

One of the first class-action lawsuits filed by a private law firm under this new law was against an Orange County, California, firm that managed more than 4,000 apartment units in Los Angeles, Riverside, San Bernardino, and Orange counties. The 1989 lawsuit charged the company with affixing a "happy face" sticker to rental applications of minority home seekers for the purpose of screening out these applicants—racism with a smile (Feldman 1989). This practice is reminiscent of the "color codes" used by real estate agents to designate neighborhoods that were open and closed to blacks (Taub, Garth, and Dunham 1984).

In the past, housing discrimination was not very costly to those who broke the law. Housing discrimination became an integral part of business, the price managers, brokers, and loan officers paid for keeping their white clients. Lawbreakers were not punished, nor were the victims adequately compensated. The prevailing view in society—from judges to real estate brokers to private citizens—was that injuries suffered by the victims of housing discrimination were minimal. This view was routinely borne out in the small compensatory damage awards made to plaintiffs—typically a few hundred to a few thousand dollars. Historically, most of the successful housing discrimination litigation efforts concluded with injunctions and consent decrees.

Intended to remedy these inequities, the new fair housing law has spurred plaintiffs and their lawyers to focus attention on compensatory damages (i.e., to make the victims of discrimination whole for the losses and injuries they have suffered) and punitive damages (i.e., to punish the defendants for egregious acts and to deter others from engaging in similar conduct). This strategy is tantamount to "hitting the lawbreakers where it hurts"—in their pocketbooks.

Fair housing and civil rights organizations have begun to target development owners and managers who discriminate. The NAACP Legal Defense and Educational Fund and Lawyers' Committee for Civil Rights Under Law have begun to push damage awards to levels where they can be felt. One of the largest housing discrimination settlements in the country came in February 1990. It was made possible by the 1988 legislation. A Los Angeles rental complex (Belford Park Apartments) agreed to pay $450,000 to settle a lawsuit that claimed the apartment owners and managers engaged in a pattern and practice of discrimination against African Americans. The lawsuit, *Westside Fair Housing Council v. Westchester Investment Company,* had been litigated by the Western Regional Office of the NAACP Legal Defense and Educational Fund for more than two years. In addition to the monetary award, the consent decree called for the owner, Westchester Investment Company, to take affirmative steps to ensure that at least one-fourth of the Belford Park's units have at least one African American resident within three years (Prentice Hall 1990).

Large settlements of this type bring new visibility to housing discrimination. The settlements send a clear message to lawbreakers that the emotional and economic damage caused by discrimination can be costly. The sooner this message becomes part of the business climate, the sooner this nation will see an end to housing discrimination.

GROWING INEQUITIES

Uneven development of central cities and suburbs, combined with the systematic avoidance of inner-city areas by many businesses, has accelerated decline and heightened social and economic inequities. For the past two decades, manufacturing plants have been fleeing central cities and taking their jobs with them. Many have moved offshore to Third World countries where labor is cheap and environmental regulations are lax or nonexistent.

Few attempts have been made by government to reverse job flight and subsequent decline of urban centers. Government-backed urban enterprise zones, special taxing districts, and economic investment incentives have amounted to more talk than action. Nevertheless, government still has an important role to play in rebuilding our cities. Clearly, housing and economic development policies flow from forces of production and are often dominated and subsidized by state actors.

The decline of central cities and the growth of suburbs are reinforced by government and corporate America. Numerous examples show how state actors have targeted cities and regions for infrastructure improvements and amenities such as water irrigation systems, ship channels, road and bridge projects, and mass transit systems. On the other hand, state actors have done a miserable job in stemming the economic disinvestment taking place in the nation's urban centers.

The absence of a coherent urban agenda in the 1980s allowed cities to become "invisible" places. The quality of life for millions of urban Americans is worse today than it was during the 1960s. Where a person lives has tremendous social, economic, and health implications. The growing economic disparity between racial/ethnic groups has a direct correlation to institutional barriers in housing, lending, employment, and education. Recent studies, for example, on the status of African Americans have uncovered a sobering truth. Little progress toward social and economic equality for African Americans has been made since the early 1970s. Although the United States made significant gains in reducing poverty during the 1960s, few gains have been made in the past two decades (Kozol 1991; Bell 1992; Hacker 1992; Pinkney 1993).

Poverty has become more persistent since the early 1970s, and the chances of poor families escaping poverty have dropped (Harris and Wilkins 1988). This fact is particularly distressing because of the alarming number of children now living in poverty. One out of every four children under the age of six in the United States lives beneath the poverty level. Fifty-eight percent of these children in poverty are people of color. Among this group, African American children are four times more likely than whites to be poor; Latino children are three and a half times as likely and other racial and ethnic children are twice as likely to be poor (Hacker 1992).

Besides acting to entrap a disproportionate number of people of color in poverty, institutional racism compounds the risks of life. There are significant disparities in life expectancy between people of color and whites (Jaynes and Williams 1989). Despite significant improvement, the life expectancy of African American males in 1985 (65.3 years) failed to equal that already achieved by white males in 1950 (66.5 years). The infant mortality rate for African Americans is twice that of whites (National Center for Health Statistics 1990).

There remain significant inequities for access to proper health care. African Americans and Latino Americans, for example, are twice as likely as white Americans to be without a regular source of health care other than a health clinic or hospital emergency room. Hospitals and clinics in inner-city neighborhoods are often overcrowded, understaffed, and underfunded. Many Native Americans live on reservations where the availability of physicians is half the national average (U.S. Department of Housing and Urban Development 1985).

Since the recession of the 1970s, manufacturing jobs and other traditional avenues of relatively high-paying employment for inner-city residents have continued to disappear. By the middle of the 1980s, the few gains that were made toward bridging the black–white income gap evaporated. The average per capita income of African Americans relative to white income fell back to the 1971 level, that is, 57 percent of white income (Jaynes and Williams 1989).

African Americans are two and a half times more likely to be unemployed than whites (Tidwell 1990). Latino Americans are far less likely to work in managerial and professional jobs. Moreover, Latino women are twice as likely as non-Latino women to be employed in service occupations (DeLaRosa and Shaw 1990). Contrary to the popular notion of Asian American economic success, the "model minority" myth, a greater percentage of Asian Americans than whites live in poverty, and the average Asian American family in poverty is significantly poorer than its white counterpart. According to the 1980 U.S. Census, 10.5 percent of Chinese families, 13.1 percent of Korean families, and 35.1 percent of Vietnamese families in the United States live below the poverty level, as compared to 6.6 percent of white families (U.S. Civil Rights Commission 1986).

When it comes to housing, African Americans—including the middle class—certainly are confronted with the harsh realities of racial discrimination. Contrary to sociologist William J. Wilson's (1978) "declining significance of race" argument, "black disadvantage resulting from housing segregation and or from white gain-motivated job discrimination is a result of racial processes, not class" (Farley 1987, 147). Race may be increasing in significance, not declining.

In *The Black Middle Class* sociologist Bart Landry offers some additional insights into the race-class debate involving housing segregation. Landry concludes that the "idea of a black middle class living in social isolation from other classes is largely a myth" (Landry 1987, 147). At the rate the country is going, it will take more than six decades for African Americans to achieve even the minimal levels of integration with whites that Asians and Latinos have now.

Some social scientists have built distinguished careers describing and analyzing residential segregation and the racial isolation of African Americans and other people of color. Most of the literature on race and the city focuses on the underclass and the underlying theoretical underpinning akin to a type of market-centered economics. Racial issues are reduced to economic issues. But race must be treated as an independent variable. The modern American city has its roots in racism. This racism can be seen in its basic ecological form. Racial segregation in housing, as well as schools and jobs, is fundamental to the geography of the modern American city.

Newly arrived immigrants to this country are more readily accepted in white neighborhoods than African Americans who have been here all along (Hacker 1992, 35). Similarly, whites and various immigrant groups have greater ease in setting up businesses in the African American community than African Americans do. The question of "who owns the ghetto" is still relevant in the 1990s.

African Americans are "faces at the bottom of the well" (Bell 1992). Law professor Derrick Bell (1992) asserts that the "very absence of visible signs of discrimination creates an atmosphere of racial neutrality and encourages whites to believe that racism is a thing of the past" (35). As a way of rationalizing racist practices, the larger society shifts its explanation of racial inequalities to individual motivation—a blaming-the-victim explanation.

Most African Americans are experts on discrimination. When they venture outside their neighborhoods seeking housing, they "can expect to receive chilly receptions, evasive responses, and outright lies" (Bell 1992, 6).

Some home seekers can even expect violence. Violence and intimidation have also been used to keep people of color out of white housing developments, neighborhoods, and subdivisions (Pinkney 1993).

The Los Angeles County Human Relations Commission (1992) documented 672 hate crimes in 1991. Residences were the most frequent site of racially motivated hate crimes, making up 50.4 percent of the cases. African Americans were the targets of 130 racially motivated hate crimes, while 67 hate crimes were directed at Latinos, 54 at Asians, 47 at other whites, 22 at Arabs, 13 at Armenians, 8 at Iranians, and 1 at an American Indian. Nine hate crimes were aimed at racially mixed households (Los Angeles Human Relations Commission 1992, 3–5).

In the period 1985–1986, there were 45 known arson and cross-burning attempts at the homes of African Americans and other people of color who had moved into mostly white residential areas across the United States (Feagin 1990). During the 1980s there were hundreds of acts of vandalism and intimidation directed at African Americans and other people of color living or traveling in white neighborhoods. The Center for Democratic Renewal (CDR) documented nearly 3,000 cases of racially motivated or hate-related violence between 1980 to 1986. CDR stated that "not a day has passed during [those years] without someone in the United States being victimized by hate violence" (Center for Democratic Renewal 1987).

Racially motivated violence is increasing both numerically and geographically, with many new crimes occurring in places where previously such incidents had not taken place. Members of far right groups such as the Ku Klux Klan, neo-Nazis, skinheads, and other white supremacist and hate groups have become increasingly ideological in their choice of targets. Racially motivated violence seems to surface most during times of economic uncertainty and in areas undergoing social transition. Today, feelings of group hostility are being exacerbated by economic insecurity, immigration, and the growing visibility of people of color communities. In many cases, individuals and institutions consciously use people of color as scapegoats during times of economic instability.

The resurgence of racially motivated violence is merely symptomatic of current racial attitudes. Studies of the present racial attitudes of white Americans toward African Americans have found that whites are far less accepting of equal treatment when it comes to the private domains of life, such as one's home or neighborhood. Even those whites who publicly espouse the principles of equality exhibit highly ambivalent attitudes and behavior in their personal lives

(Bobo, Schuman, and Steeh 1986). Where close intimate contact is involved, most whites do not accept African Americans as equals (DeFrancis 1989).

The nature of racism is best characterized by its very persistence and pervasiveness. This fact challenges the often articulated notion that race is no longer a major determining factor in the quality of life of people of color in the United States. In the 1960s, the Civil Rights Movement challenged our society to make serious strides toward alleviating racial injustice. After a short period of apparent support for racial equality, the national mood seemingly reverted to one of indifference and even hostility. The system of racial oppression and exploitation has been nurtured and strengthened for several hundred years. Merely a quarter of a century has transpired since the Civil Rights Movement, and we as a nation have only begun to address racism and its full effects.

By the 1980s, broad public support for racial progress had mostly dissipated. The reversals by the U.S. Supreme Court of legal decisions in affirmative action, equal protection, and civil rights paralleled a similar reversal of America's commitment to justice for cities and their inhabitants.

CHANGING DEMOGRAPHICS

As the twenty-first century nears, demographic conditions will increase Americans' awareness that indeed we are a multiracial and multiethnic society. The U.S. Census Bureau projects that the African American population will increase from 11.7 percent of the U.S. total in 1980 to 15 percent in 2020. At the same time, immigration trends are also increasing the numbers and proportions of Asians and Latinos in the U.S. population (Jaynes and Williams 1989). By the year 2020, the racial and ethnic population in the United States will have more than doubled, to 115 million. By the middle of the twenty-first century, whites will no longer be the majority in the United States (Henry 1990).

In the context of these demographic changes, a climate of racial intolerance can easily escalate into more extreme and divisive forms of racism in the near future. Even today, a major manifestation of contemporary racism in American society is the backlash on the part of some whites against the growing number of people of color in the United States. The "English only" and "English as the official language" initiatives, for example, openly prey upon the present majority's fear of "foreigners" and losing its own dominant position in society.

These initiatives seek to perpetuate the established patterns of society, which reflects an implicit or explicit white or Eurocentric value system that judges non-European cultures, accomplishments, and spiritual or moral standards to be innately inferior. Efforts to establish rules requiring the use of English in workplaces and to curtail educational programs for English as a second language will have more than symbolic consequences (Mydans 1990). In an increasingly pluralistic urban society, efforts must be made to strengthen education in English as well as bilingual language skills.

It is imperative that Americans accept and adjust to these demographic changes. The well-being of American society will be more and more dependent upon the vitality and productivity of people of color. This is readily evidenced by the fact that by the year 2020, African Americans will be nearly one of five children of school age and one of six adults of prime working age (Jaynes and Williams 1989).

Continued economic prosperity will depend largely upon how well the U.S. economy absorbs the growing numbers of immigrants, groups who are becoming residentially segregated in our cities. Immigrants from the Caribbean, Latin America, Asia, and Africa, at the rate of nearly 100,000 per year, played a vital role in helping to sustain economic growth in New York City during the 1980s (Levine 1990). Paralleling the growing numbers of working-age people of color is an increasingly older white population.

California, where Latinos alone account for nearly 35 percent of the population, provides a test case for a multiethnic society of the future, where people of color will bear the burden of support for an aging white population. In the year 2030, whites may account for nearly 60 percent of persons over 65 years of age while people of color may make up the majority of persons of working age (Hayes-Bautista, Schnick, and Chapa 1988).

LESSONS LEARNED

What lessons have we learned from the past? How is the nation coping with the "new" urban crisis of the 1990s? How can we dismantle residential apartheid? Ownership of property, land, and business is still a central part of the American dream of success—a dream that has eluded millions of Americans. Generally, the housing owned and occupied by people of color continues to be of lower value than that of whites. Racial barriers limit ownership options to older central city areas and suburban areas experiencing economic decline. Many older suburban neighborhoods now mirror the physical decay, crowding, poverty, and general neglect of their inner-city counterparts.

The health of cities is still important to the nation's overall health. Civil rights organizations, such as the NAACP, NAACP Legal Defense and Education Fund, and Lawyers' Committee for Civil Rights Under Law, have long been involved in cutting-edge fair housing litigation. New challenges are being raised to address imbalances resulting from redlining. For example, the civil rights community recently won an important victory against insurance redlining. In *NAACP v. American Family Mutual Insurance Co.,* the U.S. Supreme Court let stand a lower court decision that the Fair Housing Act prohibits denying or charging higher rates for home owners' insurance to residents in specific areas because of race or other illegal biases. The court decison opened the way for a group of eight African American borrowers in Milwaukee to proceed with a suit against American Family Mutual Insurance Company. The case is scheduled to go to trial in 1995.

Urban housing and economic problems can no longer be swept under the rug. Moreover, these problems are not likely to go away without some renewed national attention and government intervention. Working together, government and private fair housing agencies can make a difference in the quality of life that all Americans enjoy. The future of the nation is intricately bound to how we address the issues of the cities and residential apartheid. The federal government and private enforcement agencies must be encouraged to utilize the Fair Housing Act to end unjust, unfair, and illegal practices.

REFERENCES

Bell, Derrick. 1992. *Faces at the bottom of the well: The permanence of racism.* New York: Basic Books.

Bobo, Lawrence, H. Schuman, and C. Steeh. 1986. Changing racial attitudes toward residential integration. In *Housing desegregation and federal policy,* edited by John Goering. Chapel Hill: University of North Carolina Press.

Bullard, R. D. 1992. Urban infrastructure: Social, environmental, and health risks to African Americans. In *The state of black America 1992,* edited by Billy Tidwell. New York: National Urban League.

————. 1987. *Invisible Houston: The black experience in boom and bust.* College Station: Texas A&M University Press.

Bullard, R. D., and Joe R. Feagin. 1991. Racism and the city. In *Urban life in transition,* edited by M. Gottfiener and C. V. Pickvance. Newbury Park, Calif.: Sage.

Center for Democratic Renewal. 1987. *They don't all wear sheets: A chronology of racist and far right violence: 1980–1986.* New York: Divison for Church and Society of the National Council of Churches of Christ in the U.S.A.

Clark, Kenneth B. 1965. *Dark ghetto: Dilemmas of social power.* New York: Harper & Row.

Darden, J. T. 1989. The status of urban blacks twenty-five years after the Civil Rights Act of 1964. *Sociology and Social Research* 73:160–73.

DeFrancis, Marc. 1989. A common destiny: Blacks and American society. *Focus* 7 (August–September): 5–6.

DeLaRosa, Denise, and Carlyle E. Shaw. 1990. *Hispanic education: A statiscal portrait—1990.* Washington, D.C.: National Council of La Raza.

Denton, N. A., and D. S. Massey. 1988. Residential segregation of blacks, Hispanics, and Asians by socioeconomic status and generation. *Social Science Quarterly* 69:797–817.

Doob, Christopher Bates. 1993. *Racism: An American cauldron.* New York: Harper-Collins.

Farley, J. E. 1987. Disproportionate black and Hispanic unemployment in U.S. metropolitan areas: The roles of racial inequality, segregation and discrimination in male joblessness. *American Journal of Economics and Sociology* 46:129–50.

Feagin, J. R. 1990. *Racial and ethnic relations.* 3d ed. Englewood Cliffs, N.J.: Prentice-Hall.

Feagin, J. R., and C. B. Feagin. 1986. *Discrimination American style: Institutional racism and sexism.* Malabar, Fla.: Robert E. Krieger.

Feins, J. D., and R. G. Bratt. 1983. Barred in Boston: Racial discrimination in housing. *Journal of the American Planning Association* 49:344–55.

Feldman, P. 1989. Suit charged large apartment firm with racial bias in rentals. *Los Angeles Times,* 26 October.

Foust, D. 1987. Leaning on banks to lend to the poor. *Business Week,* 2 March.

Gallup, George, and Larry Hugick. 1990. Racial tolerance grows, progress on racial equality less evident. *Gallup Poll Monthly,* June, 23–32.

Glastris, P., and S. Minerbrook. 1989. A housing program that really works. *U.S. News & World Report,* 27 February, 26–27.

Goering, J. M. 1986. *Housing desegregation and federal policy.* Chapel Hill: University of North Carolina Press.

Hacker, Andrew. 1992. *Two nations: Black and white, separate, hostile, and unequal.* New York: Scribner's.

Harris, Fred R., and Roger W. Wilkins, eds. 1988. *Quiet riots: Race and poverty in the United States.* New York: Pantheon Books.

Hayes-Bautista, David E., Werner O. Schnick, and Jorge Chapa. 1988. *The burden of support: Young Latinos in an aging society.* Stanford, Calif.: Stanford University Press.

Henry, William A. 1990. Beyond the melting pot. *Time,* 9 April, 28–31.

James, F. J., B. I. McCummings, and E. A. Tynan. 1984. *Minorities in the Sunbelt.* New Brunswick, N.J.: Rutgers University Center for Urban Policy Research.

Jaynes, G. D., and R. M. Williams, Jr. 1989. *A common destiny: Blacks and American society.* Washington, D.C.: National Academy Press.

Jones, J. M. 1981. The concept of racism and its changing reality. In *Impact of racism on white Americans,* edited by Benjamin P. Bowser and Raymond G. Hunt. Beverly Hills, Calif.: Sage.

Kozol, Jonathan. 1991. *Savage inequalities: Children in America's schools.* New York: Crown.

Kushner, J. A. 1980. *Apartheid in America: An historical and legal analysis of contemporary racial segregation in the United States.* Frederick, Md.: Associated Faculty Press.

Landry, B. 1987. *The new black middle class.* Berkeley: University of California Press.

Levine, Richard. 1990. Young immigrant wave lifts New York economy. *New York Times,* 30 July.

Los Angeles Human Relations Commission. 1992. *Hate crimes in Los Angeles County, 1991.* Los Angeles.

Massey, D. S. 1987. Trends in the residential segregation of blacks, Hispanics and Asians, 1970–1980. *American Sociological Review* 52:802–25.

Massey, D. S., and M. L. Eggers. 1990. The ecology of inequality: Minorities and the concentration of poverty, 1970–1980. *American Journal of Sociology* 95:1153–88.

Momeni, J. A. 1986. *Race, ethnicity, and minority housing in the United States.* Westport, Conn.: Greenwood Press.

Mydans, Seth. 1990. Pressure for English-only job rules stirring a sharp debate across U.S. *New York Times,* 8 August.

National Advisory Commission on Civil Disorders. 1968. *Report of the National Advisory Commission on Civil Disorders.* New York: E. P. Dutton.

National Center for Health Statistics. 1990. *Advance report of final mortality statistics.* Washington, DC: National Center for Health Statistics.

Pinkney, Alphonso. 1993. *Black Americans.* Englewood Cliffs, N.J.: Prentice Hall.

Prentice Hall Law & Business. 1990. Rejection of black roommate brings $450,000 settlement in Los Angeles lawsuit. (April 1): 1–3.

Rosenblatt, Robert A., and James Bates. 1991. High minority mortgage denial rates found. *Los Angeles Times,* 22 October.

Taub, R. P., D. Garth, and J. D. Dunham. 1984. *Paths of neighborhood change: Race and crime in urban America.* Chicago: University of Chicago Press.

Tidwell, Billy D. 1990. The unemployment experience of African Americans: Some important correlates and consequences. In *The state of Black America 1990,* edited by Janet Dewart. New York: National Urban League.

Tobin, G. A. 1987. *Divided neighborhoods: Changing patterns of racial segregation.* Newbury Park, Calif.: Sage.

Updegrade, W. L. 1989. Race and money. *Money* 18:152–72.

U.S. Civil Rights Commission. 1986. *Recent activities against citizens and residents of Asian descent.* Washington, D.C.

U.S. Department of Health and Human Services. 1985. *Report of the secretary's task force on black and minority health: executive summary.* Washington, DC: U.S. Government Printing Office.

Willie, Charles V. 1989. *Caste and class controversy on race and poverty: Roundtable of the Willie/Wilson debate.* Dix Hills, NY: General Hall.

Wilson, W. J. 1978. *The declining significance of race: Blacks and the American institutions.* Chicago: University of Chicago Press.

Yang, C. M., M. Oneal, and R. Anderson 1988. The "blackmail" making banks better neighbors. *Business Week,* 15 August.

CHAPTER 1

A House Is Not a Home:
White Racism and U.S. Housing Practices

by Joe R. Feagin

THE FLIGHT FROM WHITE RACISM

White racism is the most fundamental if the least discussed of the causes of black-white tensions and conflict in U.S. cities. By *white racism* I mean the entrenched prejudices of white Americans, the subtle and blatant acts of discrimination by these whites, and the institutionalized system of oppression created by nearly 400 years of that prejudice and discrimination. White racism is antiblack prejudice added to the power of whites, acting on that prejudice, to change black lives—in workplaces, schools, and neighborhoods.

In April 1992 in Southern California the verdict of a suburban jury that included no black citizens exonerated four white Los Angeles police officers of police brutality. Several urban rebellions were triggered by this jury decision, and for a brief time the black urban rebellions brought issues of urban racial relations back into national media and policy discussions. Surveys of the black residents of central city areas where rebellions occur, in the 1960s as well as the 1980s and 1990s, have consistently found that those residents cite poor housing conditions, including racial discrimination in housing, as a major underlying cause of the uprisings (National Advisory Commission on Civil Disorders 1968; Feagin and Hahn 1973).

In recent years the news media treatment of white racism has been poor. I recently searched for the term white racism in Mead Data Central's Lexis/Nexis database of more than 160 magazines and newspapers. *Not one* of the many thousands of articles in the period February–May 1992 (before and after the Los Angeles rebellion) had a headline that included "white racism." This neglect of the centrality of white racism today extends from the mass media to social science research.

Of course, there have been some important shifts in mainstream social science thinking about racial issues since the 1960s. For example, as a result of the 1960s' Civil Rights Movement and ghetto riots, many influential white social scientists, together with journalists and politicians, supported new civil rights laws and reconceptualized U.S. racial relations in relatively radical terms. The new intellectual discourse moved away from terms blaming black families and black culture to mostly new terms blaming whites. The latter included sharp terms, such as *white racism* and *institutional racism*. For example, the final report of the 1968 presidential Commission on Civil Disorders, drawing on research by social scientists, concluded that "our Nation is moving toward two societies, one black, one white—separate and unequal" and minced no words about white responsibility: "White society is deeply implicated in the ghetto. White institutions created it, white institutions maintain it, and white society condones it. . . . White racism is essentially responsible for the explosive mixture which has been accumulating in our cities." The report added that one of the major ingredients in white racism is "pervasive discrimination and segregation in employment, education, and housing, which have resulted in the continuing exclusion of great numbers of Negroes from the benefits of economic progress" (National Advisory Commission on Civil Disorders 1968, 1, 5).

In the 1970s there was discontent among influential whites in academia, the media, and government over affirmative action remedies and the growing power of blacks in traditionally white institutions. Since then there has been a significant shift in how most influential white scholars, journalists, politicians, and jurists view black–white issues. Recent media articles have concluded that the "two societies" verdict of the 1968 riot commission was much too harsh. For example, the authors of a March 1988 *Newsweek* article argued that "mercifully, America today is not the bitterly sundered dual society the riot commission grimly foresaw" (19). Terms such as institutional racism have mostly been eliminated from white media and government analyses, and from the most influential academic policy analyses, largely because they represent analytical concepts too uncharitable to white America.

STUDYING WHITE RACISM IN THE HOUSING SPHERE

Yet, tragically, the reality of racial discrimination in the United States is much different than this commonplace white portrait suggests. In my own work on the discrimination faced by middle-class blacks, I have found that one must leave the ivory tower and go out and talk to those most directly affected about their lived experience with everyday racism. Many recent studies of black American problems, adopting a neo-conservative approach, have *not* gone into the field to observe what is happening to black Americans in housing or other important institutional arenas.

To ascertain the current conditions of this black middle class, I undertook a study, using black interviewers, of 209 middle-class black respondents in sixteen cities across the country. The in-depth interviews consisted mostly of open-ended questions that elicited experiences with racial barriers on the street and in public accommodations, employment, housing, and education.[1] In this chapter I will explore the panoply of dimensions of racial discrimination in housing that is faced by black Americans, with illustrations from some of the interviews.

THE BLACK AMERICAN DREAM OF HOUSE AND HOME

The right to a decent apartment or house is considered by most Americans, white and black, to be a central part of the American dream, one lived out in residential areas in every U.S. city. Middle-class black Americans clearly consider that part of the American dream to be very important; as one my respondents, an experienced teacher, expressed it: "I would like to have my dream home in the next year, and I'm serious." Similarly, in a recent survey of 1,500 Americans the polling firm Peter Hart and Associates found large percentages of Americans, black and white, viewing home ownership as a central part of the American dream, one worth sacrificing for. In an interview Peter Hart concluded: "Homeownership is really at the heart of middle-class values, of what America is about. . . . It is really all their dreams and all their hopes." John Buckley, a senior vice president of the agency Fannie Mae, commented on the survey's findings of strong black orientation to home ownership: "What was so significant about [these] findings for us was it made crystal-clear that the intensity of desire to own a home increases in inverse relationship to your ability to do it." He added that even those of moderate income in central cities do not need to be persuaded to desire home ownership (*American Political Network Hotline* 1992).

For most Americans, black and white, housing is more than a matter of a place to live. Housing represents not only pride of ownership of property but also a visible manifestation of accomplishments, one's standing in society, even one's character. Indeed, in the case of black Americans it is very important to understand just how important the home haven really is.

A BLACK PERSON'S HOME AS A PLACE OF SAFETY

A black middle-class respondent working in a western state articulated this point: "Once we have a nice place to live, maybe we can think about becoming successful. Before we can move ahead, we have to have a place to go home to. You cannot be a doctor or a lawyer if you're worried about where you're going to be staying, and if you have a meal or a warm bed."

For most families, black and white, one's housing is usually one's *home,* one of the important anchors against the turbulence of daily life. Yet not all groups in this society are alike in the significance of places of refuge. For middle-class blacks pioneering in white institutions, home often represents the only reliable anchor available to them in a hostile white-dominated world.

Let me document how home is a central fortress for those black Americans I interviewed. Putting the subject succinctly, a corporate executive in the Northeast was clear about the only place he did not encounter racial discrimination:

> The only place it probably doesn't affect me, I guess, is in my home; specifically, actually, in the interior portions of my home.

The duality of the black daily experience was explained by a manager at an electronics firm:

> Well, I think you really kind of lead dual lives. You live a life that you can be black when you go home, and then a life you live white being at work.

In other words, one cannot be oneself in the white world.

But what of one's white friends? Supposedly the desegregation of the traditionally white worlds has opened up other places of refuge outside home. But very few whites can really relate to blacks in the intimate way that family and close black friends can, as an airline manager said:

> So I can't discuss it with white friends, and I do have white friends, but they're just, I mean, like I said, in the industry, the neighborhood, the situations that I'm in, there just aren't that many black people. So my husband and my family become the stabilizing force for bouncing off situations.

A college student at a predominantly white university explained that it is hard to make close friendships with whites outside the home:

> I said number one, that white people, an example is that, when you have a white person and a black person who are friends, and this comes from my own personal experience, the black person cannot be a true, whole person with that white person without offending them, without embarrassing them, without putting them on the defensive because, I'm sorry, friendship to me is when you share your whole self. And if I have to leave my black self at home somewhere so the white person doesn't see it, that's not a friendship.

One respondent explained the problem of having to be superficial in white social networks:

> So, you just keep on a level where everything's pretty much on the surface, and you don't have to delve into a lot of the personal characteristics, and you can get along easier I think. And most of the time black people have to be almost plastic in their own personal opinions just to go with the opinions of most white folks, just to get along, to do certain things, like going to movies, or just listening to bands. If you're with a large group of whites and there's a small number of blacks, you pretty much will get outvoted on where to go, so you pretty much pretend, or will put up with it just to go with the evening, when you'd rather possibly be someplace listening to a real good jazz, or whatever, black-oriented music place. So, I think most black people have hold to back their, the stuff that they really like, the stuff that would identify them and make them black, just so they can be accepted and get along and work with the white people, since they're going to have to be in a situation a majority of the time.

He then added sharply that home, the black family and friends network, is where you can be yourself as a black person:

> I guess when they come home, is when they really become, that's when they're really black, and it's just a shame, because they have to hold that back when they're around white people because white people just probably won't be able to understand it, or really accept it or maybe

they don't even want to accept it because it's something they don't want to do.

Another respondent discussed how he separates home from social interaction with coworkers:

> I deal with it [racial discrimination] by basically being able to have my own home and my own circle of friends and communicating that with my several friends as to my experiences. When I have that in combination, I think that I'm able to have a normal lifestyle. When I say this, too, I don't really like to get involved with inviting my coworkers to my home or whatever. It's a funny thing that I feel this way.

Home is a place where blacks can retreat from racial discrimination and not have to deal with white America. This is a critical problem for middle-class black Americans, who must spend large amounts of time with white Americans as a consequence of their middle-class stature.

One respondent spoke of how quickly one may turn to the haven of one's home:

> And sometimes you can get enraged, and then you have to go home. You call and say, I'm going home now, and you just leave, because you know if you don't leave, you're not going to be very professional in your behavior and you just leave.

Speaking in lucid language, yet another saw home as a healing place:

> My family helped me by giving me a strong sense of self-awareness. And my friends the friends that I have, we talk and we're able to process some things and be mutually supportive. But I think that's basically the way I am, I have a strong sense of community. One of the things that we have as black folk is that when the white world bites us, we know that we can come home and find some healing there. And when I say home, I mean community.

Home here has connotations of the larger black community. One's personal network broadens out to include many other networks, and ultimately the local black community.

An attorney described how home is used to discuss the solutions to specific white discrimination encountered during the day:

> With my husband, I guess, he's got a lot of little situations that may crop up mostly at work, and he would come home and tell me, and I would think about it and say, "You know, this is the way you should have handled it, because I've been in that situation before. And what they expect is typically the way you did. So why don't you do this at the next group meeting you have, or say this at the next, and see what their reaction is or something?" So we just work out a strategy to deal with them. The next time, it's totally not what they expected.

Another respondent discussed her husband and detailed the problems that she and the home must handle:

> He would bring home, and times, you know, you could say, "Did you have a nice day?" and he'd chew you up, you know what I'm saying? You can have dinner on the table and that's not what I want. And at first, my feelings would be hurt, you know, 'cause I'm trying to be a good wife. . . . I learned how to deal with that. I owe it to the times learning how to not bring it home, because I found myself jumping back on him, "Listen, I had a rough one, too. I left that stuff at work, and that's where you better leave yours, and you get that door again, you pick it back up and go ahead off." You know, home's where you can come and relax and, you know, don't have to worry about that outside world right now.

A school board member in an eastern city made it clear what letting down one's guard and "being real" at home entails:

> My mother laughs now, because when all of us are home—I have five sisters and brothers—when we're all home—we're college educated, we speak distinctly, and we enunciate and enumerate our words appropriately—but when we're home, it's "get down." You know you don't care about how you say things, it's "dis" and "dat." And my mother laughs and says, "you wouldn't believe [it] if you came in here, they're all college graduates. Why do you speak that way?"

Middle-class black Americans live a dual life—one way with whites and one way in the home place. Even, or perhaps especially, well-educated and successful black Americans face a hostile white world that has allowed only one-way integration. The traditional corporate and government workplace is white-normed and white-dominated; as a result, blacks must constantly be on guard and regularly find themselves, even subconsciously, on the defensive. The reason seems to be that societal integration has not meant radical institutional change, or personal change on the part of most whites. Whites in power have rarely restructured the warp and woof of their organizations to incorporate black subculture, values, or interests.

The importance of home puts the problem of blacks' getting decent housing in hospitable neighborhoods in the proper perspective. "Fair housing" must be more than a matter of getting a decent house. It must come to encompass the whole process of getting housing for one's family, including all contacts with whites involved in the housing selection and choice process and with whites in the neighborhood once one has the house or apartment. Only then can a house truly become a home.

THE STRUGGLE FOR DECENT HOUSING

U.S. cities have historically segregated black Americans from white Americans. Seen from a distance, the racial ecology of U.S. cities today is not much different from the segregation geography of the past, with most blacks living in mostly black areas and most whites living in almost all-white areas. Recent research using 1990 census data shows that blacks only became slightly less segregated during the 1980s. Black Americans are still the most segregated of all U.S. racial and ethnic groups, with nearly two-thirds today residing in residential blocks that are heavily black in composition (Vobejda 1992, A7). In addition, most white Americans still live in mostly white neighborhoods. Another analysis of 1990 census data found that black residents were highly segregated in most of the 47 large cities, such as Detroit, Chicago, and Miami, where they constituted at least one-fifth of the population (*USA Today* 1991).

The housing racism of the late twentieth century is somewhat different from the housing racism of earlier decades, in that a few black families now live, or have tried to reside, in many historically white areas in virtually every city in the United States. State and federal laws make official discrimination illegal. But this does not mean that there is no longer serious housing discrimination. There are still the informal patterns and mecha-nisms of housing discrimination.

A free choice in housing is part of the American dream of housing. For the average American family the choice of where to live is based on several factors, including cost of housing, personal taste, suitability to family needs, and proximity to employment and other facilities. As a family's ability to pay increases, so do their options for housing—if the family is white. The great degree of residential segregation along racial lines to be found in the United States, even into the 1990s, is evidence that this formula does not apply to black Americans. For black families numerous direct and indirect institutionalized discriminatory restrictions intervene to limit housing options regardless of the ability to pay. In the previously mentioned Hart survey, 30 to 40 percent of black respondents viewed housing discrimination as a serious barrier to their securing the dream of home ownership. As Hart commented on his own survey, "When you have as large a minority within the black community feeling that they are being shut out or discriminated against it's not something that society can turn a blank eye to" (*American Political Network Hotline* 1992).

STRUGGLING FOR DECENT RENTAL HOUSING

In cities or suburbs, blacks are less likely to own their homes than whites because of past and present racial discrimination (U.S. Census Bureau 1985). As a result, rental housing is very important. Equal housing opportunity has been a major goal of the Civil Rights Movement, but the passing of fair housing legislation in 1968, and follow-up legislation since then, has not brought an end to discrimination. Housing audit studies show that a primary cause of residential segregation is racial discrimination by white landlords, home owners, and real estate agents. The 1989 national Housing Discrimination Study sent white and black testers to 3,800 randomly selected realty offices in two dozen cities. The survey found great discrimination in housing. During the course of several interactions with real estate salespeople, the study found that black home seekers would face racial discrimination at least half the time, and they were shown fewer housing units than whites. Most of the housing offered to whites was not offered to the black home seekers. Significantly, the Bush Administration delayed the official release of these findings for nine months, doubtless because of the political implications. As housing researcher Douglas Massey put it, "Rather than cracking down on discrimination when it found it and beginning to attack a condition that undoubtedly helped produce the rage unleashed in Los Angeles, the Bush administration swept evidence of persisting racism under the rug and hoped no one would notice" (Massey 1992, C2).

Housing discrimination cuts across a variety of institutions and includes white landlords, home owners, bankers, real estate agents, and government officials. It is well institutionalized for both renters and home owners. *Institutional* discrimination can be viewed as referring to actions prescribed by the norms of organizations and social networks of the dominant racial group, actions that by intention have a differential and negative impact on members of a subordinate racial group (Feagin and Feagin 1986, 1–42). The concept of institutional discrimination was developed in the 1960s to capture the organized, interconnected, and systemic character of modern racial discrimination. Norms guiding antiblack discrimination in the area of housing can be formal and written or they can be informal and unwritten. Institutionalized discrimination is not isolated and sporadic; it is carried out repeatedly by numerous whites guided by the norms of their social networks. Some early analysts contrasted a concept of impersonal institutional discrimination with "individual discrimination," but empirical work on racial discrimination in housing and other areas of this society has shown clearly that this is an artificial distinction. All institutional discrimination is carried out by individuals, who implement the shared norms of their organizations and social networks. Racial discrimination persists, not because of isolated bigots and small Klan groups, but because a majority of white Americans still harbor some strong antiblack stereotypes.

Rental Restrictions. Black renters seeking housing in white areas face antiblack attitudes in their search for housing. Like other renters, middle-class blacks often search first by phone. Black renters sometimes do not take the first answer as the true answer but respond to initial discrimination with great determination. Aware of this problem, savvy whites may listen carefully to the accent of the potential renter, as in this example given by a high school teacher of a friend of hers:

> She wanted an apartment, and she saw one in the paper. She called, and they told her that the apartment was rented. And she called me on the phone and said, "I'd like for you to call them." I said, "Why?" And she said, "Because you sound like a white person." And I called, and the apartment was still unrented.

Here the excluded friend did not accept on-the-phone discrimination quietly but had a friend check to ascertain if the apartment was rented. The intentional use of a white-sounding voice, either one's own or that of a friend, is one strategy middle-class blacks have developed to deal with racial discrimination.

A successful entrepreneur in a southwestern city described how landlords create other barriers to renting in white areas:

> So, we moved here, to move into the apartment we had to put up seven-hundred-and-some dollars. . . . After we had been there for six months, our next-door neighbor, who happened to have been a white male—we were just talking out by the pool. Somehow we got on a discussion, and we found out that none of the white tenants had to do that. He said that they were only using that when blacks would come there, because most blacks would not have that kind of money to pay first and last months' rent plus the deposit.

There is a clear suggestion here that the housing discrimination laws have had an effect on white landlords, by making outright exclusion less likely. Somewhat more subtle tactics have replaced the older door-slamming responses. Another dimension of this last story is the color of money. A teacher in a northern city noted this aspect of breaking into traditional white housing complexes:

> And when I lived in an apartment, I lived in an apartment in the suburban areas. And if you live there, they assume that you've got money. Money means all the difference in the world. That's another factor, besides the color of your skin, is how much money you've got. So, they [whites] assume that if you live there, you've got a good income, so that means that you're OK. So, I did not have a problem. I did not do a lot of socializing with them, but I did not have a problem.

A lawyer in an East Coast city noted that he had not faced direct discrimination himself because he has not ventured out into the housing market himself. Yet he has knowledge of racial discrimination from other middle-class blacks:

> No, I've lived in the same apartment complex for a number of years and I have had not any direct, I have not been out in the

housing market, either looking to buy property or to rent some-place else. So, I've not experienced anything directly. I've represented a client within the last five years involved in a housing discrimination case. I recognize that as a practical matter, living in the real world, that discrimination in housing continues to be a problem today.

No black person is an island. One dimension of the black middle-class experience is the interlocking character of that experience. Even when one has not had direct encounters with discriminatory whites in a particular arena of life, one may interact with black acquaintances, relatives, or clients who have faced that discrimination. The racial discrimination that happens to one person has a domino-like effect, in that the knowledge and pain spread through networks and have a serious social and community impact.

HOUSING BARRIERS FOR HOME OWNERS

Blatant denial of access to a home is perhaps the most basic of the discriminatory constraints facing black Americans seeking housing in formerly white areas. Home ownership in the United States has long been substantially controlled by the real estate industry, through such organizations as the National Association of Realtors (NAR), previously called the National Association of Real Estate Boards (NAREB), and its local real estate boards. One of the major methods of protecting property values has been the assurance of what these organized real estate agents view as "stable and compatible" neighborhoods, which in a white perspective has meant maintaining homogeneity of race. Historically, it was the official position of the NAR that brokers should not interfere with local preferences in regard to neighborhood homogeneity. Thus in 1924, Article 34 was written into the official NAREB Code of Ethics: "A realtor should never be instrumental in introducing into a neighborhood a character of property or occupancy, members of any race or nationality, or any individual whose presence will clearly be detrimental to property values in that neighborhood" (Helper 1969, 224). To this organizationally embedded discrimination was added the widespread use of deed restrictions and other informal practices prohibiting the sale of property to blacks. Some of the middle-class respondents commented on the situation in the 1960s, as this professor in a major western city:

When we moved to this city, we could not buy a house in the neighborhood that we wanted to buy in. Not because we did not have the money, but because blacks just didn't live in that neighborhood and the developer would not sell it. And there were no laws on the books that said you could not discriminate in housing. So, it was overtly said, we will not sell to blacks. So, we had to buy a house in a black neighborhood.

The significance of these practices, even in western cities with no history of legal segregation, is that the informal segregation set a pattern that has persisted to the present day. The earlier real estate practices were a deeply ingrained coding that, in spite of legal changes, shaped the racial future of this and other U.S. cities.

Analyzing interview data from white real estate brokers in Chicago in the 1960s, Rose Helper (1969) found that the economic gain to be realized from "the primary control of land and property" was fundamental to the ideology of brokers. White brokers have often been convinced that once property passed into black or other minority control, there is little or no future possibility of profit for whites from the property (Helper 1969).

EXCLUSION TODAY

Although the fair housing laws of the 1960s ended such official practices, local real estate operations are still overwhelmingly white-dominated. Indeed, the previously mentioned federal study of metropolitan areas found that black home seekers still face a fifty-fifty chance of encountering discrimination in white housing markets. In all regions of the nation white landlords and home owners cooperate with white real estate agents in excluding blacks from certain residential areas. In particular cases the attempts to exclude blacks can be complex, as in this one described by a black health-care professional:

My first encounter with discrimination in my present location ironically had to do with a very basic thing that most people look forward to, and that's their home. . . . That evening she [the white real estate agent] called me at home and said she thought she'd accidentally stumbled onto something that might interest me and would I be interested in looking? I said yes. . . . It was a home owned by a major insurance company executive who had been transferred to another city a hundred miles away. . . . We contacted the owner by phone. She conveyed an offer; he countered. I countered; he accepted it. I signed the papers; we sent them to him. We never got them back. The real estate owner that she [our salesperson] worked for was totally uncooperative with assisting her. Days went by; weeks went by; over a month went by. . . . Well, she knew at that interest rate, and having known what the owner [now in another city] accepted, that house would be sold to someone else out from under me in a matter of seconds. And she wanted to keep her word. It was only after about five, six weeks I said to her: "Don't bother to hide the key any more. Put it back in the office. I'll handle it." And it was at that time that I formulated a letter, and I sent a copy of it to the president of that insurance company, explaining what had happened and stating that we could not understand why there was a delay.

He added that he made a point of sending a copy to the national NAACP office. In this case a supportive white real estate agent was blocked by other white forces—the white owner and the agent's boss. Clearly, the invalidation of overt and official real estate discrimination practices resulting from court cases and fair housing laws at the local, state, and national level has not meant a radical change in housing patterns or practices, for the straitjacket of the past constrains contemporary behind-the-scenes practices; this may be difficult for white observers to see, but the practices still seem as blatant to the black targets and victims.

Sometimes it is difficult for black home seekers to know whether they have indeed faced racial discrimination. Several of my respondents were uncertain about how much racial discrimination they had faced in housing, or they simply said they were not aware of any. An audit research study in the Detroit metropolitan area by Diana Pearce found considerable persistence and increased subtlety in the character of housing discrimination directed against blacks among 97 different real estate agents. Yet, significantly, one black auditor/home seeker (with spouse) who was sent by researcher Pearce to a suburban real estate firm was told his income and savings were insufficient to buy housing in that white suburb. The man came back and asked if the researcher had made a mistake, not recognizing that a discriminatory act had, in fact, occurred. Pearce notes that a white couple/auditor had been "sent out with the same income and savings; in their interview, in contrast, no mention was made to them of inadequate resources for the community, and they were both urged to buy and were shown houses in the same community as the firm in question was located in" (Pearce 1976).

Surprisingly few of the respondents I interviewed have fil
complaints with state or federal agencies or have take any legal action. I ne
resignation that housing discrimination generated is suggested in this comment
from a law professor:

> Right around this campus, there's one community that's pre-
> dominantly white, has been for years. And the major real estate
> agents in the area take great pride in discriminating against black
> folks. . . . I remember one of my colleagues was looking for a house,
> and he came to relay this story because this realtor was showing
> him houses. And this realtor proudly told him how he had kept
> blacks out of there for a number of years. Proudly. Told him
> because he was white, and he didn't think he'd be offended. . . .
> I live in a nice neighborhood. It's near here, predominantly black.
> And I've had colleagues come who wouldn't even look in my area.
> Wouldn't even look in my area as close as it is.

Part of the story of the racism of the 1980s and 1990s is the unwillingness of
many black Americans with resources to take aggressive legal action against
illegal discrimination for fear of the pain, energy drain, and money it may
cost—and a concern for the futility of using institutionalized remedies in the
larger society.

REAL ESTATE PRACTICES

Since the 1960s significant numbers of the growing group of middle-class black
Americans have looked for better housing in predominantly or entirely white
areas. These middle-class black Americans are confronted by subtle discrimination in real estate practices that seek to circumvent the law and that rely on
the difficulty of proving intent to discriminate.

There is the persisting practice of "steering" black customers to segregated
or mixed areas and discouraging them in a variety of ways from considering
white areas, while steering white customers to those white areas. For example,
such steering was the major device cited when white and black residents of
northwest Detroit brought a famous court suit against real estate agencies for
violations of the federal Fair Housing Act of 1968. A black client testified that
a real estate agent had refused to show him housing in a white suburb, saying
he would be uncomfortable with no black neighbors. Instead, he was steered
to an area which was 43 percent black. And a few white home seekers testified
that white real estate agents steered them away from housing areas blacks had

entered, giving such reasons "housing values are down and will continue to drop" (Foundation for Change 1974, 7).

My interviews indicate that the times have not changed in regard to subtle steering practices. The owner of a company described the neighborhood he had lived in since the 1970s:

> And this neighborhood—I was open to move into any neighborhood, and what ended up happening is that we were somewhat directed, or steered, out to this neighborhood. And when we moved out into this neighborhood, it was one-third black and 60 percent white, with the remaining percentage being Hispanics.

He continued by explaining that there was a shift from majority white to mostly minority in the area as a result of steering practices. In similar fashion, another middle-class home buyer discussed his treatment at the hands of a white agent:

> The area I live in is called Stonebridge, which is predominantly white. Right across the street is Stonebridge Heights, which is 85 percent black, and across the street from there is Stonewoods, which is 99 percent black. So after she [the real estate agent] got through showing us this one house, she drove all the way to the other side into Stonebridge Heights to show us another house. The house that I bought eventually was right around the corner from the original house we saw, which is a 99 percent white neighborhood. We're the only blacks in the neighborhood, on the corner. And the other thing that made me realize that it was discrimination—how many of you have ever seen a real estate agent who has never called back a prospective buyer? This woman *never* called us back, never wanted to know if we were still looking or interested.

This type of racial steering can range from blatant to relatively subtle. After replying that she herself had not faced housing discrimination in recent years, a university administrator commented on the experience of friends with white real estate brokers:

> Just a matter of people saying things like, for instance, "you really don't want this house," once you've decided that's the house you want. Now, a realtor's job, if you decide that's the house you want, it's quite the opposite: "Oh, let's do everything we can to close the deal." But

to be told, "you really don't want this house, I've got ar
think you'll like better." In the back of the your mind, you ɪᴄ ᴋᴜᴜ ᴜ
going, "I think I know why we don't want this house." And this friend
I was talking to pretty much said, "Well, OK, we'll just take a look at
this other house that you want to show us." And eventually bought the
second house, which I thought was really strange. . . . I think it was just
the neighborhood that the realtor had decided that they were best
suited for. And without this person ever having said, you probably
want to be with your own kind.

This type of channeling often helps to shift a mixed residential area to one
that is predominantly black, as white families move out and black families
replace them. A successful entrepreneur in a southwestern city explained that
she liked that transition of her area to a greater black proportion:

When we first moved out there, it was younger. What you would have
considered the [white] yuppie group. And they were very friendly
when you first moved in. . . . It was a new neighborhood, so we were
not the first people to move into that neighborhood. . . . But then after
that the yuppies were making more money, so they were able to move
out of the neighborhood to . . . the larger houses. And then you get
in another group of white people who are just a cut above you in terms
of income, they are the blue-collar kind. They considered the
neighborhood to be middle class. . . . I see the neighborhood color
changing, the complexion of the neighborhood changing, very much
so. And it doesn't disappoint, it doesn't bother me, because all the
black people that are moving in there, they're keeping up their
properties and it looks nice. The problems we have are the whites that
live in the community. . . . I see the complexion changing, it's a
younger, black professional people moving into the neighborhood.

This description of a middle-class residential area that went through two
stages of white residents but now is seeing mostly black middle-class families
moving in is very typical across the United States.

Manipulation of white fears by white brokers further complicates this
housing picture. Once a residential neighborhood develops some natural
integration—that is, once a few black families have moved in—white brokers
may act to destroy natural integration, at the same time often significantly
increasing the price of available housing for blacks, using the technique of *block*

busting. Brokers have exploited the racial fears of whites in neighborhoods undergoing racial change. In one litigated case a mail solicitation stated "We think you may want a friend for a neighbor . . . know your neighbors," while another informed owners that the real estate firm had paid cash for a certain property in the neighborhood and would "do the same for you" (Bisceglia 1973). Thereby real estate agents fuel property value decline and other stereotypes that sustain direct discrimination in housing. In my study an engineer described how areas become black reserves:

> When I first moved. . . . It was about fifteen white families and five black families. As the neighborhood grew and the homes began to close out throughout that building [area], I saw a tendency of—it seemed that the realtors were only selling to black people.

The short time in his case, just two and a half years, signals active cooperation among real estate agents to use block busting in the area. For decades white firms have worked to concentrate blacks in certain areas of cities, including this particular city, which has a hopscotch pattern of black-white segregation in suburban areas.

Such rapid resegregation even of middle-class black Americans has created resignation and pessimism about the future, and not just in my interviews. A recent report in *USA Today* quoted Michael Lomax, the black chair of the Fulton County Commission, who lives in a very affluent south Atlanta neighborhood that was once a mixed black-white neighborhood. Yet since the 1970s it has become almost all black. Lomax was quoted as saying he is much more pessimistic today than in the 1970s. He contrasted that optimism of his youth with the situation of his seventeen-year-old daughter: "I grew up in a generation that was encouraged to integrate, that was led to believe that if you worked hard and performed well, you could benefit from an integrated existence. I think in her generation, blacks and whites are much more balkanized, much more segregated and much less tolerant of those who are different, and that does not bode well for the kind of tolerance that it takes to create a civilized society" (*USA Today* 1991).

LOAN AND BANKING BARRIERS

For many years official policies of mortgage-granting institutions have paralleled those of the real estate industry in establishing a pattern of institutional discrimination affecting black Americans. Nearly two decades ago, the U.S. Commission on Civil Rights underscored this point in a major report: "For minorities and women, the mortgage finance system is a stacked deck—stacked sometimes inadvertently, often unthinkingly, but stacked nevertheless" (U.S. Commission on Civil Rights 1974, 33). Even today the governing policies of lending institutions are often rationalized in terms of "sound business principles," such as the desire to protect investments against loss. In applying these policies, however, lending organizations make certain requirements favoring whites. Since black Americans are rare among the local and national decision makers of the nation's major housing, lending, and insuring institutions, the rules are for the most part written by whites and tend to favor whites.

Moreover, for decades the federal government, ostensibly the guarantor of decent housing, intentionally fostered racial discrimination in lending. In the last two decades federal housing regulations have banned discrimination in lending. Title VIII of the 1968 Civil Rights Act and the Equal Credit Opportunity Act prohibit discrimination in lending. Still, questions about discrimination in lending remain, if only because virtually all lending to black Americans is controlled by white lenders. A 1989 report of the federal Office of Thrift Supervision found that nationwide, black mortgage loan applicants have been rejected by savings and loan associations at twice the rate as white applicants (Office of Thrift Supervision 1989, 2). These and other recent data have pressured white lenders to admit high loan rejection rates for black applicants are linked to lenders' underwriting criteria: assuming borrowers fit the image of the ideal white middle-class family—a nuclear family in which the chief breadwinner has had a long-term work history with one firm and no credit problems—and are buying in areas that fit the image of a stable white middle-class area, similar to the real estate standard of no "detrimental" features affecting property values that I cited earlier (Byrne 1992, 1).

Today blacks face some direct discrimination in exclusion from loans for homes and businesses, but they also face more subtle and covert discrimination in the form of runarounds and added restrictions for loans, as well as the indirect discrimination of regulations favoring whites. In my interviews a number of respondents spoke of problems like these recalled by a black professor:

> From a personal standpoint, one of the major sources of discrimination is in the housing market and in the mortgage financing aspect in trying to buy houses. Now, we're skilled home buyers, we're skilled lookers. And we recognize as African American people that any time we approach a mortgage company to buy anything that exceeds $60,000 in cost we're going to have a problem. And we're going to have a problem in the arena of a black moving into a white neighbor-

hood, so to speak. Redlining is not uncommon in this city, just like it is in Atlanta and a lot of other cities that have upwardly mobile African American families. And that's one of the things that we have to deal with, and on a number of occasions in the process of purchasing six homes we've had to challenge that issue. . . . We were denied information about housing, the threat of denial of the mortgage, of [not] being able to purchase a particular home for various and sundry reasons, none of which had to do with our ability to pay the mortgage or our credit rating.

Differential treatment in the search for housing is often more than a matter of just one incident, for it can appear in one setting after another, especially in traditionally white neighborhoods.

A research administrator in a southern city noted that he had not faced overt discrimination recently, except for certain assumptions about his financial situation:

And it's kind of interesting, too, when we did come down and look for houses, the people wanted to know immediately, "Let's go in and look at your expenses to see how much house you can afford." And we said, "No, we don't need to do that. It's not a question of how much house we can afford, it's what kind of house we want." So they didn't get the opportunity to send us through this whole little game that they play.

In determining the credit worthiness of borrowers like these black respondents, white loan officers are often guided by criteria set forth in standard texts such as this:

In judging a borrower's reasons for requesting a loan, the lender should consider the strength of his attachment to the property and his probable future attitudes toward it. . . . A borrower's relationship to his family and friends is a significant element of risk although it is difficult to rate. Evaluators usually consider whether a borrower has an established reputation, a harmonious home life, associates with good reputations, and if he is active in civic affairs or whether he has been dishonest and untruthful in the past, has a troubled family life, and associates of doubtful reputation. (Grezzo 1972, 14)

This viewpoint allows much room for the introduction of racially biased probing and assumptions. Lenders place heavy emphasis on the credit record of applicants and in addition prefer to make new loans to applicants with past mortgage experience. Such practices lead to past-in-present discrimination against for black Americans who historically had much less opportunity to establish credit and secure loans.

HARASSMENT FROM WHITE NEIGHBORS

Middle-class blacks who have braved the screening of discrimination may face new forms of poor treatment. The repertoire of responses by white neighbors is broad and spans actions of violence, surveillance, and peaceful accommodation. Indeed, accounts of violence against black families moving into white neighborhoods have not been uncommon in the late twentieth century. Some of these black families have been home owners. In both North and South, black families moving into white areas have been shot at, windows have been broken in their homes, and they have fled when their houses were firebombed. In our interviews, a former secretary recounted the experiences of a friend in a midwestern city in the 1970s:

> I had a girlfriend. When they bought in the same area that we were buying in, their house got fired on three times, you know, before they even got a chance to move in. Her husband had to sit there and sleep with a shotgun. And we are still talking about the 1970s in that city. So you knew, you knew your place.

Some black home owners have fled such attacks, while others have responded by arming themselves and standing their ground.

Sometimes the opposition of whites, while not violent, is blatantly hostile. After recounting the hate stares he and his wife encountered at a local restaurant, a manager for an electronics firm continued with an account of graffiti encountered while he and his wife were walking in his predominantly white neighborhood:

> There was this big brick wall and all across this wall were negative slurs: "Go home, nigger," "Jews die," the German swastika all over the place.

Most after-the-move situations do not involve direct violence or threats of violence, such as the graffiti. For many black home owners, prejudiced reactions range from white flight to petty misconceptions and harassment.

Some white neighbors express great fear about the crime and status contamination that they think will come with black residents. New hurdles for black residents include excessive surveillance by suspicious neighbors, as one professor who now teaches at an Ivy League university indicated:

> I think when we first moved in it was pretty clear that they were a little bit nervous. And once they saw that people weren't driving up to our house at midnight, you know, purchasing small packages of white powders, then they relaxed.

Stereotyping again seems to involve notions about blacks as drug dealers and criminals. This image of blacks as criminals is deeply embedded in many white minds, thanks in part to the skewed media focus on blacks in crime.

Sometimes white neighbors' behavior is not overtly racist, but it makes a black person suspect something negative is going on. The research administrator we quoted earlier made this observation:

> The only neighbor that I know that we've had problems with is the lady who lives directly across the street. They have never said "hi" or anything. In fact, when we first got here, she would throw trash out in the middle of the street. She wouldn't throw it *at* us, but she would throw it out in the *middle* of the street.... When we were outside she'd do that.

The negative attitudes of white neighbors can often be manifested in ways that might be hard for a white observer to perceive as racist. To take another example, a teacher commented on interaction with a white neighbor, whom she clearly regards as a racist individual:

> Just, I guess, subtle things that she's done, in a sense. Like trying to ignore me. Looking right in your face and not speaking to you. I mean, those kind of things like that. Speaking to you only when she *needs* something. If she needs something, that's when maybe I would get spoken to.... And I think the misconception ... [of] white bigots is that they really think that you have a need to be in their space. And I think what I'm trying to portray to her is that I have no need to be in her space. She doesn't have anything that I want. White skin, to me, does not mean anything. I think she still lives in the days of "I've got white skin, so I'm better than you."

Part of being black in the United States is the development of a sensitivity to negative attitudes on the part of whites. The negative treatment here did not involve racist epithets, but something much more subtle, the timing of the white neighbor's comments and of what she does not say. Indeed, for an outside white observer there may be little here that seems racist. Yet living with a certain white attitude for a long period of time has enabled black Americans to be right in their judgments of white attitudes most of the time.

Integrated housing can also make for good neighbor relations. A teacher in a northern city noted that she had a friendly white neighbor who had been helpful:

> I have a very lovely lady. She's an older lady. And I don't know whether she's nice because she's old and there's not very much she can do, but she's very dependable. She exemplifies what I think a neighbor should be. She's very watchful of my house, and yet she's not nosy. I can call her in an emergency.

Protecting the Children. Black children bear a heavy burden as their parents integrate white neighborhoods. A university manager spoke of a white neighbor's hostility to his children:

> When they were smaller and they were out on the sidewalk riding their bicycles and throwing the ball and things like that, if they happened to kick the ball into his yard or something, he would get into a heated [rage]. . . . And it only happens with the Hispanic and black kids.

Here barriers were put up by a white adult, but in other cases the discrimination comes both from adults and children. A high school principal spoke of a dangerous white neighbor:

> I found out he's a KKK'er, but as I told him, I was here before you came. . . . My son was on his bike out there. And he [my neighbor] had three boys and a girl. And he [my son] was riding up and down the sidewalk. And the wife would be standing inside the screen porch watching them push him off the bike. I said: "I don't want to talk to you; I'll wait until your husband comes."

The price in terms of personal energy, however, was high, for this principal was risking violent reprisals. People think of home and neighborhood as places where they can relax and enjoy the fruits of their labors. For blacks coming to a home and neighborhood selected for comfort and other personal reasons can mean not peace and enjoyment, but frustration and stress-induced illness.

STAYING IN BLACK AREAS

In *The Declining Significance of Race,* William J. Wilson, like other recent commentators, has argued that affluent blacks have been moving out of traditionally black residential areas into white areas for some time, and thus very large numbers are living in isolation from other blacks (Wilson 1978, 1987). Yet this view is misleading, for research has shown that while housing segregation decreases for most American ethnic groups as education and income increase, it does not for black Americans (Jaynes and Williams 1989, 144–46; Massey and Denton 1987). Most middle-class blacks live in predominantly black areas. A supervisor of vocational education programs described her East Coast neighborhood:

> I've lived in a black neighborhood that's at least a hundred years old. And there's no discrimination in my neighborhood.

A financial planner noted that he had long lived in a house in a predominantly black community without problems from his neighbors. He put some general comments about housing discrimination in this context:

> I do know that in this city it still exists. . . . There is no doubt about that. . . . I've always wanted to live where blacks were. I've never wanted to live with whites. It's just, never thought about it! Not that I probably *couldn't,* but just that I don't want to. I want to be able to go across the street, and if I want to go over there and say, "I need a cup of sugar." That's where I came from, you know, and I like that environment, so that's where we are. But we *have* fought it in this city. and still know that there's still those vestiges here. That they still have in the agreements that minorities or blacks are not to be there. I know that's still facing us.

The advantages of a black neighborhood lie in the ability not to have to deal with at least one type of racial discrimination.

Some middle-class black Americans intentionally seek out predominantly black areas, but they pay a price for that choice, a successful entrepreneur noted:

When I first moved to this city, I wanted to live in the [black] east side, because it was inner-city, close to downtown, and [had] all the things that I wanted to do. However, there were only like two apartment houses and all the rest were public housing. There were no decent houses, and you couldn't get a loan to build a house. And then, what community were you going to put it in? You going to borrow, fifty, seventy-five thousand dollars to build a house and then put it next to something that's condemned?

Her problem was the absence of adequate housing in the area that was most desirable from her point of view. She notes, too, the difficulty of getting a loan to build in that area. Then she added her thoughts on absentee white landlords:

And then that's another part of racism—absentee landlords. White owners who own property in those communities, they own it, they desert it, they don't do any improvements. It's just like, if you move into an apartment in other sections of town, the property manager's planting flowers and trees and making it beautiful, where people can feel good about themselves and where they live. Well, in the deep areas of the east side, none of that goes on. It's just like we don't care anything about the environment, we don't like to smell flowers, and we don't like to see green leaves on a tree?

White landlords in black areas can make the choice of housing for renters even more difficult. Still, the choice of an integrated versus a segregated neighborhood creates serious personal and family dilemmas, as was poignantly described by a judge who is a home owner in a southern city:

I guess that one of the problems of being black [is that] I stay in a black neighborhood. And you know, staying in a black neighborhood, that's discrimination. Well, what I'm saying is, I think it's important being a black judge, being a black person, that I identify with the black community and that I reside in the black community. But with regard to services, not so much city and government services, but [with] regard to private services, in terms of grocery stores, department stores, and that type of thing, that is not available in the black neighborhoods.

The black community is his political anchor, yet his choice condemns his family to inferior services. Wherever they live, the lives of middle-class blacks remain constrained by patterns of institutionalized discrimination. There are other problems for those living in black residential areas, as well. These include loan problems. A study by the *Los Angeles Times* in September 1992 found that black home seekers trying to buy in black residential areas of Los Angeles County often encountered intentional discrimination on the part of lenders and appraisers. These include a too "stringent scrutiny of past credit problems, disappointing appraisals and a reluctance on the part of private mortgage insurers to provide the insurance that lenders demand" (Bates 1992, A27). Those working-class and middle-class black Americans who choose to buy houses in stable residential areas of central Los Angeles can find themselves in the added predicament of not being able to secure loans. Indeed, the 1992 rebellion has apparently made many white lenders, appraisers, and insurers even more unwilling to facilitate housing choices in traditional black residential areas than they were before.

CONCLUSIONS:
WHITE RACISM AND WHITE ILLUSIONS

In 1944 the Swedish social scientist Gunnar Myrdal summed up the forces then responsible for the housing segregation faced by black Americans in *An American Dilemma*: "Probably the chief force maintaining residential segregation of Negroes has been *informal* social pressure from the whites. Few white property owners in white neighborhoods would ever consider selling or renting to Negroes; and even if a few Negro families did succeed in getting a foothold, they would be made to feel the spontaneous hatred of the whites socially and physically" (622).

While there are now more whites willing to rent or sell to blacks, this comment is still largely correct. Today residential segregation and racial polarization are still basic to the fabric of U.S. towns and cities. The reason for this is that white Americans have a serious "attitude problem." Recent opinion surveys still show many white Americans believe housing discrimination by white home owners should be permitted, even legally sanctioned. In a 1990 nationwide poll, 44 percent of whites said they favored a law giving a white home owner the right not to sell a house to a black person over a law prohibiting such discrimination. The overwhelming majority of whites have a negative reaction to the idea of blacks as neighbors, especially when the numbers increase beyond modest levels to a substantial proportion. In the same 1990 survey, only one in ten whites said they had a favorable reaction to the idea of living in a neighborhood that was even half white and half black (National Opinion Research Center 1990).

The consequences of these white attitudes are many, and we have seen what happens to those black Americans who try to break out of traditional confines of housing segregation. The picture is complex, confusing, and depressing, with some whites fleeing as blacks move in, with real estate brokers having too much power over black housing alternatives, and with lenders limiting neighborhood choices. These and other white discriminators limit the life choices, even the life expectancies, of middle-class black Americans. They make a house into an even more troubled home than would otherwise be the case for those who must deal daily with American apartheid. A house in a decent neighborhood is a critical anchor for blacks in a racially oppressive world. Most whites have little awareness of what owning a home means to black families and little understanding of the devastating toll taken on black families whose attempts to buy are blocked by racial factors over which they have no control.

The reality of discrimination today is very different from the common-place portrait of a declining significance of race. There is anger and rage over white racism in every black income group, from millionaires to day laborers. The *first* black person I interviewed in the 1988–1992 research project was the owner of a successful contracting firm in the Southwest. Well-educated and clearly middle class, this woman described numerous examples of discrimination she faced in doing business. In her opening words she captured what it is like to be a black person confronting discrimination in a white business world:

> One step from suicide! What I'm saying is the psychological warfare games that we have to play every day just to survive. We have to be one way in our communities and one way in the workplace or in the business sector. We can never be ourselves all around. I think that may be a given for all people, but for us particularly, it's really a mental health problem. It's a wonder we haven't all gone out and killed somebody or killed ourselves.

This frustration and anger are not limited to a few of the middle-class respondents. Anger and rage are common in the interviews. White racism has created great rage in black America. And the recent riots are only the beginning of many more riots, if that white racism is not confronted and dealt with.

What is to be done? There is much that can be done to rid the United States of white racism and its many consequences in housing, neighborhoods, workplaces, and other arenas of daily life. We must put some real teeth into our fair housing and other civil rights laws, so that white discriminators will suffer greatly for their discrimination crimes.

Fair housing laws and agencies clearly mark a change from the past, but they are insufficient to the task of bringing large-scale changes. A professor at a western university spoke of a central concern in regard to housing and other services:

> Take any of the services—housing. They say there's no discrimination in housing. Yet, many blacks will show up to buy housing, or to rent an apartment, and they will be told it's filled. Banks will redline certain neighborhoods because the developer has said they don't want blacks to live there. . . . And it's just the whole gamut that legislation and policy says one thing, but in reality it's not.

Middle-class black Americans nationwide complain about the lack of aggressive enforcement of the laws on the books. The same situation can be seen in many states. In New York, for example, the secretary of state controls the licensing of real estate brokers and can force compliance with fair housing laws, yet the office is poorly funded and does not have the staff to check out discrimination by real estate agents. In addition, the New York Division of Human Rights is chartered to take and remedy discrimination complaints, but in 1990 it had a backlog of 12,000 racial complaints, including those involving housing. Local housing agencies in New York also have the power to investigate complaints, but as a *Newsday* (1990) editorial put it, "they work in an atmosphere where the prevailing public will is less than enthusiastic about removing racial barriers" (40).

For these reasons we must go beyond current government fair housing programs to focus on white racism itself. What is missing not only in the media but in the nation is the picture of white Americans, especially middle-class whites and powerful white leaders, taking responsibility for the widespread prejudice and discrimination that generate rage and protest among black Americans. It was white Americans who created the slavery and segregation of African Americans. And it is white Americans who today are the responsible for most continuing discrimination against African and other nonwhite Americans. White Americans created the artificial concept of race to justify this exploitation and discrimination and now use such vague concepts as "race divides" as a way of describing conditions in an impersonal way. But the conditions of racial discrimination do have creators. And the creators are mostly white Americans.

As a nation we have been lied to in recent years by a gaggle of right-wing analysts who have told us that the primary cause of persisting racial tensions and problems in this country is not white racism, but rather the black underclass, or black families, or black dependency on welfare. These apologists, including Presidents Ronald Reagan and George Bush, have blamed the underclass for its immorality and the black middle class for not taking responsibility for the underclass. A favorite phrase is the "declining significance of race." A denial of white racism and a blaming of the black victims of racism have become intellectually fashionable in the last decade.

To fight this denial we need to create a cradle-to-grave educational program for all Americans, but especially white Americans, that teaches the real racial history of the United States, including genocide, segregation, and present-day discrimination. We must create many television programs in prime time to teach white Americans about their sordid racial history, about their own prejudices and acts of discrimination, and about strategies for eliminating that racism. Most white Americans still deny that they are racist and that there is much serious racism in America. We must educate white Americans to see the racism in their attitudes and actions and to recognize that racism in others.

Most whites have no understanding of the aches of black Americans facing racial discrimination in housing, neighborhoods, workplaces, and public accommodations. Most whites, including virtually all current white policy analysts and policy makers, prefer not to "see" the massive racism black Americans face; instead, they blame continuing black problems on blacks themselves. Only the occasional white intellectual or policy maker ventures beyond the white ghetto to find out what life is like on the nonwhite side. One of these brave men is Illinois Senator Paul Simon who, in September 1990 confirmation hearings for Supreme Court Justice David Souter, challenged then-nominee Souter with these comments:

> We don't have Indian reservations in Illinois. I know there are serious problems. And while we have some Native Americans in the city of Chicago, relatively, it's a handful of people. I took the time to go to the Pine Ridge Indian reservation in South Dakota, found 73 percent unemployment, 65 percent of the homes with no telephones, 26 percent of the homes with no indoor plumbing. . . . when an issue

about American Indians comes up, it's not an abstraction for me. . . . And I don't mean this disrespectfully to your fine background: I want you to understand perhaps a little more than you now do some of the aches of America. (U.S. Senate 1990, 354)

Beyond this educational step, we must create a large group of white *antiracists* who fight aggressively against the racism they encounter in housing and other sectors of daily life. It is the rare white American today who will speak up against another white person who discriminates in a neighborhood or housing complex or who will challenge a white boss who discriminates. Until whites deal with their racist inclinations and speak out against white racism everywhere, there is no real hope of eradicating the racist foundation of the white–black tensions and conflict in neighborhoods across the United States.

NOTE

1. Using a snowball sample, I interviewed 209 black respondents in 1988–1990. About 65 percent of the respondents were residents of cities in the South and Southwest; about 6 percent were in West Coast or Midwest cities; and 29 percent were in Northeast or Middle Atlantic cities. Many have lived in several regions, and some comments refer to places other than where the individual resides now. Just over half are in the 36-to-50-years age bracket, with 32 percent in the 18-to-36 bracket and 16 percent in the 51-plus age bracket. Some are heads of their own businesses, and a few are students who probably will hold white-collar jobs. Most are corporate managers, doctors or other health care professionals, lawyers, electronic and computer professionals, teachers, government officials, college administrators, journalists or others in mass media, or clerical or sales workers. Eight percent reported household incomes of $20,000 or less, while 22 percent reported incomes in the $21,000–35,000 range; 23 percent in the $36,000–55,000 range; and 47 percent in the $56,000 or more range. All but a handful, mostly students, had household incomes above the black median family income for 1989. The sample is well educated. All have at least a high school degreee, and 96 percent have completed some college work. About 80 percent have a college degree. Most are thus in the upper reaches of the black middle class.

REFERENCES

American Political Network Hotline. 1992. Interview: Hart and Buckley on home ownership survey. In Lexis Computer Database (June).

Bates, James. 1992. Obstacle course. *Los Angeles Times,* 6 September.

Bisceglia, Joseph G. 1973. Blockbusting: Judicial and legislative response to real estate dealers' excesses. *De Paul Law Review* 22 (Spring): 818–38.

Byrne, James. 1992. Lenders set plans to eliminate unintentional discrimination; more bad numbers expected. *American Banker-Bond Buyer,* 21 September.

Feagin, Joe R., and Clarece B. Feagin. 1986. *Discrimination American style.* 2d ed. Malabar, Fla.: Kriege.

Feagin, Joe R., and Harlan Hahn. 1973. *Ghetto revolts.* New York: Macmillan.

Foundation for Change. 1974. *Fact sheets on institutional racism: White control and minority oppression.* New York: Foundation for Change.

Grezzo, Anthony D. 1972. *Mortgage credit risk analysis and servicing of delinquent mortgages.* Washington, D.C.: U.S. Department of Housing and Urban Development.

Helper, Rose. 1969. *Racial policies and practices of real estate brokers.* Minneapolis: University of Minnesota Press.

Jaynes, Gerald D., and Robin Williams, Jr. 1989. *A common destiny: Blacks and American society.* Washington, D.C.: National Academy Press.

Massey, Douglas S. 1992. Shrugging off racism. *Washington Post,* 17 May.

Massey, Douglas S., and Nancy A. Denton. 1987. Trends in segregation of blacks, Hispanics and Asians, 1970–1980. *American Sociological Review* 52:802–25.

Myrdal, Gunnar. 1944. *An American dilemma.* New York: McGraw-Hill.

National Advisory Commission on Civil Disorders. 1968. *Report of the National Advisory Commission on Civil Disorders.* Washington, D.C.: U.S. Government Printing Office.

National Opinion Research Center. 1990. *General social survey.* Chicago: University of Chicago.

Newsday. 1990. The walls between us. 15 October.

Newsweek. 1988. Black and white America. 7 March.

Office of Thrift Supervision. 1989. *Report on loan discrimination.* Washington, D.C.: Office of the Treasury.

Pearce, Diana M. 1976. Black, white, and many shades of gray: Real estate brokers and their racial practices. Ph.D. diss., University of Michigan.

USA Today. 1991. World of difference. 11 November.

U.S. Census Bureau. 1985. *American housing survey.* Washington, D.C.: U.S. Government Printing Office.

U.S. Commission on Civil Rights. 1974. *Mortgage money: Who gets it.* Washington, D.C.: U.S. Government Printing Office.

U.S. Senate. 1990. Transcript of Confirmation Hearings for David Souter, 14 September.

Vobejda, Barbara. 1992. Neighborhood racial patterns little changed. *Washington Post,* 18 March.

Wilson, William J. 1987. *The truly disadvantaged: The inner city, the underclass, and public policy.* Chicago: University of Chicago Press.

———. 1978. *The declining significance of race.* Chicago: University of Chicago Press.

CHAPTER 2

Are African Americans Still Hypersegregated?

by Nancy A. Denton

As a result of the analysis of trends and patterns of residential segregation following the 1980 U.S. census, the term *hypersegregation* became part of American public parlance (New York Times editorial 1992). Hypersegregation describes the extreme, multidimensional, cumulative residential segregation experienced by African Americans in some large metropolitan areas, mainly in the Northeast and Midwest. Statistically, it is based on the measurement of five underlying dimensions of residential segregation: evenness, isolation, concentration, centralization, and clustering (Massey and Denton 1989). Conceptually, it means that any way you look at it, African Americans are more highly segregated on more dimensions simultaneously than any other contemporary or historical group in American society.

Release and analysis of the detailed 1990 census data are just beginning. Early summary tabulations of the 1990 census show that the African-American population has grown by 13.2 percent since 1980, now numbering 30.0 million (Barringer 1991). Suburban areas also have many more African American residents than in the past; however, only about one-fourth of African Americans live in suburbs, so they are still the least suburbanized of any of the major racial/ethnic groups (Usdansky 1991). A recent analysis of the proportion of the African American population living in neighborhoods where more than 90 percent of the population was black revealed almost no change from 1980—30 percent in 1990 compared to 34 percent in 1980 (*Doig* 1991). While detailed analysis of residential patterns for all groups is currently under way, the importance of hypersegregation to the well-being of African Americans warrants prompt investigation of whether their hypersegregation has abated or worsened during the 1980s.

African American hypersegregation is important because no other major race/ethnic group was hypersegregated in 1980 (Massey and Denton 1989). Issues of the underclass are still with us (Wilson 1991a, 1991b; Jencks and

Peterson 1991; Lynn and McGeary 1990), and the deterioration of many inner-city areas continues. While the achievements and growth of the black middle-class are frequently noted (Nathan 1991; Landry 1987), the size of the African American middle class is small (Massey and Eggers 1990; Landry 1987). A related issue is the amount of discrimination even middle-class African Americans continue to experience in the course of their daily lives (Feagin 1991, 1992, this volume). Nationally, discrimination in housing continued to be extremely high, especially for African Americans, at the end of the 1980s (Turner, Struyk, and Yinger 1991). Thus, while it is important to not devalue what progress has been made, it is equally important to focus on the majority of the African American population that has been little affected by much of this progress.

Examination of hypersegregation is important to our knowledge of African American life because it combines many issues related to African American population distribution into a single analysis. Feagin and his respondents argue persuasively for the "pyramiding" and cumulative effects of the daily experiences of racial discrimination that whites tend to view as isolated incidents (Feagin 1991, 114–115). Hypersegregation suggests a similar pyramiding at the spatial level, implying drastic isolation, and describes the difficulty of escaping the effects of multidimensional layers of segregation piled on top of one another. It is one thing to be unevenly distributed across metropolitan neighborhoods and another to be denied access to the suburbs. Similarly, it is hard to interact with people different from oneself if one's neighborhood is filled only with people of one group, but it is harder still if all the neighborhoods in which your group lives are tightly clustered together to form a large ghetto. If these neighborhoods are small in area, the effects of crowding need to be examined. Not only do these five aspects of segregation interact to compose an extremely gloomy picture of life in the hypersegregated neighborhoods, they also raise extremely important moral questions in a free society. Questions of fairness, equity, and justice abound (e.g. Ryan 1981; Hochschild 1984, 1981), but fundamentally, hypersegregation poses an enormous challenge to the American Dream of "working one's way up."

For the reasons just outlined, this chapter will focus only on the segregation of African Americans. It will address two main questions: First, what is the hypersegregation status of African Americans in 1990? And second, what is the relationship between hypersegregation in 1980 and African American well-being during the 1980s? Investigation of the first question involves several parts: first, checking on the metropolitan areas where African Americans were hypersegregated in 1980 to see if they remain hypersegregated in 1990; second, looking at changes in the different dimensions of segregation in these metropolitan areas during the decade; and third, examining segregation scores for the nonhypersegregated metropolitan areas to see if any new areas became hypersegregated by 1990. These analyses will make up the first part of this chapter.

The second main question, the relationship of segregation and hypersegregation to African-American well-being, is important because we want to explore the negative effects of multidimensional segregation. While many people, particularly those active in fair housing, see integration as a fundamental goal (Saltman 1990), there are clearly two sides to the question. Some argue that segregation in and of itself is not bad and point to "zones of emergence" of middle-class black settlement (Nathan 1991). Others point to the advantages of segregation for maintaining culture and community (Leigh and McGhee 1986), as well as developing political power (O'Hare 1990). To look at this issue demands that we show the impact of segregation and hypersegregation on African American well-being.

Statistically, this question requires that we expand the logic in many of the analyses presented for the 1980 segregation indices. Those analyses sought to explain the high rates of segregation as owing to the characteristics of minorities, as well as characteristics of the metropolitan areas themselves. These spatial attainment models find that for blacks, personal characteristics are not very important in predicting their segregation (Massey and Denton 1987, 1988b). African American segregation does not decline as socioeconomic status rises (Denton and Massey 1988b). However, there is also a dynamic element to be considered: Living in segregated neighborhoods restricts opportunities to improve personal status characteristics such as jobs, school quality, and income.

Earlier studies of Philadelphia (Massey, Condran, and Denton 1987) and San Francisco (Massey and Fong 1990) have shown that living in segregated neighborhoods is associated with poorer housing, higher crime, worse health—in general, a worse living environment. Given that the metropolitan areas were segregated at this level in 1980, we can ask if it will make any difference down the road? It is one thing to be hypersegregated in a statistical sense and another if that hypersegregation adds a further negative impact to your life, over and beyond the normal effects of segregation.

DATA AND METHODS

Data for this analysis come from several sources. The 1980 segregation indices and SMSA characteristics are from the Massey-Denton segregation file, which covers sixty large metropolitan areas and matches census tract boundaries between 1970 and 1980. This file has been extensively analyzed and reported on elsewhere (Massey and Denton 1987, 1988b, 1989), so no further detail is needed here. For the 1990 segregation indices, I am indebted to the U.S. Bureau of the Census, which has calculated twenty indices of segregation for all the major race and ethnic groups for all metropolitan areas currently defined in the United States. The bureau shared the preliminary calculations of these indices with me for use in this chapter. In computing the indices for both years, the African American population was defined as non-Hispanic persons who reported their race as black on the census. The comparative group is non-Hispanic whites, so the segregation indices in this chapter report spatial patterns between African Americans and the numerical majority of persons in the United States. The areal units used in both years are census tracts, which are small, neighborhoodlike units with an average population size of five thousand to seven thousand persons.

As noted above, hypersegregation involves measuring residential segregation in different ways and then looking for patterns of high segregation across the different underlying dimensions. While these dimensions, their indices, and the mathematical properties thereof have all been explained in detail in other research (Massey and Denton 1988a, 1989), it is important that the basic concepts be reviewed here. Table 2.1 lists the dimensions, index names, and formulas for each of the five indices used to measure hypersegregation. Basically, the indices measure the concepts implied in their names, and a higher score on the index indicates a worse outcome or more segregation.

The first dimension, *evenness,* refers to each neighborhood or tract having the same proportion of African Americans as the metropolitan area as a whole (Duncan and Duncan 1957). It is usually interpreted as the proportion of either group that would have to move in order to reach an even distribution across neighborhoods. Note that *even* is defined by the metropolitanwide proportion of African Americans and thus varies substantially from one place to another. A score of zero on this index would mean that each neighborhood had the same proportion of African American residents as the metropolitan area as a whole. The more people that would have to move, the higher the segregation.

Table 2.1
Dimensions of Hypersegregation

Concept	*Index*	*Formula*
Evenness	Dissimilarity	$D = .5 * \sum_{i=1}^{n} |(x_i/X) - (y_i/Y)|$
Isolation	P-star	$P^* = \sum_{i=1}^{n}(x_i/X) * (y_i/t_i)$
Clustering	Spatial proximity	$SP = \dfrac{(XP_{xx} + YP_{yy})}{TP_{tt}}$
Concentration	CO	$CO = \dfrac{[\sum_{i=1}^{n} x_i a_i/X) / (\sum_{i=1}^{n} y_i a_i/Y)] - 1}{[\sum_{i=1}^{n1} t_i a_i/T_1) / (\sum_{i=1}^{n2} t_i a_i/T_2)] - 1}$
Centralization	CE	$CE = (\sum_{i=1}^{n} X_{i-1}A_i) - (\sum_{i=1}^{n} X_i A_{i-1})$

Symbols:

x_i = number of members of group x in tract i
y_i = number of members of group y in tract i
X = metropolitanwide total of group X
Y = metropolitanwide total of group Y
t_i = total population of tract i
T = total population of metropolitan area
a_i = area, in square miles, of tract i
n = number of census tracts
n1 and n2 refer to number of largest and smallest tracts
P_{xx} and P_{yy} and P_{tt} refer to average proximity between groups x, y, and t

For more detailed explanation of the symbols and formulae, see Massey and Denton, 1988a, 1989.

Note: All indices range from 0 to 1 in these date.

The second dimension, *isolation*, refers to just that—a lack of contact with people different from oneself, in this case non-Hispanic whites (Lieberson 1980). It is interpretable as the average probability that the first person you meet when you go outside in your neighborhood is of the same group as you. The more usual reporting of this index is to measure interaction between groups and, in the two-group case, the sum of the interaction and isolation probabilities is one (Massey and Denton 1989, 1988a). However, using the isolation index underscores a distinct experience of segregation and makes higher scores on all the indices mean greater segregation.

The third index, *clustering*, addresses the issue of contiguity among the black neighborhoods (White 1986). It measures what can be thought of as the checkerboard problem: Segregation is worse if all the red squares are on one side and all the black ones on the other than if the individually segregated neighborhoods are mixed up like the squares on a checkerboard. Clearly, interaction and integration with the larger society, as well as participation in jobs and amenities of the metropolitan area, are harder to achieve for people living in a large, contiguous ghetto rather than in an isolated ghetto neighborhood.

The fourth dimension, *concentration*, is essentially a density measure. It measures the group's share of the urban environment, intuitively making the comparison that a group which represents X percent of the population in a metropolitan area should occupy X percent of its physical land area, all else being equal. Since we know that segregation has traditionally restricted minorities to small, densely packed communities (Spear 1967; Hirsch 1983), we measure relative concentration by comparing the ratio of the actual African American-to-non-Hispanic whites proportion of the metropolitan land to the ratio that would be obtained if African Americans were maximally segregated and non-Hispanic whites were maximally dispersed (Massey and Denton 1989, 1988a). Thus an index of 1 would imply that concentration is as bad as the worst case scenario.

Centralization, the last index, refers to nearness to the central business district or downtown area. In most larger and older urban areas, much of the housing surrounding the downtown area is old, rundown, and creating what Park and Burgess (1925) called the zone of transition. Furthermore, as industry moves to the suburbs and new growth nodes with their own business and service centers grow up there (Garreau 1991), location near the downtown central business district is disadvantageous to African Americans, a fact researched as the spatial mismatch hypothesis (Kasarda 1988). This index also captures some of the lack of suburbanization of the African American population (Massey and Denton 1988b).

To examine the dynamic effects of hypersegregation in 1980 on the lives of African Americans requires socioeconomic data for a later date than the 1980 census. Detailed data on African American social and economic well-being at the metropolitan level are not yet available from the 1990 census. While much metropolitan-level data are available intercensally, little of it is for specific race/ethnic groups. Furthermore, in order to see if hypersegregation makes any difference, we need to know segregation and socioeconomic status of black Americans in metropolitan areas other than those in which they are hypersegregated. Fortunately, by pooling waves of the American Housing Survey (AHS), we can construct a data set that contains a variety of well-being indicators specifically for black Americans and covers most of the hypersegregated metropolitan areas plus a good number of others. With these data it is possible to measure African American well-being in the later part of the 1980s.

The AHS covers eleven metropolitan areas each year and has a four-year rotation schedule, so a total of forty-four metropolitan areas are included. A complete list of these Metropolitan Statistical Areas and some summary characteristics for them can be found in the appendix. The sample size for each metropolitan area was approximately 4,250, with the sample constructed to have equal numbers of owners and renters. All information is collected by personal interview. While the data are of extremely high quality, they are not precisely comparable to 1980 and 1990 census data. In particular, the sample size is much larger in the census, the census is not conducted in person, and there is a much broader range of questions asked on the AHS. While the differences will not matter for this chapter, interested readers are referred to the technical documentation found in the appendices to each volume of Current Housing Reports (U.S. Bureau of the Census 1985, 1986, 1987, 1988).

Two points should be noted about the use of the AHS data in this chapter. First, the data cover a four-year span from 1985 through 1988. To the extent that economic conditions changed during that period, and since the socioeconomic status conditions are measured at varying intervals following the measurement of hypersegregation in the 1980 census, the analysis is confounded. However, the small sample size each year and the association among particular metropolitan areas, survey year, and level residential segregation—that is, Chicago and New York are not in the same wave—means that normal statistical controls for these intervals/years are not possible and do not really measure period effects. Second, of the forty-four MSAs covered in the survey, only forty-one are used in the analyses reported here. Two (northern New

Jersey[1] and Hartford, Connecticut) were dropped because they were not part of the Massey-Denton data set; and one (Fort Worth, Texas) was combined with another (Dallas) to match the geography on the Massey-Denton data set. The combination was done with weighted averages to control for the different population sizes of the two MSAs. However, all regions and MSA sizes are represented so no substantial bias should result from these deletions, although just as the original Massey-Denton data set referred to only large SMSAs, so does this analysis. Anaheim, California, and Salt Lake City, Utah, do not appear in selected analyses that require knowing the ownership status of black households, since they had an insufficient number of blacks in the sample to protect the confidentiality of the respondents and provide reliable statistical estimates.

The AHS collects a wealth of information about persons, homes, and neighborhoods, more than could possibly be used in a single research paper. Since we are interested in African American social and economic well-being, I operationalize well-being to refer to housing, neighborhood, and personal measures of socioeconomic status. The exact variables chosen to represent these three areas of life quality may be seen by looking ahead to table 2.3. Quality of urban life has been variably measured in the literature (Blomquist, Berger, and Hoehn 1988; Pacione 1990), and defining it is not the focus of this chapter; therefore, these indicators will serve well here. A wide range of measures allows the exploration not only of the effects of residential segregation on well-being, but also the investigation of whether different dimensions of segregation relate to different aspects of well-being.

HYPERSEGREGATION IN 1990

We begin to answer the simple question posed in the title of the chapter by examining segregation scores for all five indices in 1990 and the change in these indices from 1980 for the sixteen metropolitan areas that were hypersegregated in 1980 (table 2.2).

The metropolitan areas are grouped by degree of hypersegregation in 1980 and criteria for determining hypersegregation. The first six were hypersegregated on all five dimensions, while the next four were hypersegregated on four of the five dimensions, using the stringent criteria applied in the original hypersegregation paper (Massey and Denton 1989). These criteria varied for each index, namely above .6 on evenness and clustering, above .7 on isolation and concentration, and above .8 on centralization. The next six are also hypersegregated if one applies a simpler criterion, namely being above .6 on at least four of the indices of segregation (Massey and Denton 1993). It may seem artificial to play with the criteria and odd to want to increase the number of metropolitan areas experiencing a bad thing. However, doing so underscores the arbitrariness of the statistical definition of hypersegregation and forces us to focus on the social and economic ramifications of the concept. Above all, it avoids the impression that an area that scores .58 on a particular index (hypersegregation) is in markedly better shape segregation-wise than some-place else scoring a score of .60 (hypersegregation).

Panel A of table 2.2 answers the title question directly: Yes, African Americans who lived in hypersegregated metropolitan areas in 1980 are still hypersegregated in 1990. Only two metropolitan areas, Atlanta and Dallas, were classified as hypersegregated in 1980 and could not be so classified in 1990. The 1990 score for concentration in Atlanta is .590, while that for isolation in Dallas is .579, both just barely outside the range categorized as hypersegregated. African Americans in the Baltimore, Chicago, Cleveland, Detroit, Milwaukee, and Philadelphia MSAs remain hypersegregated in 1990. Their segregation indices are above .6 on all five dimensions of segregation. Even if we use the more stringent criteria for hypersegregation, five of these six metropolitan areas remain high on all five indices, and Chicago—the one that does not—has a centralization score of .791, just barely below the more stringent cutoff of .800, but well above the simpler criteria of .6.

The remaining eight metropolitan areas in table 2.2 also remain hypersegregated in 1990. African Americans in Gary, Indiana; Los Angeles; Newark, New Jersey; St. Louis; Buffalo, New York; Indianapolis, Kansas City, and New York are highly segregated on at least four of the indices using the .6 criteria. Using the more stringent criteria, Newark joins the metropolitan areas in group one because in 1990 it is highly segregated on all five criteria, due to a 9-point increase in black isolation there. In New York, African American isolation increased by nearly 19 points, so it is hypersegregated in 1990 under the more stringent criteria, as well. St. Louis is not hypersegregated under the stringent criteria because its isolation index declined to .695, and Buffalo, Indianapolis, and Kansas City would not be hypersegregated using the stringent criteria, just as they were not in 1980.

The nearly total lack of change in classification of hypersegregation among those metropolitan areas so classified in 1980 does not address the issue of improvement in segregation. Given the extremely high values for the segregation indices in many of the SMSAs in 1980, it is possible for segregation to decline substantially but still remain above the cutoff criteria for hypersegregation. Panel B of table 2.2 presents the absolute value change in the indices over the

Table 2.2
Hypersegregation in U.S. Metropolitan Areas, 1980 and 1990

Panel A: 1990 Indices

	% Black	Evenness	Isolation	Clustering	Concentration	Centralization
Hypersegregated according to stringent criteria:						
Criteria:		>.6	>.7	>.6	>.7	>.8
All five dimensions:						
Baltimore	25.7	.714	.706	.602	.766	.849
Chicago	21.7	.858	.841	.770	.834	.791
Cleveland	19.3	.851	.809	.791	.921	.889
Detroit	21.4	.876	.823	.864	.943	.916
Milwaukee	13.6	.828	.725	.739	.933	.944
Philadelphia	18.8	.772	.722	.700	.714	.830
Four dimensions:						
Gary	19.2	.899	.842	.484	.892	.843
Los Angeles	10.5	.731	.690	.659	.717	.819
Newark	22.4	.825	.785	.786	.935	.887
St. Louis	17.2	.770	.695	.501	.896	.916
Hypersegregated according to less stringent criteria:						
Criteria:		>.6	>.6	>.6	>.6	>.6
All five dimensions:						
Buffalo	11.2	.818	.638	.487	.931	.928
Indianapolis	13.7	.743	.610	.398	.919	.922
Kansas City	12.7	.726	.617	.396	.876	.897
New York	23.2	.822	.816	.464	.875	.778
Four dimensions:						
Atlanta	25.8	.678	.665	.469	.594	.770
Dallas	15.8	.631	.579	.331	.692	.825
Average	18.3	.784	.723	.591	.840	.863

Table 2.2 continued
Hypersegregation in U.S. Metropolitan Areas, 1980 and 1990

Panel B: 1980–1990 Differences

	% Black	Evenness	Isolation	Clustering	Concentration	Centralization
All five dimensions:						
Baltimore	.5	-.033	-.017	-.020	.003	-.008
Chicago	1.8	-.020	.013	-.023	-.053	-.081
Cleveland	1.3	-.024	.005	.048	-.006	-.009
Detroit	1.1	.009	.050	.018	.101	-.008
Milwaukee	2.9	-.011	.030	.050	-.011	-.007
Philadelpia	.3	-.016	.026	.027	-.043	-.025
Four dimensions:						
Gary	-.3	-.007	.069	-.077	.023	-.044
Los Angeles	-1.8	-.080	.086	-.106	.022	-.040
Newark	1.5	.009	.093	.031	.016	.028
St. Louis	-.2	-.044	-.034	.237	.003	-.015
All five dimensions:						
Buffalo	.2	.024	.003	.044	.049	.044
Indianapolis	.3	-.019	-.013	-.013	.115	-.020
Kansas City	-.4	-.063	-.072	-.065	.019	-.024
New York	2.9	.003	.189	-.004	-.017	-.017
Four dimensions:						
Atlanta	-1.3	-.084	-.049	.071	-.092	-.057
Dallas	1.8	-.140	-.066	-.003	-.001	.076
Average		-.031	.020	.013	.008	-.013
Average Decline		-.045	-.042	-.039	-.032	-.027
Average Increase		.011	.056	.066	.039	.049

decade. The data do not allow for an optimistic interpretation. Not only are many of the magnitudes of the changes small, but nearly half (34 out of 80 or 43%) of the changes are positive, indicating that segregation on that dimension worsened between 1980 and 1990. Every single metropolitan area on the list, including those that were discussed above as no longer being hypersegregated, showed an increase on at least one dimension of segregation. In Newark and Buffalo, segregation increased on all five dimensions, and in Detroit it increased on four dimensions. Among the sixteen metropolitan areas on the list, isolation increased in ten, concentration in nine, clustering in eight, evenness in four, and centralization in three.

The bottom lines in table 2.2 list average changes, with the overall average showing that three dimensions—isolation, clustering, and concentration—increased slightly between 1980 and 1990, while evenness and centralization declined. This pattern of changes implies that while African Americans were able to move to more neighborhoods and possibly more suburban neighborhoods in total, the number of them who were able to do so was small relative to their total population. In particular, the increase in isolation and clustering belies any dismantling of the large urban ghettos. Instead, it implies a continuation of the pattern seen between 1970 and 1980, a period when the number of neighborhoods with no minority residents declined precipitously, but the level of minority presence in many of these neighborhoods remained quite low, resulting in integration from the neighborhood perspective but segregation from the population perspective (Denton and Massey 1991).

Given that the changes were not overwhelmingly in the same direction, I also list the average positive and negative changes for each index, representing gains or declines in segregation. For all dimensions except evenness, the average segregation increase is larger than the average decrease, and for clustering and centralization the average increase is nearly twice the average decrease. If we arbitrarily consider changes of .050 points or less as simply random fluctuations, then Baltimore, Cleveland, Philadelphia, and Buffalo had no change in their segregation patterns at all between 1980 and 1990. Atlanta, Dallas, Kansas City, and Los Angeles had changes of this magnitude on at least three of their dimensions, and the majority of these represent improvements in segregation. Detroit changed on two dimensions, but increased on both, while Chicago decreased on two, and Gary had one positive and one negative change of this magnitude.

A more detailed look at the change over the decade in the indices for specific areas suggests some startling findings, especially if one calculates the percent change (data not shown). Evenness declines nearly 6 percent on average, with particularly large declines in Dallas (-18.2%), Atlanta (-11%), Los Angeles (-9.9%), and Kansas City (-8%). Clearly, new areas were "opened" to African American settlement in these communities. For centralization, the other index that showed overall improvement during the last decade, the largest declines were in Chicago (-9.3%) and Atlanta (-6.9%). It will take more detailed analysis of the 1990 census data to be sure, but it is possible that African American suburbanization is increasing in these cities. However, unlike the situation with respect to evenness, where the gains were all quite small in percentage terms, two metropolitan areas show large gains in centralization: Buffalo (+5%) and Dallas (+10.1%).

For the indices that show an overall worsening during the decade, the percentage changes point to some particularly disquieting results for particular metropolitan areas. African American isolation increased 30 percent in the New York metropolitan area, a change that overwhelms the small declines or insignificant change on the other dimensions of segregation there. Isolation also increased nearly 15 percent in Newark, which mirrors New York's pattern of modest changes on the other indices, albeit all upward. Isolation also increased over 14 percent in Los Angeles, but clustering declined by nearly the same percent, suggesting the jockeying for places between the black and Mexican communities there. Isolation increases of this magnitude, on top of base indices that were already in the high range, can only imply drastic separation from the rest of society for African Americans in these metropolitan areas.

Changes in the clustering index are perhaps the most interesting of all the dimensions. Overall, it changed about 2 percent, but when it declined it was by nearly 7 percent, and when it increased it was by 17 percent on average. Clustering dominates the story for St. Louis, where a huge (89.8%) increase is a function of its moderate clustering in 1980 and hence the low base from which the change was computed. Other areas with large increases in clustering include Atlanta (+17.8), Buffalo (+9.9), and Milwaukee (+7.3%). Increases in clustering imply that the ghetto is becoming more densely packed. Decreases in clustering indicate either that there are holes opening up inside the ghetto, possibly as a result of gentrification, or that minority neighborhoods have leapfrogged to other parts of the urban landscape. A decline in clustering of 13.7 percent is found in Gary, though the positive effect is counterbalanced by a nearly 10 percent increase in African American isolation there.

Changes in concentration were more moderate, either a 4 percent decline or a 5 percent increase, on average. Concentration is most important for the segregation pattern in Detroit, where it increased 12 percent, and Indianapolis, where the increase was 14.3 percent. However, in the latter, the other dimensions of segregation declined, while Detroit also had a 6.5 increase in isolation. Increases in both isolation and concentration imply growth in densely packed all-African American neighborhoods. Concentration declined by 13.4 percent in Atlanta and by about 6 percent in Chicago and Philadelphia, indicating some abatement of density in the minority neighborhoods in these cities.

The only possible conclusion from these data is that hypersegregation persists and often is worsening in nearly all the metropolitan areas that were hypersegregated in 1980. Atlanta's and Dallas's paths out of hypersegregation involved having low indices on some of the dimensions to start with, as well as substantial declines in evenness and concentration in Atlanta and evenness and isolation in Dallas, declines which were not offset by their respective rises in clustering and centralization.

The next issue to be addressed in the examination of hypersegregation of African Americans in 1990 is whether they have become hypersegregated in any new metropolitan areas since 1980. Unfortunately, as shown in table 2.3, the answer is yes, African Americans can be classified as hypersegregated in 15 additional metropolitan areas, using the simple criteria of greater than .6 on at least four dimensions of segregation. None of them would be classified as hypersegregated using the more stringent criteria, although Birmingham, Alabama, and Miami-Hialeah are extremely close, with indices of .696 for the cutoff of .7.

Overwhelmingly these new areas are located either in the South or the Midwest. Five of them—Birmingham; Cincinnati, Ohio; Miami-Hialeah; New Orleans; and Washington, D.C.—were part of the original Massey-Denton data set of sixty metropolitan areas. Thus they were included in the original analysis of hypersegregation (Massey and Denton 1989) and represent true additions to the list of hypersegregated metropolitan areas. One, Oakland, California, was combined with the San Francisco metropolitan area in the original analysis since it was based on 1980 definitions of metropolitan areas. Thus it is not clear whether it represents an addition to the hypersegregated list. The remaining nine areas hypersegregated in 1990 are Albany, Georgia; Baton Rouge, Louisiana; Beaumont-Port Arthur, Texas; Benton Harbor, Michigan; Flint, Michigan; Monroe, Louisiana; Saginaw, Michigan; Savannah, Georgia; and Trenton, New Jersey. Since they were not included in the original data set used to assess hypersegregation, it is not known whether they are newly hypersegregated metropolitan areas in 1990 or if they remain so since

Table 2.3
New Hypersegregated Metropolitan Areas, 1990

Metropolitan Area	Evenness	Isolation	Clustering	Concentration	Centralization
Albany, GA MSA	.631	.719	.400	.642	.826
Baton Rouge, LA MSA	.639	.643	.341	.606	.745
Beaumont-Port Arthur, TX MSA	.707	.661	.335	.784	.665
Benton Harbor, MI MSA	.745	.642	.379	.829	.712
Birmingham, AL MSA	.717	.696	.455	.771	.847
Cincinnati, OH-KY-IN PMSA	.758	.610	.328	.895	.852
Flint, MI MSA	.812	.741	.518	.893	.869
Miami-Hialeah, FL PMSA	.718	.748	.489	.696	.832
Monroe, LA MSA	.714	.725	.456	.624	.830
New Orleans, LA MSA	.688	.719	.388	.708	.830
Oakland, CA PMSA	.680	.604	.405	.763	.774
Saginaw-Bay City-Midland, MI	.821	.705	.362	.907	.692
Savannah, GA MSA	.612	.675	.317	.662	.872
Trenton, NJ PMSA	.680	.619	.326	.751	.764
Washington, DC-MD-VA MSA	.661	.667	.569	.628	.831

1980.[2] Either way, they are definitely hypersegregated now, with all the concomitant disadvantage that implies for African Americans living there.

To summarize, the phenomenon identified as hypersegregation in the analyses of the 1980 residential segregation data has not abated during the last ten years. Fourteen of the original 16 metropolitan areas categorized as hypersegregated remain so, and 15 additional ones are hypersegregated based on 1990 segregation indices. The addition of cosmopolitan places with large African American populations, such as Washington, D.C., and New Orleans, to the list of hypersegregated metropolitan areas is cause for grave concern. Regarding the separate dimensions of segregation, on average, increases were greater than decreases for all dimensions except evenness, and for clustering and centralization the average increase is twice the average decrease. We now turn to an examination of the linkage between hypersegregation and African-American social and economic well-being.

Effect of Hypersegregation

As noted above, it is one thing to argue that hypersegregation is worse than simply high levels of segregation overall, and another to establish that it makes a difference in people's lives. Previous efforts to link hypersegregation to African American social and economic well-being have focused on individual metropolitan areas (Massey and Fong 1990; Massey, Condran, and Denton 1987). While the spatial attainment model postulates that the segregation is caused in part by characteristics of the segregated group, prior research found that the characteristics of African Americans explained far less of their segregation than did the characteristics of others groups (Massey and Denton 1987, 1988b). Furthermore, the link between segregated living conditions and poor quality of life is well established (Massey, Condran, and Denton 1987; Massey and Fong 1990), and the reciprocal influence of segregation on socioeconomic status and vice versa is part of the endogenous nexus of segregation documented by Galster and Keeney (1988). While it is beyond the scope of this chapter to propose a structural model of hypersegregation, especially given the lack of 1990 census results and the concomitant limitation on sample size, some preliminary investigations of the link between hypersegregation and African American social and economic well-being are warranted.

One way to ask whether hypersegregation makes a difference is simply to compare measures of social and economic well-being in metropolitan areas that are hypersegregated and not hypersegregated. Table 2.4 lists an assortment of such measures, chosen from the AHS and grouped into three categories: housing, neighborhood, and socioeconomic status. As noted above, the AHS contains a wealth of information, and these particular variables were selected both to reduce the number to a manageable size and to provide a broad array of information about African American well-being. Eight metropolitan areas are coded as hypersegregated, representing all those that were hypersegregated according to the stringent criteria except Newark and Gary, which are not included in the AHS sample. Choosing the more stringent criteria defines hypersegregation as clearly as possible.[3]

Four of the housing variables differ significantly between the hypersegregated and nonhypersegregated metropolitan areas: the proportion of blacks living in housing built after 1970, the median age of the housing, the mean number of years the housing was owned, and the relative housing value (measured as the ratio of black median housing value to median housing value for the MSA). In hypersegregated metropolitan areas, most blacks live in housing that was built

Table 2.4
Selected Indicators of African American Social and
Economic Well-Being, 1985–1988 (Means)

Indicator	Hypersegregated	NOT Hypersegregated
Housing		
% Home owners	42.9	41.7
% Built 1970 or later	10.2	29.7**
Median year built	1940	1955**
Mean years owned	14.3	12.3**
% Structure good	41.4	40.5
% Structure has severe problems	2.7	2.4
% Structure has moderate problems	8.7	11.5
Relative value	0.59	0.73**
Neighborhood		
% Neighborhood good	32.0	38.3**
% Owners say neighborhood good	37.4	44.5*
% Renters say neighborhood good	27.9	33.4*
% Neighborhood has problems	46.6	41.3*
% Poor city services	3.3	2.4
% Near commercial property	12.2	16.0
% Problems with people	22.3	17.3*
% Government displacement	34.7	16.0**
% Center city	72.5	63.4
Socioeconomic Status		
% Income > $50,000	9.6	9.9
% Income < $10,000	35.4	29.3*
% Poverty (< 99%)	29.8	24.5
Estimated labor force participation		
(LFP) household head	51.8	62.8**
% Moved in last year	19.7	27.4**
% College four or more years	11.2	15.4**
% No savings	71.4	66.4
% Washing machine	57.4	54.9
N	8	33

* = p < .10   ** = p < .05

Note: Ownership, years owned, relative housing value, and owners' and renters' opinions of the neighborhood are based on only thirty-one nonhypersegregated cases, as Salt Lake City and Anaheim did not have enough blacks to separate them into owners and renters.

around 1940, and only 10 percent live in housing built since 1970; in other cities, most blacks live in housing built about 1955, and 30 percent live in post-1970 housing. African Americans have owned their homes on average two years longer in the hypersegregated metropolitan areas; in hypersegregated metropolitan areas, their homes are worth only 60 percent of the median value, compared to 73 percent in nonhypersegregated metropolitan areas. Ignoring for the moment criticisms of the current practitioners of the building trade compared to the craftspeople of yesteryear, new housing tends to imply better living conditions. Post-1970 housing also means that its occupancy was subject to the provisions of the 1968 Fair Housing Law, which explicitly banned discrimination in housing. New housing can also imply social mobility—that is, the reward for hard work is often a newer, better house. Before accepting this difference at face value, however, one must also remember that smaller, fast-growing metro areas in the South and West also have more post-1970 housing than the older ones in the Northeast and Midwest. So some of the difference picked up by the housing variable is reflecting location as well.

The variables that do not show a significant difference reinforce this interpretation. Just over 40 percent of the householders own their home in both types of metropolitan area, and there are no significant differences in how they feel about their particular structure. While we cannot adjudicate between them, two scenarios are suggested here: One is that the hypersegregated metropolitan areas have historically had a more heterogeneous black population, some of whom were able to buy houses a while ago, but little progress has been made of late.

> While blacks of all classes kept to themselves during the 1930's, 1940's, and 1950's, middle-class blacks especially were diligent in avoiding situations that reminded them of the dilemma of their status. Not only would they not attempt to have dinner at white restaurants downtown, they eschewed alike movies in the segregated balconies of white theaters and the substandard black theaters, preferring parties and dinners at home. In this context, a home assumed greater importance among blacks than whites. It was the symbol of success in a society that allowed them precious few opportunities for conspicuous achievement, and it was an oasis in a hostile environment. (Landry 1987, 79)

A second scenario is that the hypersegregated cities represent both the best and worst of worlds for blacks—while the majority of the black population is hypersegregated in places like Chicago or Philadelphia, these are also large cosmopolitan cities where highly skilled and highly educated Blacks are best able to "make it."

When we look at characteristics of the neighborhood, many more differences emerge. African Americans in nonhypersegregated metropolitan areas are more satisfied with their neighborhood and more likely to describe it as "good"; the difference is about 6 percentage points for both owners and renters. More specifically, persons in nonhypersegregated metropolitan areas are less likely to report that one of their neighborhood problems is the people who live there (17% vs. 22%). Two of these measures can be interpreted to tap a dimension of discrimination or "targeting"—lack of city services and being displaced by the government. While the former shows no difference, government displacement is reported as the reason for moving nearly twice as often in hypersegregated metropolitan areas (35% vs. 16%). The fact that there is no difference between the proportion of African Americans living in the center city in the two types of metropolitan areas is evidence that restrictions on black housing choice are universal. In both types of metropolitan area, African Americans overwhelmingly live in the center city.

Differences in socioeconomic status add few surprises to the picture painted thus far—the proportion of blacks with high incomes doesn't differ much, but the percent with incomes less than $10,000 does—indicating that economic opportunities for poor people are somewhat better in the nonhypersegregated cities. Other indicators that imply what I call "mobility potential"—the ability to affect one's own situation—also differ by type of area. African Americans in nonhypersegregated metropolitan areas are more likely to be employed (63% vs. 52%),[4] to have completed four or more years of college (15% vs. 11%), and to have moved in the last year (27% vs. 20%). While in some circles moving is seen as a sign of instability, and certainly the poor move more frequently than the rich, changing residence can imply social mobility when one is considering the circumstances of a group that has historically been confined to ghettos.

While differences between the hypersegregated and nonhypersegregated metropolitan areas are clear from the analysis of the means, the distinction between being hypersegregated and not hypersegregated is one of degree, as discussed above. Many of the metropolitan areas included in this analysis have substantial African American versus non-Hispanic white segregation. We can use multiple regression to explore the link between hypersegregation, segregation, and African-American well-being. A further analysis will examine the role of each of the five dimensions of segregation separately to see if particular dimensions relate more strongly to one aspect of social and economic well-being than another. If they do, it will provide further evidence of the multifacetedness of segregation.

Table 2.5 presents the unstandardized OLS[5] regression coefficients showing the effect of hypersegregation, represented as a dummy variable coded 1 for the eight hypersegregated cities, and 0 otherwise, and the mean of the segregation indices for all five dimensions on measures of African-American well-being. Though hypersegregation is measured using the other dimensions of segregation, the correlation between hypersegregation and the mean segregation score is moderate ($r = .598$).

While the mean segregation score is often significant, hypersegregation is significant over and above segregation for only three outcomes: percent living in center city, percent earning more than $50,000 per year, and percent who report severe structural problems with their structure. The fact that living in a hypersegregated metropolitan area significantly *lowers* the percent of African Americans living in the center city at the same time it significantly *raises* the proportion with high household incomes at first seems contrary to expectations that hypersegregation worsens an already bad situation. But examination of the whole equation shows that hypersegregation is working in the opposite direction from the mean segregation, and thus is adding information about the lives of African Americans in these metropolitan areas. Statistically, it is reflecting multicollinearity to some degree, but it is also interpretable as showing that in these large cosmopolitan cities, African Americans who "make it" do well.

Mean segregation is an unsatisfactory summary measure for the reality of segregation, however, because it does not take advantage of the information contained in the indices representing each of the separate dimensions. In table 2.6, I regress the well-being indicators on the hypersegregation dummy variable, plus the indices for each dimension separately. Again, the indices are frequently working against each other because of their interconnection, but hypersegregation remains significant for severe structural problems and proportion living in the center city. It also lowers the labor force participation of household heads and increases the percentage reporting that one of the problems with their neighborhood is the people who live there.

When we look at the separate dimensions, however, an interesting set of patterns emerges. First, the evenness dimension, measured by the index of dissimilarity, the most widely used measure of segregation, is only significant for a few outcomes. In particular, it lowers home ownership, the percentage who think the structure is good, the percentage who think the neighborhood

Table 2.5
OLS Regressions of MSA Mean Segregation and Hypersegregation on Selected Indicators of African American Social and Economic Well-Being

Outcome		Mean		
	Hypersegregation	Segregation	Intercept	R^2
Housing				
% Owners	5.97	-22.92*	55.10***	.03
% Built 1970 or later	0.06	-85.07***	77.59***	.63
Median age	-2.59	-56.88***	1987.3***	.42
% Structure good	2.09	-5.09	43.37***	-.03
% Structure severe problems	-1.47*	7.52***	-1.79	.20
% Structure moderate problems	-4.89	9.34	6.22	-.02
Years owned	0.63	6.19	8.71***	.14
Relative housing value	-0.02	-0.62***	1.10***	.46
Neighborhood				
% Neighborhood good	-2.79	-15.20*	46.86***	.21
% Owners say neighborhood good	-2.63	-21.49*	57.34***	.16
% Renters say neighborhood good	-2.66	-13.65	41.34***	.12
% Neighborhood has oroblems	3.36	8.42	36.56***	.09
% Poor city services	-0.13	4.24***	0.05	.16
% Near commercial property	-3.33	-2.30	17.32***	.01
% Problems with people	2.94	9.00	12.22***	.13
% Government displacement	6.22	54.29***	-14.57	.26
% Center city	-14.47**	8 0.75***	22.95**	.30
Socioeconomic Status				
% Income > $50,000	5.31**	-24.34***	23.58***	.22
% Income < $10,000	-0.86	30.09***	12.43**	.20
% Poverty (< 99%)	-2.11	32.13***	6.45	.21
Estimated LFP household head	-6.13	-20.82	74.48***	.16
% Moved in last year	-1.05	-28.67***	43.48***	.29
% College four or more years	0.72	-21.61***	27.59***	.27
% No savings	-2.47	32.37***	48.25***	.23
% Washing machine	2.14	1.58	54.02***	-.04

*p < .10.   **p < .05.   ***p < .01.

Note: Ownership, years owned, relative housing value, and owners' and renters' opinions of the neighborhood are based on only 39 cases, as Salt Lake City and Anaheim did not have enough blacks to separate them into owners and renters.

Table 2.6
OLS Regressions of Hypersegregation, Five Dimensions of Segregation on

Outcome	Hypersegregation	Evenness	Isolation	Clustering
Housing				
% Owners	6.98	-42.52*	26.93***	-8.46
% Built after 1970	-0.76	30.40	-4.54	-28.98*
Median age	-1.75	10.45	12.12	-26.85
% Structure is good	3.36	-28.97**	11.93*	-3.14
% Structure has severe problems	-1.79*	4.80	-1.99	3.12
% Structure has moderate problems	-3.22	-34.07	25.86**	-2.78
Years owned	1.74	-8.01	6.27**	-2.46
Relative housing value	0.004	0.30	0.038	-0.033**
Neighborhood				
% Neighborhood is good	0.92	-38.25***	22.28***	-15.53*
% Owners say neighborhood is good	-0.61	-41.58**	21.81**	-10.48
% Renters say neighborhood is good	1.28	-25.94	17.72**	-17.71*
% Neighborhood has problems	1.75	25.57	-20.57***	8.39
% Poor city services	0.27	-0.29	2.43	-0.72
% Near commercial property	-2.00	43.96**	-2.10	-14.36
% Problems with people	4.85*	18.28	-14.89**	-3.09
% Government displacement	6.59	-27.77	77.39***	-2.16
% Center city	-16.49*	-0.65	-16.04	35.74
Socioeconomic Status				
% Income > $50,000	1.71	3.47	-10.64	6.51
% Income < $10,000	4.41	-9.34	10.86	-8.93
% Poverty (< 99%)	3.93	-12.97	15.11	-11.47
Estimated LFP household head	-10.87*	50.96*	-2.57	-1.73
% Moved last year	-0.18	30.82	-26.13***	-10.41
% College four or more years	-2.39	8.77	-16.66***	6.50
% No savings	-0.31	-21.28	21.17**	1.03
% Washing machine	5.24	-82.86***	32.40***	-3.11

Selected Indicators of African American Social and Economic Well-Being

Concentration	Centralization	Intercept	R^2
-11.45	-8.80	74.56***	.24
-42.22***	-2.07	45.90**	.66
-32.63***	1.24	1968.22***	.44
3.33	-8.86	60.54***	.06
2.92*	-1.38	-1.35	.20
7.15	-21.19*	36.03**	.12
5.02*	-2.27	14.02***	.20
-0.367***	0.098	0.75***	.49
2.17	-16.03**	69.41***	.47
-2.53	-16.31	80.25***	.30
5.39	-17.03*	57.71***	.28
0.41	18.55**	16.17	.28
1.04	0.60	0.56	.09
-11.54*	10.72	-10.88	.07
8.87*	8.60	0.18	.36
-8.68	-17.39	18.74	.48
27.45*	41.92**	16.70	.33
-16.36***	14.77**	8.93	.37
24.89***	-19.96*	33.78**	.33
25.45***	-19.21*	29.12**	.36
-36.99***	25.85*	31.53*	.35
-4.57	4.47	20.35	.39
-12.11**	14.73**	11.11	.43
13.30*	-7.56	68.78***	.24
4.33	14.87	82.19***	.29

*p < .10   **p < .05   ***p < .01

Note: Ownership, years owned, relative housing value, and owners' and renters' opinions of the neighborhood are based on only thirty-nine cases as Salt Lake City and Anaheim did not have enough blacks to separate them into owners and renters.

is good, and the percentage of households with washing machines. Dissimilarity raises the percentage who live near commercial property and the labor force participation of the household head.

Second, isolation is significantly related to many more outcomes than evenness, and it is particularly significant, in a negative direction, for indicators of "mobility potential"—namely, moving, four or more years of college, savings, and having a washing machine. For the housing indicators, high isolation increases ownership, thinking the structure is good or has only moderate problems, and the number of years it has been owned. The impact of isolation on the neighborhood outcomes is interesting in that many of the signs of the significant coefficients are opposite what would be expected. The isolation dimension is closely linked substantively and statistically to the evenness dimension and thus isolation is working in conjunction with evenness. For the likelihood of being displaced by the government, isolation is the only dimension that is significant, and it raises the chance of that outcome substantially. Clearly, the political opportunity to disrupt only one part of the electorate is tempting in many metropolitan areas.

Clustering, the third dimension of segregation, significantly lowers the relative housing value ratio, that is the ratio of African American median housing value to that for the metropolitan area as a whole. It is also negatively related to the proportion of housing built after 1970 and to thinking that the neighborhood is good. While it is hardly surprising that in metropolitan areas with large, contiguous ghettos, African Americans are more likely to say their neighborhood is not good, these results show that little new housing is built there, and the ghetto effectively isolates the African American home owner from the larger real estate market.

The fourth dimension of segregation, concentration, is particularly linked to the well-being of African Americans through their socioeconomic status. It significantly lowers the proportion with incomes over $50,000, labor-force participation, and college degrees, while raising the percent in poverty and with incomes less than $10,000. It also significantly lowers relative housing value and implies living in significantly older housing. Looked at in light of the focus on the underclass, one interpretation of this pattern of effects for concentration is an identification of underclass areas.

Centralization, the last dimension of segregation, is clearly linked to concentration, and its effect is to temper the effects of concentration for many of the outcomes where it is significant. It is hardly surprising that centralization is significantly related to percentage living in the center city, and going along with the idea that the suburbs represent a higher quality of life, it increases the percentage who say their neighborhood has problems and decreases the percentage who say their neighborhood is good.

Overall, then, this descriptive analysis has enabled us to specifically link hypersegregation to severe structural problems, problems with people in the neighborhood, center-city residence, labor force participation, and high household income. It has also shown how the various dimensions of segregation, even though they are conceptually and statistically related, do link to specific aspects of well-being and thus are not all measuring the same thing. I will draw upon some of these specific linkages in the discussion and conclusion section that follows.

DISCUSSION AND CONCLUSIONS

This analysis has focused on only one group, African Americans, defined as persons who reported to the census that their race was black and that they were not of Hispanic origin. While they represent the largest U.S. minority group and are important to study in their own right, it is hard to portray their situation accurately until the situation of other groups is also known. Given that no metropolitan areas had hypersegregated Hispanic or Asian populations in 1980, it is unlikely that any will in 1990. But a good guess, even if accurate, does not substitute for the actual data. Furthermore, the rate of Asian and Hispanic immigration (and migration in the case of Puerto Ricans) has been substantial during the 1980s, a factor that makes increases in their segregation somewhat likely.

It will be interesting to see the dimensional structure of their segregation to gauge how metropolitan areas are coping with the influx. Their increasing numbers not only provide an important context in which to interpret the results for African Americans discussed here, but make the study of interminority segregation of great interest as well. Racial issues arise for groups other than African Americans, particularly Caribbean Hispanics (Denton and Massey 1988a). But however these results inform and flesh out those for African Americans, the pattern is clear, and the news is not good.

This investigation of the hypersegregation of African Americans in 1990 raises serious concerns about the well-being of the African American population in contemporary U.S. society. While a full examination of their residential patterns will be forthcoming as the 1990 census data are more fully analyzed, the total African American population of the metropolitan areas listed in table 2.2 is nearly 10 million. For them, and for those living in the metropolitan areas newly listed as hypersegregated in 1990 and shown in table 2.3, residential segregation at such high levels is a matter of grave concern. Specifically, only two of the hypersegregated metropolitan areas in 1980 are no longer classified as hypersegregated in 1990, and both of these experienced increases on at least one dimension of segregation. Furthermore, fifteen more metropolitan areas can be so classified in 1990. Hypersegregation is not abating.

It bears reiterating here that every single metropolitan area on the list, including those that were discussed above as no longer being hypersegregated, showed an increase on at least one dimension of segregation. In Newark and Buffalo, segregation increased on all five dimensions, and in Detroit it increased on four dimensions. Among the sixteen metropolitan areas on the list, isolation increased in ten, concentration in nine, clustering in eight, evenness in four, and centralization in three. Thus—albeit to different degrees and on different dimensions—segregation is actually *increasing* in the hypersegregated metropolitan areas.

Taken together, this lack of change in hypersegregated metropolitan areas and the increases in segregation seen there yield an unambiguous conclusion: *Whatever we are now doing to combat residential segregation is not nearly enough and in many cases is not working at all.*

One factor that merits comment here is the role of public policy. We would be deceiving ourselves to not realize that while the segregation indices reported here are for metropolitan areas, further research is going to show that much of it is found in the central cities of the metropolitan areas. The link between federal policies that drastically reduced money to cities and the ensuing decrease in city services (Cole, Taebel, and Hissong 1990) and the increases in segregation needs exploration. As we more often invest in "private solutions to public problems" (Massey, quoted in Terkel 1992, 96), those who are least able to "vote with their feet," due not only to current poverty but to the cumulative effects of past discrimination, are those left to face the segregated urban environment.

A related question raised by these data is: What will it take to dismantle the ghetto and change the hypersegregation of African Americans in the United States? Clearly, a solution based solely on the continued heroic efforts of the nation's many fair housing groups, while important, is inadequate to address a problem of this magnitude. The 1988 Amendments to the Fair Housing Law greatly enhanced the enforcement capability of the 1968 Act. Vigorous enforcement of the law has certainly not ever been tried and is to be strongly encouraged. The well-documented role of government policies in creating the situation (see, for example, Massey and Denton forthcoming; Hirsch 1983) and the magnitude of the problem both demand the involvement of the federal government.

But this analysis raises individual-level issues, as well, particularly regarding racism in U.S. society. But merely blaming white Americans for the problem does not suggest actions to combat it, particularly for those people who are interested but feel powerless to confront established government and business practices. New analyses of racism by Hacker (1992) and Terkel (1992) focus on what it means to be an African American in contemporary America. A greater understanding of how even the subtle acts of daily exclusion cumulate and take a toll can lead to widespread and concerted individual-level "affirmative civility" (Terkel 1992, 18). The days of overt racism are thankfully behind us in many areas, but efforts to overcome subtle marginalization and victimization are required as well. The first step is to learn to recognize these characteristics in our own daily behavior.

On another level, research has shown that integrated neighborhoods are rare but possible (Lee and Wood 1990), though they require work to maintain (Saltman 1990). As individual citizens we need to make neighborhood integration a goal, whether we are moving to a new neighborhood or remaining in our current one. If the latter, we can evaluate our neighborhood organization and block group activities for racist impacts and challenge them. Likewise, challenging neighbors who make restrictive housing statements about who they'd like to see move in or who they'd like to sell or rent to would help educate people to the ramifications of their beliefs. These types of challenges directly attack what is reported in many probes into the reasons for attitudes toward integration and real estate steering. People say "I am not prejudiced but..." and give a rationale that depicts the prejudice of their neighbors or customers.

Moving to a new neighborhood, whether integrated or not, offers the opportunity to change the climate of real estate transactions. People should demand to be shown all houses or apartments in their desired price range, specifically stating prointegration intentions, and they should challenge any hints of racism. Moving is a difficult and harried time for everyone, but would it really add that much of a burden to demand a full range of options? Where people choose to live is ultimately an individual decision, but the decision is made no less one's own by looking at all the available options. The potential power of repeated demands by consumers to see housing in integrated neighborhoods has the potential to go a long way toward changing the behavior of real estate practitioners and the climate of real estate transactions.

Note that these are also fairly low-cost options, particularly for white home seekers, but for African American home seekers, too. Discussions of integration frequently get waylaid by concerns of minorities who do not want to be the first to integrate a hostile neighborhood, who hesitate to be social isolates because of small numbers in nonhostile ones, or who value all the culture and comforts associated with retreating to African American settings after fighting subtle discrimination all day in the larger world. Whites voice similar fears. But the levels of segregation shown here serve to put these fears into perspective. We are currently in no danger of experiencing a shortage of single-race neighborhoods, particularly where African Americans are concerned. People who wish to live in them will be able to do so for a long time to come. Survey data consistently show a diversity of opinion in both the African American and the white community on neighborhood integration (Sigelman and Welch 1991; Schuman, Steeh, and Bobo 1985). Perhaps only some will want to make the moves toward integration. But all can help to make those moves possible.

By suggesting these individual actions, I seek to involve concerned citizens in the process of fair housing and neighborhood integration, but do not suggest that their actions will solve the problem. The enormity of the segregation and its deep historical roots will demand cooperation and action at all levels. Hypersegregation clearly denies African Americans access to the "bundle of amenities" associated with living in a good neighborhood. We now have the necessary laws, but we seem to lack large quantities of federal, state, local, and individual will. The question is not *can* we rise to the challenge, but rather *will* we?

Notes

1. While it does include Newark, northern New Jersey does not correspond well enough to the previously defined Newark SMSA which was in the Massey-Denton data set.

2. Forthcoming work by the Census Bureau will make it possible to answer this question.

3. The analyses were also done including the other hypersegregated metropolitan areas listed in table 2.2, and no substantial differences emerged.

4. A rough estimate of labor force participation was obtained by taking the number of workers divided by the population age 15 to 64.

5. While logit is technically the correct estimation method with a limited-range dependent variable, few of the percents lie near 0 or 100. OLS is appropriate for the middle of the distribution and OLS coefficients are much more easily interpretable.

REFERENCES

Barringer, Felicity. 1991. Census shows profound change in racial makeup of the nation. *The New York Times,* 11 March, p. A1, A12.

Blomquist, Glenn C., Mark C. Berger, and John P. Hoehn. 1988. New estimates of quality of life in urban areas. *The American Economic Review* 78:89–107.

Cole, Richard L., Delbert A. Taebel, and Rodney V. Hissong. 1990. America's cities and the 1980s: The legacy of the Reagan years. *Journal of Urban Affairs* 12:345–60.

Denton, Nancy A., and Douglas S. Massey. 1991. Patterns of neighborhood transition in a multi-ethnic world: U.S. metropolitan areas 1970-1980. *Demography* 28:41–63.

———. 1988a. Racial identity among Caribbean Hispanics: The effect of double minority status on residential segregation. *American Sociological Review* 54:790–808.

———. 1988b. Residential segregation of blacks, Hispanics, and Asians by socioeconomic status and generation. *Social Science Quarterly* 69:797–817.

Doig, Stephen K. 1991. Neighborhoods show small gains in integration. *The Miami Herald,* 9 April, p. 1A, 13A.

Duncan, Otis D., and Beverly Duncan. 1957. *The Negro population of Chicago.* Chicago: University of Chicago Press.

Feagin, Joe R. 1992. A house is not a home: White racism and U.S. housing practice. Paper read at the Commission for Racial Justice Fair Housing Symposium, December, Atlanta, Georgia.

———. 1991. The continuing significance of race: Antiblack discrimination in public places. *American Sociological Review* 56:101–16.

Galster, George C., and W. Mark Keeney. 1988. Race, residence, discrimination, and economic opportunity: Modeling the nexus of urban racial phenomena. *Urban Affairs Quarterly* 24:87–117.

Garreau, Joel. 1991. *Edge city: Life on the new urban frontier.* New York: Doubleday.

Hacker, Andrew. 1992. *Two nations.* New York: Macmillan.

Hirsch, Arnold R. 1983. *Making the second ghetto: Race and housing in Chicago 1940–1960.* Cambridge: Cambridge University Press.

Hochschild, Jennifer. 1984. *The new American dilemma: Liberal democracy and school desegregation.* New Haven, Conn.: Yale University Press.

————. 1981. *What's fair? American beliefs about distributive justice*. Cambridge, Mass.: Harvard University Press.

Jencks, Christopher, and Paul E. Peterson, eds. 1991. *The urban underclass*. Washington, D.C.: The Brookings Institution.

Kasarda, John D. 1988. Jobs, migration, and emerging urban mismatches. In *Urban change and poverty*, edited by Michael G.H. McGeary and Lawrence E. Lynn, Jr. Washington, D.C.: National Academy Press.

Landry, Bart. 1987. *The new black middle class*. Berkeley: University of California Press.

Lee, Barrett, and Peter Wood. 1990. The fate of residential integration in American cities: Evidence from racially mixed neighborhoods, 1970–80. *Journal of Urban Affairs*, 12:425–436.

Leigh, Wilhelmina A., and James D. McGhee. 1986. A minority perspective on residential racial integration. In *Housing desegregation and federal policy*, edited by John M. Goering. Chapel Hill: University of North Carolina Press.

Lieberson, Stanley. 1980. *A piece of the pie: Blacks and white immigrants since 1880*. Berkeley: University of California Press.

Lynn, Laurence E., Jr., and Michael G.H. McGeary, eds. 1990. *Inner city poverty in the United States*. Washington, D.C.: National Academy Press.

Massey, Douglas S., Gretchen A. Condran, and Nancy A. Denton. 1987. The effect of residential segregation on black social and economic well-being. *Social Forces* 66:29–56.

Massey, Douglas S., and Nancy A. Denton. 1993. *American apartheid: Segregation and the making of the underclass*. Cambridge, Mass.: Harvard University Press.

————. 1989. Hypersegregation in U.S. metropolitan areas: Black and Hispanic segregation along five dimensions. *Demography* 26:373–91.

————. 1988a. The dimensions of residential segregation. *Social Forces* 67:281–315.

————. 1988b. Suburbanization and segregation in U.S. metropolitan areas. *American Journal of Sociology* 94:592–626.

————. 1987. Trends in the residential segregation of blacks, Hispanics, and Asians. *American Sociological Review* 52:802–25.

Massey, Douglas S., and Mitchell L. Eggers. 1990. The ecology of inequality: Minorities and the concentration of poverty, 1970–80. *American Journal of Sociology* 95:1153–88.

Massey, Douglas S., and Eric Fong. 1990. Segregation and neighborhood quality: Blacks, Hispanics, and Asians in the San Francisco metropolitan area. *Social Forces* 69:15–32.

Nathan, Richard P. 1991. A new agenda for cities. Paper prepared for a colloquium sponsored by the Ohio Municipal League and Research Fund.

New York Times editorial. 1992. Can Democrats do better on race? 17 March.

O'Hare, William. 1990. City size, racial composition, and election of black mayors inside and outside the South. *Journal of Urban Affairs* 12:307-13.

Pacione, Michael. 1990. Urban liveability: A review. *Urban Geography* 11:1-30.

Park, R. E., and E. W. Burgess. 1925. *The city*. Chicago: University of Chicago Press.

Ryan, William. 1981. *Equality*. New York: Pantheon Books.

Saltman, Juliet. 1990. *A fragile movement: The struggle for neighborhood stabilization*. New York: Greenwood Press.

Schuman, Howard, Charlotte Steeh, and Lawrence Bobo. 1985. *Racial attitudes in America*. Cambridge, Mass.: Harvard University Press.

Sigelman, Lee, and Susan Welch. 1991. *Black Americans' views of racial inequality*. Cambridge: Cambridge University Press.

Spear, Allan H. 1967. *Black Chicago: The making of a Negro ghetto*. Chicago: University of Chicago Press.

Terkel, Studs. 1992. *Race: How blacks and whites think and feel about the American obsession*. New York: The New Press.

Turner, Margery Austin, Raymond J. Struyk, and John Yinger. 1991. *Housing discrimination study: Synthesis,* Contract HC-5811. Washington, D.C.: U.S. Department of Housing and Urban Development.

U.S. Bureau of the Census. 1988. *Current housing reports*. Washington, D.C.

———. 1987. *Current housing reports*. Washington, D.C.

———. 1986. *Current housing reports*. Washington, D.C.

———. 1985. *Current housing reports*. Washington, D.C.

Usdansky, Margaret L. 1991. Segregation: Walls between us. *USA Today,* 11–13 November (reprint).

White, Michael J. 1986. Segregation and diversity measures in population distribution. *Population Index* 52:198–221.

Wilson, William Julius. 1991a. Poverty, joblessness, and family structure in the inner city: A comparative perspective. Paper presented at the Chicago Urban Poverty and Family Life Conference, October 10–12, 1991, University of Chicago.

———. 1991b. Studying inner-city social dislocations. *American Sociological Review* 56:1–14.

Appendix:
Listing and Characteristics of American Housing Survey MSAs Included in Study

Metropolitan Area	1980 Population	% Black	% Hispanic	Region	AHS Year	Hyper-segregated	Evenness	Isolation	Clustering	Concen-tration	Central-ization	Black Median Income, 1980
Anaheim	1,933	1.2	14.8	West	1986	NO	0.458	0.038	0.018	-0.442	0.576	18,084
Atlanta	2,030	24.3	1.1	South	1987	NO	0.762	0.714	0.398	0.686	0.827	11,232
Baltimore	2,174	25.2	0.9	South	1987	YES	0.747	0.723	0.622	0.763	0.857	12,397
Birmingham	847	28.0	0.7	South	1988	NO	0.419	0.496	0.059	0.775	0.830	9,369
Boston	2,763	5.6	2.4	Northeast	1985	NO	0.774	0.550	0.491	0.799	0.871	11,099
Buffalo	1,243	9.2	1.3	Northeast	1988	NO	0.794	0.635	0.443	0.882	0.884	9,181
Chicago	7,104	19.9	8.2	Midwest	1987	YES	0.878	0.828	0.793	0.887	0.872	12,609
Cincinnati	1,401	12.2	0.6	Midwest	1986	NO	0.723	0.543	0.158	0.669	0.883	10,652
Cleveland	1,899	18.0	1.4	Midwest	1988	YES	0.875	0.804	0.743	0.927	0.898	12,068
Columbus	1,093	12.1	0.7	Midwest	1987	NO	0.724	0.571	0.321	0.854	0.933	11,821
Dallas-Fort Worth	2,975	13.9	8.4	South	1985	NO	0.771	0.645	0.334	0.693	0.749	11,792
Denver	1,621	4.7	10.8	West	1986	NO	0.685	0.410	0.211	0.385	0.719	13,633
Detroit	4,353	20.3	1.6	Midwest	1985	YES	0.867	0.773	0.846	0.842	0.924	13,684
Houston	2,905	18.0	14.6	South	1987	NO	0.695	0.593	0.238	0.569	0.840	13,775
Indianapolis	1,167	13.4	0.8	Midwest	1988	NO	0.762	0.623	0.411	0.804	0.942	12,878
Kansas City	1,327	12.9	2.4	Midwest	1986	NO	0.789	0.689	0.461	0.857	0.921	12,162
Los Angeles	7,478	12.3	27.6	West	1985	YES	0.811	0.604	0.765	0.695	0.859	12,423
Memphis	913	39.8	0.9	South	1988	NO	0.695	0.737	0.440	0.550	0.817	8,986
Miami	1,626	16.7	35.8	South	1986	NO	0.778	0.642	0.344	0.565	0.463	11,356
Milwaukee	1,397	10.7	2.5	Midwest	1988	YES	0.839	0.695	0.689	0.944	0.951	12,187
Minneapolis	2,114	2.3	1.1	Midwest	1985	NO	0.693	0.306	0.102	0.890	0.944	12,274
New Orleans	1,187	32.2	4.1	South	1986	NO	0.683	0.688	0.327	0.584	0.906	9,382

Appendix continued:
Listing and Characteristics of American Housing Survey MSAs Included in Study

Metropolitan Area	1980 Population	% Black	% Hispanic	Region	AHS Year	Hyper-segregated	Evenness	Isolation	Clustering	Concentration	Centralization	Black Median Income, 1980
New York	9,120	20.2	16.4	Northeast	1987	NO	0.819	0.627	0.468	0.892	0.795	10,979
Norfolk	807	29.5	1.3	South	1988	NO	0.628	0.625	0.199	0.559	0.712	10,615
Oklahoma City	834	8.9	2.3	South	1988	NO	0.710	0.560	0.250	0.546	0.886	11,635
Philadelphia	4,717	18.5	2.5	Northeast	1985	YES	0.788	0.696	0.673	0.757	0.855	11,369
Phoenix	1,509	3.1	13.3	West	1985	NO	0.594	0.225	0.041	0.548	0.945	11,938
Pittsburgh	2,264	7.6	0.5	Northeast	1986	NO	0.727	0.541	0.272	0.821	0.812	10,640
Portland	1,243	2.7	1.9	West	1986	NO	0.685	0.316	0.168	0.826	0.956	11,707
Providence	919	2.6	2.0	Northeast	1988	NO	0.731	0.253	0.120	0.803	0.818	10,024
Riverside, CA	1,558	4.7	18.7	West	1986	NO	0.488	0.160	0.048	0.212	0.896	12,942
Rochester	971	7.9	2.0	Northeast	1986	NO	0.679	0.437	0.321	0.792	0.874	12,831
St. Louis	2,356	17.2	0.9	Midwest	1987	YES	0.814	0.729	0.264	0.893	0.931	11,365
Salt Lake City	936	0.8	5.0	West	1988	NO	0.533	0.041	0.006	0.384	0.443	12,466
San Antonio	1,072	6.3	46.0	South	1986	NO	0.641	0.358	0.229	0.544	0.523	10,605
San Diego	1,862	5.0	15.0	West	1987	NO	0.643	0.263	0.171	0.537	0.902	12,244
San Francisco	3,251	11.8	10.8	West	1985	NO	0.717	0.511	0.282	0.687	0.836	12,631
San Jose, CA	1,295	3.2	17.5	West	1988	NO	0.487	0.066	0.032	0.177	0.795	18,379
Seattle	1,607	3.5	2.0	WEST	1987	NO	0.682	0.294	0.137	0.791	0.952	13,752
Tampa	1,569	9.1	5.1	South	1985	NO	0.735	0.507	0.246	0.493	0.581	9,193
Washington, DC	3,061	27.6	3.0	South	1985	NO	0.693	0.672	0.450	0.441	0.850	16,484

CHAPTER 3

African American Residential Segregation:
An Examination of Race and Class
in Metropolitan Detroit

by Joe T. Darden

Some observers believe that the significance of race as a factor in residential segregation has declined since passage of the federal Fair Housing Act of 1968, which declared racial discrimination in housing illegal (Wilger 1988). This belief may be related to (1) the change in white attitudes toward the principle of open housing, and (2) the decline (although small) in residential segregation between 1970 and 1980.

The percentage of whites who agreed that "black people have a right to live wherever they can afford to" rose from 65 percent to 88 percent between 1964 and 1976 (Schuman, Steeh, and Bobo 1985). Studies of residential segregation suggest average declines between 1970 and 1980 of 10 percentage points, especially in middle-size and small metropolitan areas (Massey and Denton 1987; Darden 1985).

Wilger (1988) attributes the decline in residential segregation to the construction of new housing and argues that as more new housing is built to replace existing housing or as African Americans continue to move to the suburbs, residential segregation will continue to decline.

Massey and Gross (1991), however, present a different view. They argue that although white racial attitudes did indeed shift during the 1970s following passage of the Fair Housing Act, such attitudes did not change enough to bring about meaningful residential integration in the metropolitan areas where most blacks live. As a result, discrimination did not decline significantly in urban areas with large African American populations, and the declines in racial segregation that occurred only serve to underscore the continued salience of race in the United States, since they occurred almost entirely in cities with small black populations, where white preferences for limited interracial contact are not threatened by racial desegregation (15).

Massey and Gross (1991) based their conclusions on the premise that although many whites may endorse open housing as a general principle, they do not accept its implications in practice. Indeed, surveys of neighborhood racial preference suggest that most whites prefer segregated neighborhoods (Darden 1987). The preference of whites for segregation can be fulfilled in areas where the black population remains small and where open housing practices can occur without threatening white preferences for limited black-white contact (Massey and Gross 1991, 16). However, in an area with a relatively large number of blacks, implying a high degree of potential black-white contact, racial segregation is generally maintained. Furthermore, when the metropolitan area has a central city that is predominantly black, the factor of race becomes even more significant, because the political boundaries separating the city from the suburbs become rigid racial boundaries. Negative images whites may have of the predominantly black city are often transferred to the black individual.

The movement of blacks across central city-suburban political boundaries results in strong white resistance. According to the customer-prejudice hypothesis of the cause of discrimination, white real estate agents tend to discriminate most against lower-income blacks, who are more likely to upset their white customers (Yinger 1987, 56). However, race is so important to many white residents that socioeconomic status differences between black home seekers become blurred, resulting in a high level of black segregation from whites, regardless of black socioeconomic status.

The question addressed in this chapter is whether, in the case of metropolitan Detroit, African Americans at high occupational, educational, and income levels are less segregated from whites residentially than are African Americans at low levels of occupation, education, and income. This chapter (1) tests the socioeconomic–racial residential segregation hypothesis, using 1980 census data for the Detroit Standard Metropolitan Statistical Area (SMSA) (Wayne, Oakland, and Macomb Counties); (2) discusses the demographic changes between 1980 and 1990 within metropolitan Detroit; and (3) considers the implications of these changes for African American residential desegregation in the nineties.

Past Research Since the 1968 Fair Housing Act

A review of the literature reveals that there have been few studies that compare and contrast racial and class segregation since passage of the Fair Housing Act (Downing and Gladstone 1989). The most extensive study that considered segregation by race and class was conducted by Farley

(1977). Farley analyzed 1970 census data for 29 urbanized areas, using the index of dissimilarity to address the question: "To what extent are blacks in a given social group residentially segregated from whites in the same social group?" Farley found that after controlling for social class, blacks were still highly segregated from whites. Black professionals, for example, were highly segregated from white professionals by place of residence. Farley concluded that racial residential segregation did not vary by occupational status, educational attainment, or income.

Massey's (1979) study was consistent with Farley's. He analyzed 29 urbanized areas using the same three measures of class—that is, education, occupation, and income. He found little or no relationship between socioeconomic variables and black–white residential segregation. Segregation was high at all levels of education, income, and occupational status. Although Massey's findings are in agreement with Farley's, both studies were based on 1970 census data—data collected only two years after passage of the Fair Housing Act.

Since 1970, several socioeconomic and demographic changes have occurred. A greater number of blacks have entered professional occupations. Furthermore, more blacks have become better educated and are earning higher incomes. According to theorists of human ecology, as minority groups move up in socioeconomic status, they tend to seek housing in higher-income areas— that is, the suburbs. This movement may result in a greater degree of residential integration (Massey and Denton 1987, 823). Of interest in this chapter is the extent to which African American socioeconomic status contributed to African American residential integration in metropolitan Detroit.

From 1970 to 1980, the median family income of African Americans in the Detroit metropolitan area increased from $8,643 to $15,931. The percentage of African American college graduates increased from 3.7 percent in 1970 to 7.2 percent in 1980. Additionally, the African American suburban population increased 36 percent—from 96,655 in 1970 to 131,478 by 1980 (U.S. Department of Commerce 1973, 1983).

DATA AND METHODOLOGY

Data for this chapter were obtained from the U.S. Bureau of the Census Population and Housing Summary Tape File 4 (1983). The data consisted of the numbers of blacks and whites by census tracts in the same occupation, education, and income categories in the Detroit SMSA. The method employed to measure residential segregation, which is defined as the overall unevenness in the spatial distribution of two racial groups, was the *index of dissimilarity*. It can be stated mathematically as:

$$D= 100 \left(1/2 \sum_{i=1}^{k} | x_i - y_i |\right)$$

Where:

x_i = the percentage of the Detroit SMSA's white population living in a given census tract;

y_i = the percentage of the Detroit SMSA's black population living in the same census tract;

D = the index of dissimilarity, or one-half the sum of the absolute differences (positive and negative) between the percentage distribution of the white and black populations in the SMSA.

The method used in this analysis consisted of cross-tabulating race and socioeconomic status statistics by census tract. Using this approach, the influence of occupation, education, and income status on residential segregation by race could be determined without estimation. Thus, instead of indirectly determining the amount of segregation explained by socioeconomic status using, for example, regression analysis, direct calculations were made of segregation of white professionals from black professionals, white college graduates from black college graduates, and so on. This method has been used effectively by others to eliminate the effects of socioeconomic disparities (see Kantrowitz 1973; Darroch and Marston 1971).

FINDINGS

RESIDENTIAL SEGREGATION BETWEEN BLACKS AND WHITES WITH THE SAME LEVEL OF OCCUPATION IN THE DETROIT METROPOLITAN AREA, 1980

In 1980, the black and white executive, administrative, and managerial workers in metropolitan Detroit were highly segregated residentially. The index of dissimilarity was 67.7 percent. Professional workers, black and white, were only slightly less segregated, with an index of 62.3 percent. Black and white technicians and sales workers and black and white administrative support workers were segregated at 68.6 and 67.3 percent, respectively (table 3.1). The level of segregation between black and white service workers was 74.1 percent. Black and white precision, production, craft, and repair workers had an index of 72.5 percent. Finally, black and white operators, fabricators, and

Table 3.1
Residential Segregation Between Blacks and Whites in the Same
Occupational Category for the Detroit Metropolitan Area, 1980

Occupational Category	No. Whites	No. Blacks	Segregation Index
Executive, administration, and managerial	31,414	1,352	67.7
Professional specialty	36,197	2,600	62.3
Technical and sales	37,505	1,736	68.6
Administrative support and clerical service	41,208	3,849	67.3
Services	27,556	3,562	74.1
Precision production, craft, and repair	28,384	1,528	72.5
Fabricators, operators, and laborers	34,156	5,098	71.4

Source: Computed by the author from data obtained from U.S. Bureau of the Census, *Population and Housing Summary Tape File 4*, 1983.

laborers also lived in separate neighborhoods, resulting in a segregation index of 71.4 percent (table 3.1).

These findings show that regardless of occupation, in 1980 in the Detroit metropolitan area, most blacks and whites did not live in the same neighborhoods. Differences in occupational status, therefore, did not explain the high level of residential segregation between blacks and whites.

RESIDENTIAL SEGREGATION BETWEEN BLACKS AND WHITES WITH THE SAME LEVEL OF EDUCATION IN THE DETROIT METROPOLITAN AREA, 1980

Like black and white workers, most Detroit area blacks and whites with the same level of education lived in separate neighborhoods in 1980. Blacks and whites with a high school education were only slightly less segregated than blacks and whites with an elementary school education. The mean index of dissimilarity for blacks and whites at the elementary level was 72.3 percent,

Table 3.2

Residential Segregation Between Blacks and Whites with the Same Level of Education for the Detroit Metropolitan Area, 1980

Education Level	No. Whites	No. Blacks	Segregation Index
Elementary			
0–4 Years	5,238	1,168	77.1
5–7 Years	10,942	1,924	70.2
8 Years	19,636	1,278	69.4
Mean			72.3
High school			
1–3 Years	57,151	7,172	70.1
4 Years	148,872	11,549	70.7
Mean			70.4
College			
1–3 Years	72,749	6,230	65.0
4 Years	36,272	1,666	66.4
5 or More Years	32,710	2,130	59.7
Mean			63.7

Source: Computed by the author from data obtained from U.S. Bureau of the Census, *Population and Housing Summary Tape File 4,* 1983.

---

compared with 70.4 percent at the high school level. The mean index of dissimilarity for college-educated blacks and whites was somewhat lower, at 63.7 percent (table 3.2).

It appears, therefore, that segregation between Detroit area blacks and whites in 1980 was high, regardless of education, although the level of segregation declined slightly with increasing education.

RESIDENTIAL SEGREGATION BETWEEN BLACKS AND WHITES WITH THE SAME LEVEL OF INCOME IN THE DETROIT METROPOLITAN AREA, 1980

Residential segregation in 1980 was uniformly high (ranging from 64.1 percent to 94.1 percent) between Detroit area blacks and whites with the same level of income, regardless of the amount. Blacks and whites earning $35,000 to $39,999 per year were more segregated from each other (at 86.1 percent) than were blacks and whites earning less than $2,500 per year (82.7 percent). Furthermore, the segregation level between affluent blacks and whites (i.e., those earning $75,000 or more) was only 5 percentage points lower than the level between blacks and whites earning $20,000 per year (table 3.3).

Black-white residential segregation cannot be explained by income, and the level of segregation between blacks and whites did not decline as the income level increased.

This section has investigated whether the level of residential segregation between blacks and whites in metropolitan Detroit in 1980 was a function of occupation, education, and income differences or of racial differences. Socio-economic status differences were controlled by direct calculations of residential segregation between blacks and whites with the same level of occupation, education, and income.

The results revealed that blacks and whites with the same levels of occupation, education, and income did not live in the same census tracts in metropolitan Detroit in 1980. Residential segregation between blacks and whites remained high, regardless of socioeconomic status. Differential socio-economic status, therefore, does not explain the high level of black residential segregation observed in 1980 in the Detroit metropolitan area.

The implications of these findings are clear. Improvements in the occupa-tion, education, and income levels of blacks in metropolitan Detroit will not necessarily result in reductions in the level of residential segregation.

THE OUTLOOK FOR RESIDENTIAL SEGREGATION IN THE NINETIES

As we move into the 1990s, racial residential segregation remains the most characteristic feature of metropolitan Detroit (Wayne, Oakland, and Macomb Counties). Census figures for 1990 reveal that most of the region's whites are living in the suburbs, while most of the region's blacks reside in the city of Detroit.

Of the 413,730 whites who resided in the city in 1980, 46 percent had left by 1990, thus increasing the black proportion of the city from 62.7 percent to 76 percent. The suburbanization process also involved a substantial number of blacks who moved, primarily to Oakland County. During the decade, Oakland County's black population increased from 47,962 to 77,488, or by 61.6 percent, compared with an increase of only 13.8 percent for Macomb County, and 2.3 percent for Wayne County. Between 1980 and 1990, the

Table 3.3

Residential Segregation Between Blacks and Whites with the Same Levels of Income for the Detroit Metropolitan Area, 1980

Family Income Level	*No. Whites*	*No. Blacks*	*Segregation Index*
Less than $ 2,500	5,405	12,014	82.7
2,500 to 4,999	9,389	17,816	88.0
5,000 to 7,499	14,138	18,377	76.7
7,500 to 9,999	14,941	14,113	73.2
10,000 to 12,499	16,515	13,029	79.7
12,500 to 14,999	15,327	10,816	88.8
15,000 to 17,499	17,628	11,636	91.1
17,500 to 19,999	18,672	11,153	81.3
20,000 to 22,499	20,767	10,906	69.0
22,500 to 24,999	18,627	9,036	94.1
25,000 to 27,499	19,357	9,042	77.9
27,500 to 29,999	16,120	7,273	84.0
30,000 to 34,999	28,719	12,125	81.4
35,000 to 39,999	20,897	8,740	86.1
40,000 to 49,999	23,644	9,783	79.6
50,000 to 74,999	17,153	4,813	71.7
75,000 or More	6,200	927	64.1

Source: Computed by the author from data obtained from U.S. Bureau of the Census, *Population and Housing Summary Tape File 4,* 1983.

percentage increase in Oakland County's black population (61.6 percent) was 20 times greater than the percentage increase in its white population (3.0 percent).

Black suburbanization was not the same, however, as black residential integration. In 1990, 80.7 percent of the 77,488 blacks in Oakland County were concentrated primarily in three suburban municipalities—Pontiac, Southfield, and Oak Park. On the other hand, only 11 percent of Oakland County's white population lived in these same three municipalities.

The overall index of dissimilarity between African Americans and whites of all occupational, educational, and income levels in metropolitan Detroit in 1990 was 87.0 percent, an increase of 1.2 percentage points from the level in 1980.

Furthermore, such a high level of segregation was not due to the inability of African Americans to pay for housing in predominantly white sections of metropolitan Detroit. Analysis of the data revealed no strong negative correlation on the spatial distribution of African Americans and the spatial distribution of housing rent and housing value. Instead, the correlation (r) was -0.53 for median contract rent and -0.50 for median housing value, with an r^2 of 0.28 for rent and 0.25 for housing value.

It appears that the housing market in metropolitan Detroit has not been allowed to operate without intervention. Race-conscious intervention to segregate the races, by means of racial steering and racial discrimination in housing, has been occurring in the market (Darden 1990). This intervention denies equal access to housing, in violation of the 1968 Fair Housing Act. Given black and white individuals of equal socioeconomic status, whites will probably reside in a better neighborhood with better schools, services, and cultural advantages.

Discrimination results in lower-, middle-, and upper-class blacks living in closer proximity on the average than do lower-, middle-, and upper-class whites. Such clustering of blacks, regardless of class, is often mistakenly attributed (by most whites) to black preference for segregated living. Most whites have a tendency to comfort themselves with the idea that most blacks want to live in black neighborhoods. Yet the evidence is strong that discrimination in housing has been the major factor in black residential segregation (Darden 1987).

THE REMEDY: RACE-CONSCIOUS INTERVENTION PROGRAMS FOR INTEGRATION

Thus, in order to correct past wrongs, to assure blacks and whites equal access to housing, and to reduce residential segregation, any effective remedy for the purpose of integration must be race conscious.

An innovative approach to intervention in the housing market must be employed for the purpose of racial integration. Heretofore, few fully developed intervention strategies for the purpose of racial integration have been used in the nation and none in the state of Michigan. Nationally, such strategies have been tried in Shaker Heights and Cleveland Heights, Ohio; Oak Park, Illinois; and University City, Missouri.

These race-conscious intervention strategies have achieved some success. Shaker Heights, for example, has been able to maintain a relatively stable racial composition for more than 30 years (see Cromwell 1990). Such programs as the one in Shaker Heights have limited impact, however, because they have been based on a single municipality. To be effective, a program should cover a geographic territory consisting of an entire metropolitan area or at least an entire county.

AFFIRMATIVE INCENTIVE LOAN PROGRAM

What metropolitan Detroit needs is an affirmative incentive program to counteract racial steering and to encourage black and white home seekers to make pro-integrative housing choices—that is, the purchase of homes in neighborhoods in which their own race is underrepresented. Such incentives may include low-interest loans to cover part of the down payment or any needed maintenance.

Unlike racial steering, which restricts choices on the basis of race, affirmative incentive programs expand the housing choices of both blacks and whites. Such programs may be initiated by local, county, state, or federal governments or by institutions in the private sector.

Affirmative incentive programs may be the last hope for metropolitan Detroit to reverse its persistent pattern of racial residential segregation. What is at stake is a future of permanent apartheid with continuous racial conflict or a future of racial integration with the prospect of increased racial harmony.

LEGAL SUPPORT FOR AFFIRMATIVE INCENTIVE PROGRAMS

Legal support for affirmative incentive programs came in a recent decision of the U.S. Court of Appeals for the Seventh Circuit. The Seventh Circuit has jurisdiction over the southern suburbs of Chicago, Illinois. The case involved the South-Suburban Housing Center and the Greater South-Suburban Board of Realtors.

In order to stem the tide of market forces and promote integrated housing patterns, the South-Suburban Housing Center attempted to influence the housing market by encouraging the sales and marketing of real estate in what it terms nontraditional ways—that is, by encouraging whites to move to black or integrated areas and blacks to move to white or integrated areas (see *South-Suburban Housing Center v. Greater South-Suburban Board of Realtors* 1988, 1075). The initial complaint in this litigation was sparked by a controversy between South-Suburban Housing Center and the Board of Realtors over the propriety of special efforts made by the Fair Housing Center to market houses in black neighborhoods to white home buyers in the Village of Park Forest.

The South-Suburban Housing Center's purpose was to "add some white traffic to the properties in addition to black traffic," not to decrease or restrict the black traffic. Thus, the court saw nothing wrong with the South-Suburban Housing Center attempting to attract white persons to housing opportunities they might not ordinarily know about and thus choose to pursue (*South-Suburban Housing Center v. Greater South-Suburban Board of Realtors,* 1988, 1085; see also U.S. Court of Appeals ruling of June 19, 1991). The Appeals Court disagreed with the Board of Realtors' argument that increased competition among black and white home buyers for the same homes constitutes a violation of the Fair Housing Act. Instead, the court stated that this is precisely the type of robust multiracial market activity which the Fair Housing Act intends to stimulate.

Recommendations

As for metropolitan Detroit, past segregation and the lingering effects of discrimination in housing have been documented in the preceding pages. A race-conscious remedy is appropriate. Any policy, however, should include the following characteristics:

1. Be metropolitan in scope in order to carry out the expansion of options and opportunities.

2. Endorse a single metropolitanwide multiple-listing service in order to provide all real estate brokers with the same listings, regardless of location of the firm.

3. Maintain high-quality city services for all neighborhoods of the municipality in order to sustain a balanced demand for housing.

4. Maintain high-quality, academically excellent, racially diverse, highly creative schools with unique programs that attract students within and outside each district within the Detroit metropolitan area.

5. Strengthen affirmative marketing efforts in order to encourage prointegrative housing choices by providing information about available housing to underrepresented racial groups.

6. Strengthen efforts to attack racial steering through strong support for a comprehensive metropolitanwide program of random testing by one or more organizations in the metropolitan area.

7. Apply governmental pressure to increase the degree of racial integration of personnel in real estate brokerage firms in all municipalities throughout the metropolitan area.

8. Avoid the use of the term *integration maintenance* and instead use *integration incentives,* so that it will be absolutely clear that the purpose of the policy is to expand and not restrict the housing options for blacks and other racial minorities throughout the cities and suburbs of the Detroit metropolitan area. The housing options of racial minorities should be equal to the options of the white majority (Darden 1990, 9).

9. Develop special steps to provide financial incentives to promote integration, since the policy must be designed to eliminate vestiges of segregation due to past discrimination. One example is to provide low-interest loans to families who purchase homes in areas where the race to which the families belong is underrepresented. Even lower-interest loans should be provided to families who keep their children in public schools, since the racial composition of public schools often influences the housing choices of home seekers.

10. Educate all Detroit-area communities concerning the policy and practice of fair housing without restriction. Equal access will help to assure areawide integration.

REFERENCES

Cromwell, B. A. 1990. Pro-integrative subsidies and their effects on housing markets: Do race-based loans work? Working paper 9018, Federal Reserve Bank of Cleveland.

Darden, J. T. 1990. *Racial residential segregation and discrimination in housing: The evidence from municipalities in three Michigan counties (Oakland, Wayne, and Macomb Counties), 1970–1990.* East Lansing: Urban Affairs Programs, Michigan State University.

———. 1987. Choosing neighbors and neighborhoods: The role of race in housing preference. In *Divided neighborhoods: Changing patterns of racial segregation,* edited by Gary Tobin. Newbury Park, Calif.: Sage.

———. 1985. The housing situation of blacks in metropolitan areas of Michigan. In *The state of black Michigan,* edited by Frances Thomas. East Lansing: Urban Affairs Programs, Michigan State University.

Darroch, G., and W. G. Marston. 1971. The social class basis of ethnic residential segregation: The Canadian case. *American Journal of Sociology* 77:491–510.

Downing, P. M., and L. Gladstone. 1989. *Segregation and discrimination in housing: A review of selected studies and legislation.* Washington, D.C.: Library of Congress, the Congressional Research Service for Congress.

Farley, R. 1977. Residential segregation in urbanized areas of the United States in 1970: An analysis of social class and racial differences. *Demography* 14 (4): 497–518.

Kantrowitz, N. 1973. *Ethnic and racial segregation in the New York metropolis.* New York: Praeger.

Massey, D. S. 1979. Effects of socioeconomic factors on the residential segregation of blacks and Spanish Americans in U.S. urbanized areas. *American Sociological Review* 44:1015–22.

Massey, D. S., and N. A. Denton. 1987. Trends in the residential segregation of blacks, Hispanics and Asians. *American Sociological Review* 52 (6): 802–25.

Massey, D. S., and A. B. Gross. 1991. Explaining trends in racial segregation, 1970–1980. *Urban Affairs Quarterly* 27 (1): 13–35.

Schuman, H., C. Steeh, and L. Bobo. 1985. *Racial attitudes in America: Trends and interpretations.* Cambridge, Mass.: Harvard University Press.

South-Suburban Housing Center v. Greater South-Suburban Board of Realtors 713 F. Supp. 1068, 1074 (N. D. Ill. 1988) Appealed to U. S. Seventh Circuit Court, Decided June 19, 1991.

U.S. Bureau of the Census. 1983. *Population and housing summary tape file 4.*

U.S. Department of Commerce. 1983. *1980 census of population: general social and economic characteristics.* Vol. 1, *Michigan.* Washington, D.C.: U.S. Government Printing Office.

———. 1973. *1970 census of population: characteristics of the population.* Vol. 1, *Michigan.* Washington, D.C.: U.S. Government Printing Office.

Wilger, R. J. 1988. Black–white residential segregation in 1980. Ph.D. diss., Department of Sociology, University of Michigan.

Yinger, J. 1987. The racial dimension of urban housing markets in the 1980s. In *Divided neighborhoods: Changing patterns of racial segregation,* edited by Gary Tobin. Newbury Park, Calif.: Sage.

CHAPTER 4

Minority Suburbanization in Denver

by Franklin J. James

A shift of minority populations from central cities to suburbs has been going on for some time, since at least 1970 (Clark 1979; Clay 1979; Clark 1987). During the 1970s, the absolute numbers of new minority residents in suburbs were frequently small, though percentage growth rates of suburban minority populations were high (U.S. Department of Housing and Urban Development 1979). Analysis of changes during the 1970s has generally challenged the significance of the migration. Galster (1991a) has shown that suburban blacks were disproportionately concentrated in suburbs closer to central cities, while whites continued to move further out. Research in New York has shown that minority suburbanites had less access to high-quality suburban communities in 1980 than did non-Hispanic whites with equivalent incomes (Logan and Alba 1993). Neighborhood segregation fell in 54 of 60 major metropolitan areas during the 1970s, at a rate "unprecedented in the history of urban America" (Massey and Denton 1988, 13). However, there was little real progress toward integration in the metropolitan areas with the largest black populations, such as New York or Detroit (Massey and Gross 1991).

The release of the 1990 census shows that the scale of minority suburbanization continued at a very rapid pace during the 1980s, both among blacks and among Hispanics (Schneider and Phelan 1993). The absolute magnitude of the growth in minority populations in suburbs appears to be far greater than was the case during the 1970s. It also proceeded at a rapid pace in all major regions. Schneider and Phelan (1993) concluded that black suburban populations tended to grow most rapidly in suburban communities with established black populations. However, they also concluded that "even more striking is the large decline in the number of suburbs that were less than 1 percent black" (277–78). Black suburban populations also grew most rapidly between 1980 and 1990 in suburban communities closer to the central city and with relatively low incomes (Schneider and Phelan 1993).

There is a great need for more research on suburbanization among minority groups other than blacks and for evaluative research on the minority suburbanization that took place during the 1980s and the issues it raises for civil rights and urban policy. This chapter presents preliminary evidence from the 1990 census regarding the scale of suburbanization among Hispanics and Blacks in a sample of 29 major metropolitan areas. It also provides a more detailed picture of minority suburbanization in the Denver metropolitan area during the 1980s and its effects on neighborhood and school integration in that area.

It presents a detailed case study of exclusionary state and local policies in the Denver metropolitan area. This case study is not meant to imply that policies in Denver are typical of those in other places, or that Denver is better or worse in this respect than most other places. The Denver case study does show a powerful and, in many cases, deliberate effort by suburban whites to segregate themselves from minorities. The chapter concludes by outlining research and policy issues raised by minority suburbanization.

In evaluating the evidence from Denver, it should be kept in mind that black suburbanization in the western United States—and thus perhaps in Denver—may differ from that in other regions. Massey and Gross (1991) found that during the 1970s, neighborhood segregation diminished most rapidly in western metropolitan areas. They concluded that "desegregation occurred primarily in areas where the percentage of blacks was so small that little or no segregation had to be imposed to keep the probability of white-black contact low" (32). In their analysis of trends during the 1980s, Schneider and Phelan (1993) found fewer indications that resegregation of suburban Blacks was occurring in suburbs of western metropolitan areas, compared to metropolitan areas in other regions.

Far more research is needed to document intrametropolitan residence patterns of minorities in places other than Denver. Research is also needed to account for the differences and to analyze their implications. As will be seen, discriminatory barriers to minority suburbanites are clearly present and strong in the West, perhaps contrary to the suggestion of Massey and Gross (1991). There are a number of other potential explanations of the apparently different patterns of segregation in the West. Perhaps the most important is that the research done so far does not consider the effects on black segregation of the existence of a second large minority group, Hispanics. Hispanic populations are especially large in many western areas (James, McCummings, and Tynan 1984). In addition, socioeconomic disparities between blacks and non-

Hispanic whites are often smaller in the West than in other regions (James and del Castillo 1992).

MINORITY SUBURBANIZATION DURING THE 1980S

Trends in a sample of 29 major U.S. metropolitan areas show that the center of gravity of minority populations in metropolitan areas shifted rapidly toward the suburbs during the 1980s. Rapid net growth of suburban black and Hispanic populations occurred during the 1980s.[1] The data to be discussed in this section measure population trends in the central counties of the 29 areas and in surrounding counties of the suburban rings. The boundaries of counties are unaffected by annexations in most though not all cases. This makes trends in the populations of counties a somewhat more reliable indicator of actual shifts in the geographic locations of population than are population trends in cities.[2] Central counties are generally larger than the central cities they contain. Population trends between central counties and suburban rings thus understate the extent of suburbanization as conventionally defined.

As can be seen in table 4.1, the 29 metropolitan areas were home to 71 million people in 1990. In 1980, slightly more than one-half—51 percent—of their populations lived outside the central county and in the suburban ring. Fully 58 percent of non-Hispanic whites lived in these suburban rings. Only slightly more than one-fourth—28 percent—of blacks lived in the suburban rings. Only 32 percent of Hispanics lived in the suburban rings. Clearly, in 1980 the overall quality of urban life for minorities was dependent much more on conditions in the central county than it was on conditions in the suburbs.

In 1990, both blacks and Hispanics remained much more highly concentrated in central counties than were non-Hispanic whites, but the numbers of minorities in the suburbs had grown remarkably. By 1990, about one-third of *both* black and Hispanic populations resided in the suburban ring. Percentage rates of growth of minority populations were very high in suburban rings (table 4.2).

Between 1980 and 1990, black populations in the central counties of the 29 areas grew by 561,000 or 8.5 percent. Black populations in the suburban rings grew by 917,000, or by 37 percent. Absolute black population growth in the suburbs thus exceeded black population growth in the central counties by two-thirds.

The rate of Hispanic population growth in the suburbs also exceeded Hispanic growth in the central counties, though by a lesser extent than for blacks, and absolute change in Hispanic population was greater in the central counties than in the suburbs. In the suburbs, Hispanic population grew two-thirds between 1980 and 1990, by 769,000 persons. In the central counties, Hispanic population grew by 54 percent or 1,321,000 persons. A major decentralization of Hispanic population is also clearly under way in U.S. metropolitan areas.

The geographic decentralization of blacks and Hispanics within urban areas is producing racial and ethnic diversity in overall suburban populations. In 1990, fully 14 percent of the populations of the suburban rings of these 29 metropolitan areas were minority: 9 percent black and 5 percent Hispanic. Only 11 percent of their populations had been minority in 1980. Minorities accounted for almost one-third—30 percent—of the population growth in the suburban rings during the 1980s.

Suburban populations grew in 27 of the 29 metropolitan areas. Together, blacks and Hispanics made up 20 percent or more of overall suburban population growth in 14 of these 27 areas. Blacks and Hispanics accounted for over half of net suburban population growth in three areas: Miami, New Orleans, and Cleveland.

Aggregate population trends may be shaped by the experiences of a few larger areas. In the 29 metropolitan areas, unweighted average percentage growth of black and Hispanic populations in suburbs outstripped unweighted average growth in central counties by over 20 percentage points. The average percentage change of black populations in the central counties during the decade was 16 percent; in the suburban rings, it was 38 percent. The rates of growth of suburban black populations outpaced those of black populations in the central counties of 22 of the 29 metropolitan areas.[3]

For Hispanics, populations in the central counties grew by an unweighted average of 42 percent, and by 61 percent in the suburbs. The rates of growth of suburban Hispanic populations exceeded those of Hispanic populations of 19 central counties.[4] Clearly, relatively rapid growth of minority populations in suburbs is the rule and not the exception.

Typically, more than one-half of black and Hispanic population growth in the 29 metropolitan areas occurred in the suburban rings. For blacks, this was true in 17 of the 29 metropolitan areas. This was true for Hispanics in 13 of the metropolitan areas.[5] In a few of the metropolitan areas, *all* net minority population growth took place in the suburban rings. For blacks, this was the case in Denver, Washington, St. Louis, and Philadelphia. The black population declined in the central county of each of these metropolitan areas. All metropolitan growth in Hispanic population occurred in the suburban rings

Table 4.1
Population in Central Counties and Suburban Rings of 29 Metropolitan
Areas, by Race and Ethnicity: 1980–1990

	1980		*1990*	
	Number (000)	*Percent of Metro Area*	*Number (000)*	*Percent of Metro Area*
Central Counties				
Non-Hispanic				
Whites	20,850	42.5	20,627	39.6
Blacks	6,589	72.5	7,150	67.7
Hispanics	2,448	68.1	3,769	66.3
Other	816	53.6	1,311	49.0
Total	30,702	48.6	32,857	46.3
Suburban Rings				
Non-Hispanic				
Whites	28,165	57.5	31,416	60.4
Blacks	2,498	27.5	3,41	32.3
Hispanics	1,147	31.9	1,916	33.7
Other	706	46.4	1,362	51.0
Total	32,516	51.4	38,109	53.7
Metropolitan Areas				
Non-Hispanic				
Whites	49,015	100.0	52,043	100.0
Blacks	9,087	100.0	10,565	100.0
Hispanics	3,595	100.0	5,685	100.0
Other	1,522	100.0	2,673	100.0
Total	63,218	100.0	70,966	100.0

*Central counties are counties including the central city. The 29 metropolitan areas are listed in Appendix A.

Source: Computed by the author from data obtained from 1980 and 1990 Censuses of Population.

Table 4.2
Population Change Between 1980 and 1990 in Suburban Rings of 29
Metropolitan Areas by Race and Ethnicity

| | *Central Counties* | | *Suburban Rings* | | *Metropolitan Areas* | |
	No. (000)	*%*	*No. (000)*	*%*	*No. (000)*	*%*
Non-Hispanic						
Whites	-223	-1.1	3,251	11.5	3,028	6.2
Blacks	561	8.5	917	36.5	1,478	16.3
Hispanics	1,321	54.0	769	67.0	2,090	58.1
Other	495	60.7	656	92.9	1,151	75.6
Total	2,155	7.0	5,593	17.2	7,748	12.3

See notes to Table 4.1.

of four areas: New Orleans, Baltimore, Cincinnati, and St. Louis. Hispanic
populations of the central county of these areas also declined in absolute terms.

As a result of these trends, the historic concentration of minorities in
central cities rapidly eroded in many places.

SUBURBANIZATION AND SEGREGATION IN DENVER

Events in the Denver metropolitan area illustrate the extent of change going on
in some places. In 1970, 1980, and even today, Denver is remarkable for the
extremely high concentration of both blacks and Hispanics in the core city.[6]
Denver is also remarkable for a rapid shift to the suburbs for both minority
groups. Denver continues to exhibit great differences in the residential patterns
of minorities and non-Hispanic whites. However, the region is making rapid
progress toward integration of its suburbs.

At the start of the 1970s, Denver's blacks were almost totally contained
within the city. In 1970, only 3,000 blacks lived in the suburbs, while 46,000
lived in Denver. Hispanics were more represented than were blacks in the
suburbs, but still only one-third lived outside Denver. Growth rates of

minorities in Denver's suburbs were extremely high during the 1970s. The suburban black population burgeoned by over 500 percent, and the Hispanic suburban population by 138 percent. In absolute numbers, however, the black population in the suburbs grew only slightly more rapidly than did the black population of Denver: a suburban growth of 16,000, and a city growth of 13,000. Hispanic suburban growth was very rapid in absolute terms, rising by 47,000, while Hispanics in the city grew by only 23,000 (James, McCummings, and Tynan 1984).

The suburbanization of minorities during the 1980s differed in a number of respects from what had occurred during the 1970s (table 4.3). Remarkably, a small but historic reversal took place in the direction of black population change in Denver. Black population in Denver actually declined slightly between 1980 and 1990, so that all net growth of black population took place in the suburban counties. By 1990, almost 40 percent of the region's blacks lived in the suburban ring. Among Hispanics, the rate of population growth in the city fell by half compared to the 1970s, to 16 percent. Almost three-fourths (71 percent) of net growth of Hispanic population took place in the suburbs.

As a result of the slowdown or reversal in minority population change in the city, Denver experienced its most rapid loss of population in any decade of the postwar period. During the 1980s, it lost 5 percent of its population. The rate of loss of non-Hispanic white population actually moderated slightly between the two periods: This group fell by 12 percent between 1980 and 1990, and by 14 percent between 1970 and 1980. There are reports that the loss of black population is producing mounting problems in the older, poorer black neighborhoods of the city. Such neighborhoods—including Cole and Five Points—are experiencing falling housing values, rising vacancy and disinvestment, and some housing abandonment.

The shift of minorities to the suburbs has produced a significant increase in the neighborhood integration of minorities in the region. For purposes of research, social scientists have defined a neighborhood exposure rate of one group to a second group (termed P* in the sociological literature) as the proportion of the population of the second group in the neighborhood of the average person in the first group (James 1986).[7]

As can be seen in table 4.4, the exposure rate of blacks to non-Hispanic whites in the city of Denver was .35 in 1990. This means that non-Hispanic whites made up 35 percent of the population in the census tract or neighborhood of the average black person in the city in 1990. The exposure rate of Hispanics to non-Hispanic whites was .44 in Denver in 1990. In the suburbs, by contrast, the exposure rates of blacks and Hispanics to non-Hispanic whites

Table 4.3

Population Trends in the Denver Metropolitan Area, by Race and Ethnicity: 1980–1991[a]

	Central County			Suburban Ring		
	No.(000)		*% Change*	*No.(000)*		*% Change*
	1980	*1990*	*1980–90*	*1980*	*1990*	*1980–90*
Non-Hispanic						
Whites	326.6	287.2	-12.1	1003.6	1186.8	18.3
Blacks	58.4	57.8	-0.1	18.2	36.4	100.0
Hispanics	92.3	107.4	16.4	81.3	118.8	46.1
Other	15.1	15.3	1.3	23.0	38.7	68.3
Total	492.4	467.6	-5.0	1126.1	1380.7	22.6

Source: Computed by the author from data obtained from 1980 and 1990 Censuses of Population.

[a]The Denver metropolitan area comprises the following counties: Adams, Arapahoe, Boulder, Denver, Douglas, and Jefferson. Denver county is co-terminous with Denver city.

---

were generally more than twice as high. Clearly, minorities within Denver are far more likely to be living in substantially minority neighborhoods than is true for minorities in the suburbs.

Exposure rates are sensitive to the overall composition of population in an area. Exposure rates of minorities to non-Hispanic whites should be expected to be higher in suburbs, because non-Hispanic whites are a larger proportion of the overall population in suburban areas. In a more fundamental sense, however, blacks and Hispanics are more highly dispersed, or less clustered, within the suburbs than they are within Denver. So-called segregation indexes have been developed to measure the dispersion of groups among neighborhoods. A value of 1.0 on these indexes indicates that minorities are totally isolated in all-minority neighborhoods. A value of zero indicates complete neighborhood integration, in the sense that all neighborhoods have the same racial and ethnic composition (James 1986).

With the exception of Adams County, segregation indexes in Denver's suburban counties were only slightly above zero in 1990, indicating very substantial spreading out of minority populations among census tracts or

Table 4.4

Indicators of Neighborhood Integration in Denver County and Its Suburban Counties: 1990

	Exposure Rates to Non-Hispanic Whites[a]		Segregation Indexes[a]	
	Blacks	*Hispanics*	*Blacks*	*Hispanic*
Denver	.35	.44	.41	.28
Suburban Counties				
Adams	.65	.71	.15	.07
Arapahoe	.78	.82	.06	.02
Boulder	.88	.85	.00	.05
Douglas	.95	.95	.00	.00
Jefferson	.87	.88	.01	.02
Metro. Area	.51	.63	.30	.19

[a] The indexes are defined in the text, and in James, 1986.

---

neighborhoods (table 4.4). By contrast, segregation in Denver was significant in 1990, especially for blacks. The 1990 segregation index for blacks in Denver was .41; the index for Hispanics was .28.

Overall, in part as a result of suburbanization, the Denver metropolitan area made remarkable progress toward racial and ethnic integration of neighborhoods.[8] At the metropolitan scale, the index of segregation of blacks declined by almost half between 1970 and 1990, from .59 to .30. Unfortunately, the index of segregation changed much less for Hispanics. In 1970, the index was .22, and in 1990 it was .19. Nevertheless, overall progress toward integration is striking and significant. Suburbanization has been an important process, undercutting segregation and increasing integration.

The suburbanization of minorities has also been a potent force for the school integration of minorities (table 4.5). The exposure rates of both black and Hispanic pupils to non-Hispanic white pupils are far higher in the major suburban school systems than they are in Denver public schools. One-third or less of the classmates of the average minority child in Denver schools are non-Hispanic whites; indeed, about one-third of the overall enrollment of the

Table 4.5

Indicators of Public School Integration in City and Suburban School Systems of the Denver Metropolitan Area: 1989–1990[a]

	Exposure Rates to Non-Hispanic Whites[b]		*Segregation Indexes*[b]	
	Blacks	*Hispanics*	*Blacks*	*Hispanics*
Denver Public Schools	.34	.30	.30	.27
Suburban School Districts				
Aurora	.63	.67	.08	.01
Cherry Creek	.84	.86	.04	.01
Jefferson County	.85	.84	.01	.05
Littleton	.90	.90	.01	.01

[a]The data described patterns in elementary schools. The school is the unit of analysis. The results of analysis of middle schools and high schools are fundamentally similar.

[b]Exposure and segregation in Indexes are defined in James, 1986.

Source: Analyses of data provided by the Colorado Department of Education.

district is non-Hispanic whites. Exposure rates are two to three times higher in the suburban districts. As will be discussed in the next section, Denver has been under a federally ordered school busing program since 1974. None of the suburban school systems are.

As discussed above, segregation indexes measure the extent of clustering of minorities and non-Hispanic whites in separate schools or neighborhoods. Segregation indexes are not affected by the overall racial or ethnic composition of an area or school district. This makes it remarkable that blacks and Hispanics in Denver's elementary schools are more highly segregated than they are in any of the suburban districts listed in the table. In the suburban systems, segregation indexes are never above 0.08, a comparatively low level. By contrast, the indexes in Denver are approximately 0.30, four times as high.

The data for middle schools and high schools suggest fundamentally similar conclusions. The relatively high segregation of Denver pupils appears to be the result of a focus of the Denver busing plan on fostering integration of minority children with non-Hispanic white pupils and an indifference to integrating youth from minority groups with one another. In Denver, as in other cities, blacks and Hispanics are as segregated from one another as they are from non-Hispanic whites (James, McCummings, and Tynan 1984).

PUBLIC POLICY AND THE SHIFT OF MINORITIES TO THE SUBURBS

As was mentioned in the introduction, some evidence suggests that blacks in the West are achieving more significant and enduring progress toward integration than they are elsewhere in the nation. Thus, the hopeful trends in Denver may not be typical of events in other places. Massey and Gross (1991) suggest that the trends in the West may be due to less opposition on the part of whites to integration because of the smaller average size of black populations in the West. Denver's progress could thus be due to weak efforts by suburban whites to deter black and Hispanic suburbanization.

Unfortunately, direct measures of exclusionary efforts and strategies by whites seeking to avoid integration are generally not available. One indicator that is available for a number of metropolitan areas is audit evidence on the probability of discrimination against minority home buyers and renters. Such audits were done in a number of metropolitan areas in 1989 by the Urban Institute (Yinger 1991). This evidence implies that Denver Hispanics encounter relatively low levels of housing discrimination compared to other places, but that blacks in the metropolitan area are about as likely as blacks in other areas to face housing discrimination (Yinger 1991, tables 18–21).

I have examined exclusionary policies in the Denver metropolitan area, focusing on policies of the state of Colorado and of governments in Denver's two largest suburban counties, Arapahoe and Jefferson. This analysis was limited to policies of the past twenty years, that is, 1970 or later. Earlier, now outmoded, or illegal efforts such as the use of racially restrictive covenants and racial zoning are not included.[9] This survey dramatically documents resistance by white suburbanites to racial and ethnic mixing. Thus, as in other places, blacks and Hispanics in Denver have had to overcome considerable barriers excluding them from the suburbs.[10]

THE POUNDSTONE AMENDMENT
In 1974, Colorado voters passed two amendments to the state constitution that severely curtailed the ability of Denver to annex surrounding unincorporated areas. One—the Poundstone amendment—was an initiative resulting from a petition drive. The other—the Boundary Control Commission—was an amendment proposed by the state legislature to head off the Poundstone

amendment. Since their passage, Denver has been able to complete only one annexation, in 1988, required for the construction of a new Denver airport.

By fixing the boundaries of the central city, these constitutional amendments probably have had the effect of increasing the proportion of metropolitan area minorities who live outside the city limits, in suburban cities or counties. However, they are early dramatic indicators of the determination and ability of white suburbanites to use public policy to limit their exposure to blacks and Hispanics. Suburban voters were motivated to a significant degree by the desire of white suburbanites to keep their children out of the Denver public schools. At the time—and still today—Denver's public schools had the largest representation of black and Hispanic students of any system in the metropolitan area. Denver's schools were also facing court-ordered desegregation.

The attention of both Denver and its suburbs became riveted on issues of racial segregation and integration when Denver public schools began formal consideration of school busing in 1968 and when litigation began the next year after a bruising school district election focusing on school busing issues. The academic year 1974–75 was the first school year following a U.S. Supreme Court decision imposing a school desegregation plan in Denver. This plan resulted from litigation that began in 1969. School busing was implemented with much less trouble and divisiveness than in most other major cities (Orfield 1981). Still, it had a major impact.

Under the Colorado constitution, Denver has a unique status. The boundaries of the city coincide with those of the county and school district serving the city. Expansion of the city also means expansion of boundaries of Denver public schools. A 1972 Denver planning department study of annexation argued: "Without annexations, Denver could soon become the ghetto of the metropolitan area" (Denver Planning Department 1972).

To avoid this fate, Denver became much more aggressive in its annexation, and Denver suburbs began a series of defensive incorporations and annexations designed to stop Denver. Aurora and Greenwood Village, both in Arapahoe County, were especially active in defensive annexations. Major suburban cities, such as Lakewood and Wheat Ridge in Jefferson County, were incorporated in large part as a result of fears that they might be annexed by Denver. Denver considered but did not act on a state constitutional amendment separating its boundary from that of Denver schools. Rather, the city began denying access to its regional water system to areas that refused to annex to the city.

In mid-1973, Freda Poundstone, a resident of Greenwood Village, began a petition drive for a constitutional amendment barring further

Denver annexation.[11] This amendment went on the ballot for the 1974 elections and was passed easily. The voters also passed a state constitutional amendment prohibiting school busing for purposes of desegregation and the Boundary Control Commission designed by the state legislature to limit Denver annexation. Poundstone was also active in pushing the antischool busing amendment.

All available evidence supports the conclusion that the issues of school desegregation and busing played a major role in the passage of the Poundstone amendment. Contemporaneous newspaper analyses reported that fears of school busing were important. In a 1990 interview, Freda Poundstone said that "busing undoubtedly did play a role" in the passage of her amendment. She went on the say that Denver could have preserved its annexation powers if the boundaries of the school district had been separated from those of the city (Poundstone, August 31, 1990). During the 1974 campaign, the press characterized Poundstone's position: "It is the neighborhoods—particularly schools and the threat of Denver busing—which she said is the main impetus in the annexation battle" (Whitbeck 1974).

Suburban school districts—particularly Cherry Creek, Littleton, and Jefferson County schools—were prominent supporters of the Poundstone amendment, as were the suburban counties of Arapahoe and Jefferson. The limits on Denver annexation passed in 1974 have had the effect of increasing the racial isolation of minority children in Denver public schools. Today, only about one-third of the students in Denver schools are non-Hispanic whites. In the absence of the Poundstone amendment, numbers of whites in the schools would have been far higher. Analysis of Denver's annexation plans and strategies suggests that in the absence of the amendments, Denver would have continued its aggressive annexation activities of the early 1970s, successfully annexing large areas to the south and southwest of the city.

Strictly speaking, limits on Denver annexation do not exclude minorities from the suburbs. However, by stopping Denver annexation, suburbanites were rejecting service by desegregated government institutions. The amendments could have left little doubt in the minds of minorities in the region that they were not welcome in many suburbs.

ASSISTED HOUSING IN DENVER'S SUBURBS

Denver's fear of being overwhelmed by growing populations of minorities and the poor also led it to take a leadership role in the early 1970s in efforts to stimulate the supply of assisted or subsidized housing in the suburbs, so as to increase the residential choices of the poor. In 1972, the city contained 82 percent of the metropolitan area's 10,438 assisted housing units (Denver Regional Council of Governments 1982).

In order to reduce the concentration of assisted housing in the city, Denver worked within the Denver Regional Council of Governments (DRCOG) to create a regional "fair share" allocation model for low-cost housing. The result was the adoption of an innovative Regional Housing Plan in 1972. The plan called for 21,000 new assisted units for the region, 73 percent of which were to be located in the suburbs.

This plan had relatively little effect. President Nixon's 1973 moratorium on all assisted housing programs robbed the program of resources, and opposition by a number of suburban governments was intense (Duff and Hardy 1978). Some decentralization of assisted housing was accomplished, however. By 1977, 73 percent of assisted housing was in Denver, down from 82 percent in 1972 (DRCOG 1982).

In 1978, as a result of President Carter's national urban policy, the federal Department of Housing and Urban Development (HUD) encouraged Areawide Regional Housing Opportunity Plans. Regions implementing such plans were offered bonus allocations of housing aid and extra planning dollars. DRCOG submitted such a plan to HUD in 1978. The result was a second effort to produce assisted housing in the suburbs of the region. Between 1972 and 1981, over half (53 percent) of the 16,748 assisted units added were located in Denver's suburbs. Moreover, so-called family housing was shifted to the suburbs more rapidly than was housing for the elderly.

Unfortunately, the new assisted units in the suburbs did not produce a commensurate increase in the supply of assisted housing for Denver's poor people, who were disproportionately minorities. In 1980, the great majority (78 percent) of the residents of assisted family housing in Denver were minority, that is, black or Hispanic. In contrast, the bulk—82 percent in 1980—of the residents of assisted family housing in the suburbs were non-Hispanic whites (Orfield 1981). It appears that assisted housing in the suburbs was not commonly available to minority families from Denver who were eligible for assisted housing.

Two policies contributed to this outcome. There was a general failure of suburban housing authorities to affirmatively market their housing to minorities. More importantly, a number of suburban housing authorities used (and continue to use) residency preferences in the selection of tenants. Because the suburban counties have relatively small minority populations, such residency preferences have given non-Hispanic white tenants priority. Suburbs wanted to serve their own poor first. Residency preferences provided the suburbs some confidence that they could serve their own people.

Racial fears contributed to the desire of suburbs to serve their own people first. Persons involved in the regional housing opportunity plan and in the establishment of suburban housing authorities to implement it report that race was very carefully avoided in discussions of the plan (Branscombe 1991; Muldanado 1991; Ratzlaff 1991). However, people did discuss fears in the suburban communities that "all of the poor people in Denver would move in" if assisted housing were built. Bill Ratzlaff (1991), the director at the time of Denver Housing Authority, reports:

> Racial motivation was always beneath the surface in Denver's dealings with the suburbs. However, representatives of the communities involved were always careful to not say anything that would reflect a racial or segregationist bias. Some communities, such as Jefferson County and Englewood (and perhaps Littleton), did express their fear of being inundated by Denver's poor if they were allowed free movement from housing projects in one community to those in others.

In the opinion of another person involved, "Race was a major concern" (Muldanado 1991). John Helm (1990) of the Denver Housing Authority reports that the prevailing attitude in the suburbs was "to contain minority families in Denver."

Another indicator of the role of racial fears in suburban housing policies is that assisted housing projects attracted intense suburban opposition in the Denver area during the late 1970s. In one remarkable case in the suburb of Arvada, a project was stymied by impassioned local protests. The developer complained to the Colorado Civil Rights Commission. The commission staff investigated and found probable cause that the opposition was racially motivated and illegal under Colorado and federal law. Conciliation efforts by the commission failed, however, and the development was never accomplished (Colorado Civil Rights Commission 1978a, Appendix C).

It should also be noted that a number of suburban communities refused to cooperate with the housing opportunity plans. For instance, DRCOG found the performance of most Arapahoe County municipalities (aside from Aurora and Littleton) unacceptable. These communities included Greenwood Village and Cherry Hills Village and the very large unincorporated areas of the county (DRCOG 1979).

EXCLUSIONARY HOUSING POLICIES IN THE DENVER SUBURBS

It is likely that researchers and courts have overstated the potential effects of exclusionary land-use controls on minority access to suburbs. It has been established again and again that income differences between whites and minorities account for only a small part of the disparities in residential patterns of the groups (Yinger 1979; Darden 1987). This suggests that differences in housing costs and characteristics, and thus zoning and subdivision controls, also may not by themselves explain very much.

It is somewhat plausible that policies which diminish the supply of rental housing may have an exclusionary effect, however. One heritage of discrimination is that minorities frequently lack the capital needed for home ownership. Moreover, minorities frequently encounter discrimination in capital markets when they seek to buy homes (James, McCummings, and Tynan 1984; Galster 1991b). As a result, rental housing is of special importance in enabling minorities to enter a neighborhood or community.

Exclusionary zoning has not been a major factor limiting the suburban housing supply in the Denver metropolitan area, though it has played a small role. Some major suburbs have encouraged a diverse housing stock. Aurora is notable, for example, for offering a mix of various housing types within neighborhoods in the city. Unincorporated Arapahoe County has enabled some large moderate-cost housing developments (Roberts 1985). Jefferson County was active from 1979 through the mid-1980s in providing home financing at tax-exempt rates to buyers of moderate-cost housing in the county. Over $200 million of such financing was provided from 1979 to 1984 (Shulruff 1985).

This is not to say that some communities do not have land-use controls that exclude high-density housing or mobile homes. For instance, research by the Colorado Civil Rights Commission and Suburban Action Inc. during the mid-1970s found exclusionary practices in some suburbs in Jefferson County, including Wheat Ridge, Arvada, and Lakewood (Colorado Civil Rights Commission 1978b). A review of the current zoning maps of Cherry Hills Village in Arapahoe County shows that no land is zoned for multifamily housing and that large lots are generally required for one-family homes. Greenwood Village, the home of Freda Poundstone, has permitted multifamily development only in areas in the northwest parts of the city, close to the Denver Tech Center, a major office development close to I-25. However, such exclusionary practices are not pervasive. High-density, moderate-cost housing is available in many of Denver's suburbs.

HOUSING DISCRIMINATION IN THE SUBURBS

Both blacks and Hispanics have been shown to encounter significant discrimination by landlords and real estate agents when they seek to rent or buy housing in Denver suburbs. Three independent research projects have used the audit or testing method to measure patterns of racial and ethnic discrimination. One, by me, found that both blacks and Hispanics encountered the most severe discrimination in predominantly white neighborhoods (James, McCummings, and Tynan 1984). Blacks ran up against the most severe discrimination in such neighborhoods of the suburbs. Both black and Hispanic renters encountered discrimination throughout the metropolitan area.

A second study by the Colorado Civil Rights Division found significant discrimination in the metropolitan area against blacks, Hispanics, Asians, Native Americans, and Moslems (Snow 1991). This study found such discrimination throughout the metropolitan area.

The third and most recent study was done in 1989, and focused on discrimination against blacks and Hispanics (Metro Denver Fair Housing Center undated). This study is a preliminary report of the fieldwork performed for the Urban Institute research cited above. This study found there was a slight tendency for discrimination to be more common in the suburbs than in Denver. For instance, non-Hispanic whites were favored over blacks in every audit of discrimination in Arapahoe and Douglas counties, both suburbs to the south of Denver, while in Denver, whites were favored in 89 percent of tests. In tests for Hispanics, whites were favored in Denver in 66 percent of tests. In the suburbs, whites were favored over Hispanics in 73 percent of the tests in Arapahoe County, 77 percent in Jefferson, and 80 percent in Douglas (Metro Denver Fair Housing Center undated).

Human relations commissions have been formed only in Denver, Boulder, and Aurora. No other jurisdiction in the metropolitan area has created such a unit (Crow 1982). There is little doubt that patterns of discrimination have in some cases channeled blacks and Hispanics into relatively narrow segments of suburban or fringe development. During the 1960s and 1970s, only one major new home development in the region announced an equal opportunity policy for minority buyers: Montbello, in northeastern Denver. Subsequently, this development has become predominantly minority in its racial and ethnic composition (Culp and Landes 1983). The city of Aurora undertook fair housing activities during the 1970s, which appear to have stimulated blacks to move into the community in large numbers (Cowan 1991). Aurora became a focus of black migration into the suburbs during the 1970s and 1980s.

EXCLUSION BY THE SUBURBAN SCHOOLS

There is some evidence that minority children in suburban public schools do better academically than they do in Denver public schools. For instance, black second graders in Denver public schools scored on average in the 35th percentile on the Iowa Test of Basic Skills in 1989-90. Blacks in the major suburban districts got average percentile scores of between 38 percentile (Aurora) and 65 percentile (Littleton). Similar discrepancies exist for Hispanic youth. Minority students in the suburbs come from more affluent, better-educated families, accounting for some of the difference.[12]

If the suburban schools really do better in educating minority children, it is not due to any special interest in meeting the needs of minorities. Indeed, it appears that virtually all the school districts in Arapahoe and Jefferson counties offer an atmosphere that is largely indifferent to affirmative action and that can be actively hostile to minority teachers and students.

The best indicator of the indifference of the suburban schools to affirmative action is their poor track record in hiring and retaining minority teachers. The failure to employ reasonable numbers of minority teachers can deny minority children access to role models and to persons in whom they can confide with confidence. Table 4.6 presents figures on the racial and ethnic composition of certificated personnel in the major school districts of the metropolitan area. Certificated personnel is the category of employees which includes teachers.

Denver is the only district in the metropolitan area that employs significant numbers of minority teachers. Even in Denver, only 25 percent of certificated personnel are black, Hispanic, or Native American. Fully 65 percent of the students in the Denver system are minority, including Asians and Native Americans, as well as blacks and Hispanics. Amazingly, the Littleton School District in Arapahoe County employs essentially no black teachers. Fewer than 1 percent of its teachers are Native American or Hispanic. This is the worst record in the metropolitan area. In Cherry Creek schools—also in Arapahoe County—only 3.6 percent of certificated personnel are minority. Only 5 to 6 percent of certificated personnel in Aurora and Jefferson County schools are minority.

Administrators in the suburban schools generally argue that a shortage of qualified minority teachers accounts for their failure to employ substantial numbers of minorities. This argument is somewhat implausible, however.

Table 4.6
Racial and Ethnic Composition of the Certificated Staff of School
Systems in the Denver Metropolitan Area: 1989 (percentages)

District	Non-Hispanic White	Black	Hispanic	Other
Denver Public Schools	74.0	12.1	12.4	1.5
Suburban School Districts				
Aurora	92.4	4.4	1.9	1.3
Cherry Creek	95.3	1.7	1.9	1.2
Jefferson County	93.6	1.2	3.5	1.7
Littleton	99.0	0.0	0.6	0.4

Source: Data from the Colorado Department of Education.

Denver schools have among the lowest pay scales in the metropolitan area. If Denver can hire minority teachers despite its low salaries, it would seem that the suburban districts could, too.

Jefferson County schools form the largest district in the Denver region. The failure of this district to hire minority teachers was identified by the U.S. Department of Justice as a serious problem in 1979. After efforts to achieve a voluntary settlement failed, the Department of Justice brought suit, alleging that Jefferson County schools "pursued and continue to pursue policies and practices which discriminate against hispanics and blacks in hiring for teaching or faculty positions" (U.S. Department of Justice 1979).

In 1980, in response to the suit, Jefferson County schools issued a revised affirmative-action plan setting a goal of making 18 percent of its new teachers black or Hispanic. These goals were exceeded in the first year of the plan, and the federal court case was stayed, then dismissed. Jefferson County's progress was mostly temporary, however. Ten years after the suit, only 5.5 percent of the district's certificated personnel are minority. Interviews with a number of teachers, administrators, and staff of the district leave little doubt that indifference or hostility toward minorities is common in the district.

It should be emphasized that Jefferson County schools are not alone with such problems. The Aurora system, which educates the bulk of suburban black children in the region, is reported to have problems recruiting and promoting Blacks. The Denver NAACP reports that it has sent "dozens" of qualified minority teachers to apply for jobs in the Cherry Creek system, and few if any have been hired.

Unequal discipline is also reported to be a problem in some suburban districts. Black students are reported to be special targets for disciplinary action in the Aurora district, the suburban district with the largest black enrollment in the region. A review of school records by the U.S. Office of Civil Rights has raised this issue for the district. The review disclosed that in one Aurora high school, blacks were 15 percent of students, yet accounted for 29 percent of total suspensions and 47 percent of suspensions for fighting. Even greater discrepancies were found in 1989, when blacks were 17 percent of enrollment and 37 percent of suspensions (Robey 1990).

Gang issues have become very significant in Aurora schools. A number of incidents of gang-related violence have taken place there.

WELFARE PROGRAMS

In Colorado, welfare programs such as Aid to Families with Dependent Children and food stamps are administered by counties.[13] There is evidence that the two largest suburban counties in the metropolitan area—Jefferson and Arapahoe—administer their welfare programs in a manner which impedes access of the needy to help. Such administrative practices would have the effect of excluding actual and potential welfare clients, a group which is disproportionately minority.

In particular, welfare application procedures frequently take far longer to complete and require more extensive documentation in Arapahoe and Jefferson counties than in Denver; the outcomes are reported to be more capricious and unpredictable. A former Legal Aid official reports that cases in which welfare clients seek to transfer into Jefferson and Arapahoe counties are treated as new applications, thus imposing considerable delay and documentation. This is clearly a potential barrier to poor Denver residents seeking to move into these counties.

Evidence from the Colorado Department of Social Services shows that it takes far longer to get welfare assistance in Jefferson and Arapahoe counties than it takes in Denver. Fully 93 percent of Denver applications were decided within thirty days. Fewer than 1 percent took sixty days or longer. By contrast, only 56 percent of Jefferson County applications are resolved within thirty days.

Fully 29 percent of Jefferson County cases took longer than forty-five days, the maximum time permissible under federal and state guidelines. Arapahoe County offers quicker dispositions than Jefferson, but considerably slower than Denver. Nine percent of Arapahoe County cases took longer than forty-five days.

Since late 1990, the state social services department has attempted to speed up application procedures. It has authorized all counties in the state to use so-called "minimum verification" procedures to facilitate applications. These procedures have speeded up applications in some places. However, a recent evaluation reported:

> Homeless service providers still report a great disparity among counties. Even within some counties AFDC processing standards continue to vary—all too often dependent upon individual technicians—whose job it is to determine eligibility, not to set policy (Colorado Coalition for the Homeless 1991).

The Colorado Coalition for the Homeless reports that progress has been substantial in Denver but largely nonexistent in Arapahoe County. The coalition reports an "apparent unwillingness of [Arapahoe County] administrators and technicians to look at the system and to change the system" (Colorado Coalition for the Homeless 1991, 8). A shelter official asserts that in Arapahoe County, "if the tech doesn't like a person they'll shuffle their case around" and create delays. This shelter operator reports that Arapahoe County procedures can force homeless persons to leave the county when application delays exceed the capacity of her shelter to house a family (ibid.).

Indicative of the power of technicians, Colorado has the highest rate in the nation of application denial for what are termed "procedural" reasons, such as failure to provide requested documentation.

RESEARCH AND POLICY ISSUES

It should be emphasized that not all of the barriers imposed on minorities by suburbs are deliberate efforts to exclude people. Some are the result of ignorance or indifference or are side effects of other policies. Moreover, available research does not provide a basis for judging or estimating the effects of such barriers on the scale of minority migration to the suburbs or on the quality of life for minorities in suburbs.

It is to be expected that the future pace of minority suburbanization will continue as at present or accelerate. The blacks and Hispanics who have moved to the suburbs have created paths that future migrants can follow, as well as support networks in suburban communities. Though the suburban barriers to new black and Hispanic residents are substantial, they are frequently not great enough to stop a determined person with the ability to pay for a suburban residence. For instance, discrimination in urban housing markets generally takes the form today of concealment of information (James, McCummings, and Tynan 1984). This makes the housing search process more costly in time and effort for minorities, but it doesn't preclude success to a determined home seeker.

The migration of increasing numbers of blacks and Hispanics to suburban residences is a profoundly hopeful trend for the people involved. As shown, the shift to suburbs is producing greater neighborhood and school integration for minorities, at least in the Denver area. It is likely to boost minority freedom of choice of where and how to live, thus increasing access to employment, quality housing, public services, and other good things. Moreover, the presence of large numbers of blacks and Hispanics in largely non-Hispanic white suburbs means that there are fewer refuges for racist whites seeking to flee integrated neighborhoods. The evidence from Schneider and Phelan (1993) is that there has been a dramatic national decline in the number of all-white suburbs. This could begin to make stable integrated neighborhoods more feasible everywhere in metropolitan areas (Yinger 1986).

The migration to the suburbs also challenges future civil rights and urban policies. The suburbanization of large numbers of blacks and Hispanics undercuts the hard-won political bases of minorities in central cities. As William Julius Wilson has emphasized, the minorities who are leaving city ghettos frequently take with them critical economic and social resources (Wilson 1987). Suburban leadership opportunities will emerge for minorities, as their presence in the suburbs grows. For instance, Aurora, Colorado, just elected the first black member of the city council this last month. However, this transition will likely be slow and uncertain. There is a danger that minority leaders could become increasingly marginalized if they focus their agendas on their existing city bases.

Clearly, much more research is needed to determine the characteristics, needs, and desires of minorities who are moving to the suburbs. We also need to know much more about the effects of these relocations on the well-being of the migrants and their new communities, as well as on the communities they are leaving behind. We need more information about the effectiveness and problems of suburban institutions in servicing the new minority suburbanites and how they can be helped.

APPENDIX A

Metropolitan Areas Included in the Analysis

Atlanta
Baltimore
Buffalo-Niagara Falls, New York
Charlotte, North Carolina
Cincinnati
Cleveland
Columbus, Ohio
Dallas-Fort Worth
Denver-Boulder
Detroit
Houston
Indianapolis
Kansas City
Miami-Fort Lauderdale
Milwaukee
Minneapolis-St. Paul
New Orleans
Norfolk, Virginia
Philadelphia
Pittsburgh
Portland, Oregon
Sacramento, California
St. Louis
Salt Lake City
San Antonio
San Francisco-Oakland
Seattle-Tacoma
Tampa-St. Petersburg, Florida
Washington, D.C.

NOTES

1. The 29 metropolitan areas are listed in the appendix. They exclude New York, Chicago, and Los Angeles, among others. The great size of these areas creates a danger that their trends might dominate those of other places.

2. The metropolitan areas were defined in conformance with census definitions as of 1990. For each metropolitan area, the same counties were included in the 1980 and 1990 population data.

3. The exceptions are Tampa–St. Petersburg, Florida; Minneapolis–St. Paul; Charlotte, North Carolina; Pittsburgh; San Antonio; Salt Lake City; and Milwaukee.

4. The exceptions are Sacramento, California; Minneapolis–St. Paul, Buffalo, New York; Charlotte, North Carolina; Cleveland; Columbus, Ohio; Pittsburgh; Houston; Salt Lake City; and Milwaukee.

5. For non-Hispanic whites, this is true in seventeen of the areas.

6. Denver county and Denver city are coterminous under the Colorado constitution, as will be described below.

7. The census tract is the basic geographic unit used in this chapter to measure neighborhood integration or segregation.

8. The 1970 segregation indexes are from James, McCummings, and Tynan 1984.

9. For a historical examination of relevant policies, see Crow 1982.

10. The negative role of state and local policies toward minority suburbanization is widely assumed, but its full dimensions are not appreciated. Rabin (1987) has described local government segregative policies in the most detail. Rabin focuses only on "land use related" policies such as zoning, clearance activities, and the construction or destruction of public projects such as housing or highways.

11. Specifically, this amendment barred annexation by a county or "city and county" without "submitting the question to a vote of the qualified electors of the county" proposed for annexation.

12. The Gautreaux program in Chicago has relocated hundreds of poor persons seeking assisted housing from Chicago to its suburbs. Studies of the performance of the children in the suburban schools have found what appears to be a generally successful adjustment. Unfortunately, this research does not document the experience of the children in Chicago schools prior to the move, nor does it investigate the performance of any control group of children. Thus,

its findings are merely suggestive (Rosenbaum, Rubinowitz, and Kulieke, 1986).

13. Some counties, including Denver, Jefferson, and Arapahoe, offer general assistance programs as well. These programs are county financed and are optional with the county.

REFERENCES

Branscombe, Bea. 1991. Interview by author, 8 November.
Clark, Thomas. 1979. *Blacks in suburbs: A national perspective*. New Brunswick, N.J.: Rutgers University Center for Urban Policy Research.
————. 1987. The suburbanization process and residential segregation. In *Divided neighborhoods: Changing patterns of racial segregation*, edited by Gary A. Tobin. Newbury Park, Calif.: Sage.
Clay, Philip. 1979. The process of black suburbanization. *Urban Affairs Quarterly* 14:405-24.
Colorado Civil Rights Commission. 1978a. *Identification, development, and demonstration of administrative strategies which can be used by state civil rights/human rights agencies for combating systemic discrimination: Strategy I—exclusionary land use and development controls*. Denver.
————. 1978b. *Supplemental report: Land use strategy*. Denver.
Colorado Coalition for the Homeless. 1991. *Aid to Families with Dependent Children Program in Colorado*. Denver: Colorado Coalition for the Homeless.
Cowan, Norris. 1991. Interview by author, 21 April.
Crow, Eleanor. 1982. *Measuring housing discrimination in Colorado*. Denver: Colorado Civil Rights Division.
Culp, Derrin, and David Landes. 1983. *Green Valley Ranch: Challenge and opportunity*. Denver: University of Colorado at Denver, Center for Public/Private Sector Cooperation.
Darden, Joe T. 1987. Choosing neighbors and neighborhoods: The role of race in housing preference. In *Divided neighborhoods: Changing patterns of racial segregation*, edited by Gary A. Tobin. Newbury Park, Calif.: Sage.
Denver Planning Department. 1972. *Denver annexation policy: Review and recommendations*. Denver.
Denver Regional Council of Governments. 1982. *Notations: Distribution of assisted housing improved*. Denver.

————. 1979. *1979 annual assessment of housing performance.* Denver.

Duff, Mary, and Kathy Hardy. 1978. *Colorado Civil Rights Commission final report: The A-95 review process and civil rights compliance.* Denver: Colorado Civil Rights Commission.

Galster, George. 1991a. Black suburbanization: Has it changed the relative location of races? *Urban Affairs Quarterly* (June 1991): 621–28.

————. 1991b. *The use of testers in investigating mortgage lending and insurance discrimination.* Washington, D.C.: The Urban Institute.

Helm, John. 1990. Interview by author, October 8.

James, Franklin J. 1990. President Carter's comprehensive national urban policy: Achievements and lessons learned. *Government and Policy* 8:29–40.

————. 1986. A new generalized "exposure-based" segregation index. *Sociological Methods and Research* 14 (3): 301–16.

James, Franklin J., and Steven del Castillo. 1992. Measuring job discrimination: Hopeful evidence from recent audits. *Harvard Journal of African American Public Policy* 1:33–53.

James, Franklin J., Betty L. McCummings, and Eileen A. Tynan. 1984. *Minorities in the Sunbelt.* New Brunswick, N.J.: Rutgers University Center for Urban Policy Research.

Logan, John R., and Richard D. Alba. 1993. Locational returns to human capital: Minority access to suburban community resources. *Demography* 30:243–68.

Massey, Douglas S., and Nancy A. Denton. 1988. Suburbanization and segregation in U.S. metropolitan areas. *American Journal of Sociology* 94:592–626.

Massey, Douglas S., and Andrew B. Gross. 1991. Explaining trends in racial segregation, 1970–80. *Urban Affairs Quarterly* 27 (September): 13–35.

Metro Denver Fair Housing Center. undated. *Housing for all.* Denver.

Muldanado, John. 1991. Interview by author, November 22.

Orfield, Gary. 1981. *Housing and school integration in three metropolitan areas: A policy analysis of Denver, Columbus, and Phoenix.* Washington, D.C.: U.S. Department of Housing and Urban Development.

Poundstone, Freda. 1990. Interview by author, 31 August.

Rabin, Yale. 1987. The roots of segregation in the eighties: The role of local government actions. In *Divided neighborhoods: Changing patterns of racial segregation,* edited by Gary A. Tobin. Newbury Park, Calif.: Sage.

Ratzlaff, Bill. 1991. Interview by author, 19 November.

Roberts, Linda Dowton. 1985. County trying to lure affordable housing. *Denver Post,* 13 March.

Robey, Renate. 1990. Feds cite racial bias in school's discipline. *Denver Post,* 22 November.

Rosenbaum, James E., and Susan J. Popkin. 1990. *Economic and social impacts of housing integration.* Evanston, Ill.: Northwestern University Center for Urban Affairs and Policy Research.

Rosenbaum, James E., Leonard S. Rubinowitz, and Marilynn J. Kulieke. 1986. *Low-income black children in white suburban schools.* Evanston, IL: Northwestern University Center for Urban Affairs and Policy Research.

Schneider, Mark, and Thomas Phelan. 1993. Black suburbanization in the 1980s. *Demography* 30:269–79.

Shulruff, Lawrence. 1985. Low-income due aid on mortgages under new policy. *Denver Post,* 13 March.

Snow, Nancy. 1991. Housing discrimination testing. *Apartment Trends,* January, 8–10.

U.S. Department of Housing and Urban Development. 1979. *Recent suburbanization of blacks: How much, who, and where?* Washington, D.C.: Office of Policy Development and Research.

U.S. Department of Justice. 1979. *Complaint,* United States of America v. Jefferson County School District, U.S. District Court for the State of Colorado.

Whitbeck, Chris. 1974. Suspicious of Denver: Poundstone unyielding. *Denver Post,* 30 June.

Wilson, William J. 1987. *The truly disadvantaged: The inner city, the underclass, and public policy.* Chicago: University of Chicago Press.

Yinger, John. 1991. *Housing discrimination study: Incidence of discrimination and variation in discriminatory behavior.* Washington, D.C.: U.S. Department of Housing and Urban Development.

———. 1986. On the possibility of achieving racial integration through subsidized housing. In *Housing desegregation and federal policy,* edited by John M. Goering. Chapel Hill: University of North Carolina Press.

———. 1979. Prejudice and discrimination in urban housing. In *Current issues in urban economics,* edited by Peter Mieszkowski and Mahlon Straszheim. Baltimore: Johns Hopkins University Press.

CHAPTER 5

African American Mobility
and Residential Quality in Los Angeles

by J. Eugene Grigsby, III

While there is some evidence that the degree of racial segregation in the United States may have diminished over the past two decades, racially segregated neighborhoods are still the predominant mode in most metropolitan areas (Goering 1986; Farley and Allen 1987; Massey and Denton 1987, 1993; Jaynes and Williams 1989; Hacker 1992; Leigh 1992). Scholars and those seeking to influence housing policy continue to be concerned about racial segregation for a number of reasons. Paramount among them is the fact that quality of life for minorities relegated to racially segregated neighborhoods is not equal to that of whites who have greater access to a variety of residential areas. In particular, it has been well documented that minorities, especially blacks, live in the oldest housing stock, often in need of substantial repair, pay a disproportionate share of their income for housing, are limited in the amount of equity accumulation, and live in the poorest quality residential environments (Grigsby and Hruby 1985, 1992; King and Mieskowski 1973; Yinger 1978; Schafer 1979).

National initiatives to alleviate these adverse conditions for minorities have not proven to be all that successful. Grigsby and Hruby (1985) found that in spite of the variety of programs initiated by the federal government during the 1970s to improve blighted deteriorating neighborhoods, increase the availability of affordable housing, and reduce discriminatory practices in the marketplace, the majority of urban African American renters did not improve their housing status. Relative to urban renters as a whole, African Americans still pay more, live in older housing of poorer quality, and face restrictions in locational choice even when their incomes make such choices possible.

The decade of the 1980s saw a retrenchment on the part of the federal government in vigorously prosecuting individuals and/or institutions whose actions, practices, or policies perpetuated racial segregation. Furthermore, the federal government has also substantially withdrawn support for building affordable housing, financing urban infrastructure, and/ or providing housing assistance. This has meant that primary responsibility for improving the opportunity for minorities to gain greater access to a variety of residential neighborhoods has fallen to local governments and community-based organizations.

Local government, however, has relied almost entirely on federal resources in attempting to redress adverse conditions found in predominantly minority neighborhoods, while at the same time trying to increase residential access. According to many local government officials, the current economic downturn, coupled with limited federal resources and a change in federal tax laws, has made it nearly impossible to significantly increase the supply of affordable housing or provide housing assistance to minority residents in need (Martinez 1991). Industry experts blame federal tax laws and the credit crunch for driving away potential investors from the multifamily construction market. As a result, builders are required to pay a higher percentage of the development costs up front and recover their money through higher rents. Equally difficult, according to these officials, is the ability to effectively sanction those who continue to perpetuate housing segregation.

Given this rather bleak picture of the past, present, and likely future status of minority access to a variety of residential neighborhoods, we have chosen to more closely examine black residential mobility and its implications for neighborhood quality. We do this in order to identify possible housing strategies that might be employed by local officials to improve residential access and subsequent residential quality for minorities. We suspect that because of the variety of settings in which housing policy must be formulated and implemented, workable local solutions for improving residential neighborhood quality may prove to be more beneficial than national efforts aimed primarily at reducing barriers to racial discrimination.

According to Leigh (1992), equal opportunity in access to housing—or fair housing—means the ability of households or any racial or ethnic group to seek out and acquire housing they can afford in any market area. Of particular importance in Leigh's definition is that access to housing does not necessarily mean in integrated neighborhoods. Her concept is broad enough to encompass the notion that "access to housing could also include residence in racially segregated neighborhoods (that is, neighborhoods in which only one racial group lives), if the decision to so reside is not coerced" (Leigh 1992, 5). This notion of black residential mobility into and out of designated residential neighborhoods is the focus of this research inquiry.

THE SETTING

The Los Angeles metropolitan area serves as a good venue for assessing how residential quality of life for blacks has been affected by residential mobility. The region experienced tremendous population and economic growth in the 1980s. Furthermore, there are a number of independent municipalities within the region responsible for formulating and implementing housing policies. For those not familiar with Los Angeles, it should be noted that the Los Angeles metropolitan area, a census-defined Standard Metropolitan Statistical Area (SMSA), is coterminous with Los Angeles County. What is often overlooked, however, is that Los Angeles County comprises 88 independent municipalities, one of which is the city of Los Angeles, as well as unincorporated territory. Because of the number of different local governments within the same housing market, we have an opportunity to assess if and how local policies might influence residential mobility as well as neighborhood quality.

In 1970, 77 of the then-78 cities within Los Angeles County had residential populations whose minority compositions were 10 percent or less. There were only 78 municipalities in Los Angeles County in 1970. This number increased to 88 by 1990. By 1990, all 88 cities within the county had minority populations exceeding 10 percent. Particularly striking is the fact that in 1970 one city, Compton, had a minority composition greater than 50 percent; by 1990, 42 cities had minority compositions of 50 percent or more (see Figure 5.1). As measured by geographic dispersal, minorities had experienced residential mobility within the Los Angeles metropolitan area over this twenty-year period.

Does this mean, however, that minorities in Los Angeles have substantially improved their residential quality of life? Or does it mean that conditions characteristic of residentially segregated neighborhoods in earlier decades prevail today because Los Angeles's minorities, while having moved out of the central city, have become resegregated within other residential locations?

THE APPROACH

In attempting to determine how residential mobility has affected housing quality for Los Angeles's black residents, we analyzed 1970 and 1990 census data to identify residential mobility patterns of African Americans, as well as to

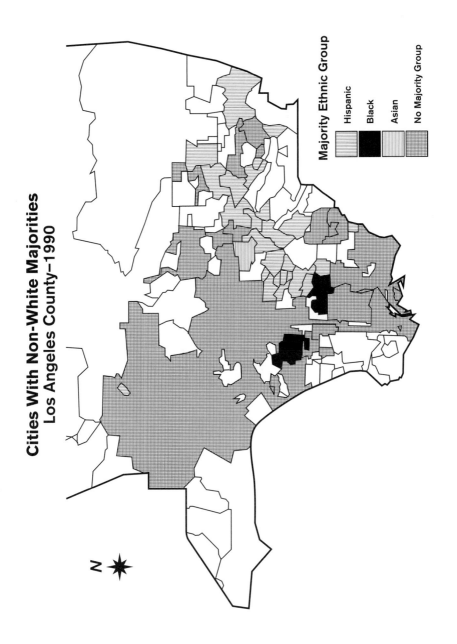

Figure 5.1

assess selected housing characteristics. Throughout this chapter the terms *black* and *African American* are used interchangeably.

Because of the tremendous population growth that has occurred within the Los Angeles region over the past two decades, as well as the seemingly greater residential mobility of blacks, we speculated that several different types of black residential neighborhoods might exist. Our primary unit of analysis was the census tract. All tracts meeting a specified set of criteria were grouped together to form unique neighborhood types.

We did not use traditional segregation indexes to assess neighborhood type for several reasons. First, unlike many other metropolitan areas, Los Angeles has a number of different ethnic groups (e.g., Mexicans, Guatemalans, Koreans, Japanese, etc.) residing in close proximity to each other. Existing segregation indexes have been built assuming a black/white dimension. Second, discussions with a number of black residents indicate they believe that ethnic immigration (particularly Latino) into traditional black residential areas adversely affects their quality of life. Finally, within the Los Angeles metropolitan area, whites are rapidly becoming the minority group, while people of color represent a plurality. Los Angeles is unique in this regard, compared to most metropolitian areas in the country.

We hypothesized that these neighborhoods could be categorized into one of three distinct types. *Declining neighborhoods* are those residential areas where the proportion of blacks declined from 1970 to 1990.[1] Out-migration and/or rapid in-migration of nonblacks accounts for this neighborhood type. Under this type, four subtypes were defined. These included:

> 1. D1—residential areas where blacks constituted more than 65 percent of the population in 1970 but declined to between 65 and 50 percent of the population by 1990.

> 2. D2—residential areas where blacks constituted between 50 and 65 percent of the population in 1970 and declined to less than 50 percent of the population by 1990.

> 3. D3—residential areas where blacks constituted more than 65 percent of the population in 1970, but less than 50 percent of the population by 1990.

> 4. D4—areas where the black population declined in terms of absolute numbers but which did not meet numeric criteria for any of the other three types of declining neighborhoods.[2]

Emerging neighborhoods are those in which the proportional size of the black residential population increased over the 1970–1990 time period. Growth of the black population within this type of neighborhood could only result from in-migration, more than likely from other parts of the metropolitan area rather than from outside the county. Two subtypes were defined as follows:

> 1. E1—residential areas in which the black population increased by 100 percent or more from 1970 to 1990, and the 1990 population was 200 or more.[3]

> 2. E2—residential areas that showed net growth in black population, but that did not meet either E1 criteria or those for declining neighborhood types.

Stable neighborhoods are those residential areas where the relative size of the black population did not change over the twenty-year time period. Three subtypes were defined for this neighborhood type.

> 1. S1—residential areas where blacks constituted more than 65 percent of the residential population from 1970 to 1990.

> 2. S2—residential areas where the proportion of the black population did not vary by plus or minus 10 percent between 1970 and 1990 and which did not meet criteria for any declining or emerging areas.

> 3. S3—residential areas in which the numeric size of the black residential population did not change over the twenty-year period and which were not included in any of the other stable neighborhood types.

Each of these neighborhood types was constructed so that they would be mutually exclusive. These measures function in two ways:

> 1. To describe quantitative changes in the size and residential location of Los Angeles County's black population.

> 2. To serve as an independent variable with which possible differences in residential quality might be associated; they can also be used to test the notion that movement to less segregated areas is associated with better residential quality, as measured by the housing data.

The objective was to determine whether or not residential mobility, as measured by neighborhood type, would have any discernable effects on housing quality.

THE FINDINGS

DISTINCT NEIGHBORHOOD TYPES EXIST

Figure 5.2 shows the location of each of the neighborhood types within Los Angeles County. It should be noted that not all of the hypothesized neighborhood subtypes could be constructed. Only three declining neighborhood, two stable neighborhood, and two emerging neighborhood subtypes met the criteria or contained enough blacks to make further analysis meaningful.

The majority of African Americans within the Los Angeles region, irrespective of neighborhood type, are clustered in fourteen cities (Carson, Compton, Culver City, Gardena, Hawthorne, Inglewood, Long Beach, Los Angeles, Lynwood, Monrovia, Paramount, Pasadena, Pomona, and Signal Hill). Using a population concentration index of segregation would undoubtably show a high degree of black/white residential segregation, particularly if all tracts within the SMSA were employed.

Unfortunately, there is no SMSA jurisdictional body with authority over the 88 municipalities in the region which can formulate or implement housing policy. Thus, while an SMSA-wide segregation index in and of itself might be interesting, its ability to inform local housing policy is rather dubious, particularly since seventy-four of the municipalities within the SMSA with housing policy responsibilities have virtually no African American residents.

The total African American residential population of 765,389 persons within the 14 cities listed above constitutes 93 percent of the African American population within the metropolitan area, whose 1990 black population was 863,411. Furthermore, regardless of the "clustering" of African Americans within the central core of the region, distinct neighborhood types do appear to exist. Finally, the data also show that new areas of African American residence are beginning to emerge throughout the region.

DECLINING NEIGHBORHOODS

Table 5.1 shows the distribution of declining neighborhood types for each of these fourteen cities. No D3 neighborhood subtypes were identified: that is, between 1970 and 1990 no city had residential areas in which the African American population declined from greater than 65 percent to less than 50 percent.

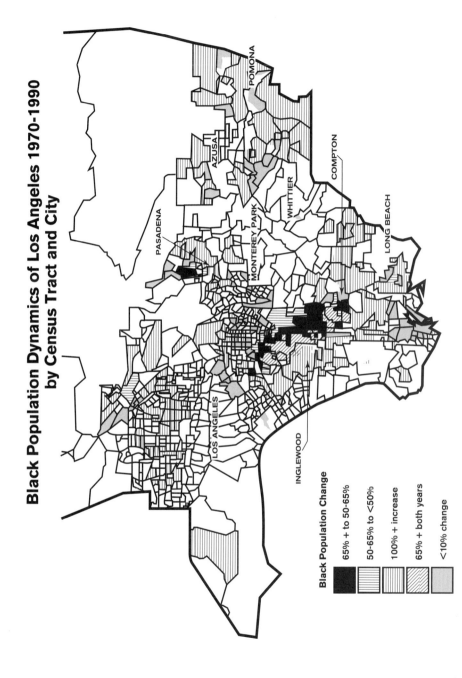

Black Population Dynamics of Los Angeles 1970-1990 by Census Tract and City

Black Population Change

65% + to 50-65%
50-65% to <50%
100% + increase
65% + both years
<10% change

Figure 5.2

Table 5.1
Percent of Black Population Living in Declining Neighborhoods by City

| | Declining Neighborhood Subtypes | | | |
City	D1	D2	D4	Total
Carson	0.00	0.00	7.77	7.77
Compton	**23.56**	**13.81**	**0.00**	**37.37**
Culver City	0.00	0.00	0.00	0.00
Gardena	0.00	0.00	0.00	0.00
Hawthorne	0.00	0.00	0.00	0.00
Inglewood	0.00	0.00	0.00	0.00
Long Beach	0.00	9.34	4.20	13.54
Los Angeles	**21.81**	**16.62**	**2.67**	**41.10**
Lynwood	0.00	0.00	0.00	0.00
Monrovia	0.00	51.24	0.00	51.24
Paramount	0.00	0.00	0.00	0.00
Pasadena	**27.53**	**14.60**	**4.93**	**47.06**
Pomona	0.00	10.73	18.53	29.26
Signal Hill	0.00	0.00	0.00	0.00
Others[a]	12.51	4.88	3.84	21.23
County[b]	15.27	11.22	3.04	29.53

[a]These data represent the aggregate total of the other seventy-four cities in the region.

[b]The aggregate total of all cities within Los Angeles County. Data for residents in unincorporated territory are not included.

Note: Boldfaced cities represent those with the largest black populations.

Source: Computed by the author from data obtained from U.S. Bureau of the Census, Census of Population and Housing, 1970 (computer file): Summary tape file 1A, 1990 (computer file): P.L. 94-171.

Over 40 percent of African Americans in Pasadena and Los Angeles live in residential areas in which the African American population has been declining. Nearly 40 percent of African Americans in Compton also lived in this type of neighborhood. These three cities have the largest black populations within Los Angeles County (65 percent of the county's total African American population). Even though 51.24 percent of Monrovia's African American population lives in D2 areas, this represents less than 1 percent of the county's African

Table 5.2
Date of City Incorporation

City	Date of Incorporation
Carson	1968
Compton	**1888**
Culver City	1917
Gardena	1930
Hawthorne	1922
Inglewood	1908
Long Beach	1897
Los Angeles	1850
Lakewood	1921
Monrovia	1887
Paramount	1957
Pasadena	1886
Pomona	1888
Signal Hill	1924

Note: Boldfaced city is that with the largest black population.

Source: Computed by the author from data obtained from the Los Angeles County Department of Regional Planning, Population Research Section.

American population. The percentage of African Americans living in this type of neighborhood throughout the county (29.53 percent) or living in cities with extremely small black populations (21.23 percent) is much smaller (see table 5.1). Cities with declining African American residential neighborhoods are among the oldest cities within the region (see table 5.2).

EMERGING NEIGHBORHOODS

Fewer blacks in Compton (25.98 percent) and Los Angeles (28.37 percent) live in emerging areas (see table 5.3). However, the majority of blacks in eleven of the other twelve cities live in this type of neighborhood. It is likely that in these other twelve cities, the majority of black residential growth occurred between 1980 and 1990 and in large measure represents black out-migration from the city of Los Angeles, as well as from other traditional areas of African American

Table 5.3
Percentage of Black Population Living in Emerging Neighborhoods by City

City	Emerging Neighborhood Subtypes		
	E1	*E2*	*Total*
Carson	57.69	31.84	89.53
Compton	**9.17**	**16.81**	**25.98**
Culver City	95.01	4.99	100.00
Gardena	96.72	3.28	100.00
Hawthorne	88.89	11.08	99.97
Inglewood	89.70	9.86	99.56
Long Beach	69.04	17.42	86.46
Los Angeles	**15.68**	**12.69**	**28.37**
Lynwood	98.81	1.19	100.00
Monrovia	40.40	7.64	48.04
Paramount	100.00	0.00	100.00
Pasadena	**26.53**	**26.42**	**52.95**
Pomona	67.13	3.61	70.74
Signal Hill	100.00	0.00	100.00
Others[a]	30.12	27.60	57.72
County[b]	32.64	16.38	49.02

[a]These data represent the aggregate total of the other seventy-four cities in the region.

[b]The aggregate total of all cities within Los Angeles County. Data for residents in unincorporated territory are not included.

Note: Boldfaced cities represent those with the largest black populations.

Source: Computed by the author from data obtained from the U.S. Bureau of the Census, Census of Population and Housing, 1970 (computer file): Summary tape file 1A, 1990 (computer file): P.L. 94-171.

residence. Between 1970 and 1990, the city of Los Angeles experienced a net decline in its African American population of 3.23 percent or 16,257 persons.

Countywide, 49 percent of all African Americans live in emerging neighborhoods while 57 percent of those residing outside of the fourteen comparison cities live in emerging neighborhoods. These figures reinforce the notion that African American residential mobility as measured by geographic dispersion has been substantial between 1970 and 1990, most noticeably in the

Table 5.4
Percentage of Black Population Living in Stable Neighborhoods by City

| City | Stable Neighborhood Subtypes | | |
	S1	*S2*	*Total*
Carson	2.70	0.00	2.70
Compton	**32.24**	**4.13**	**36.37**
Culver City	0.00	0.00	0.00
Gardena	0.00	0.00	0.00
Hawthorne	0.00	0.00	0.00
Inglewood	0.00	0.00	0.00
Long Beach	0.00	0.00	0.00
Los Angeles	**28.78**	**1.58**	**30.36**
Lynwood	0.00	0.00	0.00
Monrovia	0.00	0.00	0.00
Paramount	0.00	0.00	0.00
Pasadena	0.00	0.00	0.00
Pomona	0.00	0.00	0.00
Signal Hill	0.00	0.00	0.00
Others[a]	13.56	0.56	14.12
County[b]	18.73	1.10	19.83

[a]These data represent the aggregate total of the other seventy-four cities in the region.

[b] The aggregate total of all cities within Los Angeles County. Data for residents in unincorporated territory are not included.

Note: Boldfaced cities represent those with the largest black populations.

Source: Computed from data obtained from U.S. Bureau of the Census, Census of Population and Housing, 1970 (computer file): Summary tape file 1A, 1990 (computer file): P.L. 94-171.

last decade. On the surface it might appear that African Americans in the emerging areas are "concentrating." Analysis of data for each of these cities shows that the pattern of African American concentration in emerging tracts mirrors the growth pattern for each city's entire population. At present, black residential concentration does not appear different from nonblack residential concentration patterns.

STABLE NEIGHBORHOODS

Over one-third of African Americans in Compton and 30 percent in Los Angeles live in neighborhoods that have demonstrated residential stability for the past two decades. This compares to just under 20 percent for African Americans throughout the region and 14 percent of African Americans in the other cities (see table 5.4). As was the case with the declining neighborhoods, only the oldest cities exhibit this neighborhood type.

SUMMARY

The majority of all African Americans (93 percent) in Los Angeles County reside in fourteen cities. Within these cities, however, African Americans live in different types of neighborhoods, declining, emerging, or stable. These findings suggest that the context in which housing policy is formulated and implemented could be quite varied. For the majority of the cities within the region, a focus on housing policy that attempts to address issues of greater access may not be deemed necessary because these cities have few African American residents. What is not known, however, is whether existing policies or practices in these cities significantly inhibit African American accessibility to their housing markets.

In the fourteen cities that house the majority of the region's African American residents, the issue of accessibility would appear to be quite different. Not only have African Americans in these cities shown a great deal of residential mobility, they also reside in very different types of neighborhoods. In these cities, the more salient policy issue may be that of improving residential quality instead of increasing accessibility. In the next section we compare the residential quality of blacks in each of the neighborhood types.

DIFFERENCES IN NEIGHBORHOOD QUALITY

DECLINING NEIGHBORHOODS

Originally we sought to examine four subtypes of declining neighborhoods. However, after census tract clusters were identified that met our criteria, we could identify only three subtypes. When we looked at the number of African Americans actually residing in these subtypes, only two had large enough populations to be analytically useful. These two subtypes were D1 and D2. Among the D1 neighborhoods only three cities, Compton, Los Angeles, and Pasadena, had sufficient clusters for analysis of census tracts in which the black residential population had declined over the past twenty years. Data presented in table 5.5 show that the number of African Americans in these tracts relative

Table 5.5

Percentage of Black Population Living in Different Neighborhoods by City

City	All Neighborhood Subtypes						
	D1	D2	D4	E1	E2	S1	S2
Carson	0.00	0.00	7.77	57.69	31.84	2.70	0.00
Compton	23.56	13.81	0.00	9.17	16.81	32.24	4.13
Culver City	0.00	0.00	0.00	95.01	4.99	0.00	0.00
Gardena	0.00	0.00	0.00	96.72	3.28	0.00	0.00
Hawthorne	0.00	0.00	0.00	88.89	11.08	0.00	0.00
Inglewood	0.00	0.00	0.00	89.70	9.86	0.00	0.00
Long Beach	0.00	4.34	4.20	69.04	17.42	0.00	0.00
Los Angeles	21.81	16.62	2.67	15.68	12.69	28.78	1.58
Lynwood	0.00	0.00	0.00	98.81	1.19	0.00	0.00
Monrovia	0.00	51.24	0.00	40.40	7.64	0.00	0.00
Paramount	0.00	0.00	0.00	100.00	0.00	0.00	0.00
Pasadena	27.53	14.60	4.93	26.53	26.42	0.00	0.00
Pomona	0.00	10.73	18.43	67.13	3.61	0.00	0.00
Signal Hill	0.00	0.00	0.00	100.00	0.00	0.00	0.00
Others[a]	12.51	4.88	3.84	30.12	27.60	13.56	0.56
County [b]	15.27	11.22	3.04	32.64	16.38	18.73	1.10

[a]These data represent the aggregate total of the other seventy-four cities in the region.

[b]The aggregate total of all cities within Los Angeles County. Data for residents in unincorporated territory are not included.

Note: Boldfaced cities represent those with the largest black populations.

Source: Computed from data obtained from the U.S. Bureau of the Census, Census of Population and Housing, 1970 (computer file): Summary tape file 1A, 1990 (computer file): P.L. 94-171.

to the number of blacks in each city ranged from a low of 21.81 percent in Los Angeles to a high of 27.53 percent in Pasadena. In the other cities, only 12.51 percent of the black population reside in declining neighborhoods, while 15.27 percent of all blacks in Los Angeles County reside in this type of neighborhood (see Table 5.6).

The first measure of residential quality employed for each of these cities was median home value. As shown in table 5.6, the median home

Table 5.6
Assessment of Neighborhood Quality in Declining (D1) Neighborhoods

City	% Black Population	Median Home Value	% Black Owned	%Single-Family Units
Compton	23.56	112,500	51.20	67.93
Los Angeles	21.81	112,500	33.92	55.39
Pasadena	27.53	162,500	47.91	74.38
Other[a]	12.5	112,500	40.49	68.92
County[b]	15.27	112,500	36.39	59.01

[a] These data represent the aggregate total of the other seventy-four cities in the region.

[b] The aggregate total of all cities within Los Angeles County. Data for residents in unincorporated territory are not included.

Source: Computed from data obtained from the U.S. Bureau of the Census, Census of population and Housing, 1990 (computer file): Summary tape file 1A, 1990 (computer file): P.L. 94-171.

value was identical in all D1 neighborhoods except for Pasadena. The percentage of black home ownership was another measure of neighborhood quality. The city of Los Angeles had the lowest incidence of black home ownership, 33.92 percent compared to 47.91 percent for Pasadena and 51.20 percent for Compton. The other cities had a black ownership rate of 40.49 percent, while the county rate was 36.39 percent. Given the size of the black population within the city of Los Angeles and the fact that it represents a significant proportion of the county's black population, it is not surprising that their home ownership rates were quite similar.

The third measure of neighborhood quality was the percentage of single-family homes within a particular neighborhood type. Among the three cities, Pasadena had the highest proportion of single-family homes (74.38 percent) while Los Angeles had the lowest percentage (55.39 percent).

A different pattern emerged in D2 neighborhoods (see table 5.7). Compared to D1 areas, fewer blacks—13.81 percent in Compton, 14.6 percent in Pasadena, and 16.62 percent in Los Angeles—reside in this declining neighborhood subtype. Median home values were lower than in the D1 neighborhoods

Table 5.7
Assessment of Neighborhood Quality in Declining (D2) Neighborhoods

City	% Black Population	Median Home Value	% Black Owned	%Single-Family Units
Compton	13.81	87,500	46.71	69.21
Los Angeles	16.62	112,500	29.67	50.03
Pasadena	14.60	225,000	28.59	47.82
Other[a]	4.88	87,500	44.17	73.38
County[b]	11.22	112,500	32.15	53.26

[a]These data represent the aggregate total of the other seventy-four cities in the region.

[b]The aggregate total of all cities within Los Angeles County. Data for residents in unincorporated territory are not included.

Source: Computed from data obtained from the U.S. Bureau of the Census, Census of population and Housing, 1990 (computer file): Summary tape file 1A, 1990 (computer file): P.L. 94-171.

for Compton and in the other cities. Home values were the same as in the D1 neighborhood subtype for Los Angeles and for the county. In Pasadena, median home values were higher in D2 than in D1 neighborhoods.

Only Pasadena showed a substantial change in the percent of single-family homes, 47.82 percent in D2 neighborhoods compared to 74.38 percent in D1 neighborhoods. Qualitatively, it would appear that residential areas in which blacks fall below the numerical majority (e.g. D2 areas) tend to exhibit characteristics traditionally associated with areas in economic decline. Historically, this has happened in white neighborhoods in which "tipping" occurred when the black population grew noticeably larger (see Goering 1978). This same phenomenon may exist when other ethnic groups move into predominantly African American residential areas. Pasadena is an exception because historically, it has been in high demand as a residential neighborhood. Consequently, housing prices within predominantly African American neighborhoods in Pasadena are more like citywide median prices, which is not true for other cities within the region with sizable declining black residential communities.

Table 5.8
Assessment of Neighborhood Quality in Emerging (E1) Neighborhoods

City	% Black Population	Median Home Value	% Black Owned	% Single-Family Units
Carson	57.69	187,500	76.19	77.51
Compton	**9.17**	**112,500**	**62.22**	**77.80**
Culver City	95.01	350,000	35.14	42.44
Gardena	96.72	187,500	45.70	44.88
Hawthorne	88.89	225,000	3.38	30.94
Inglewood	89.70	162,500	31.05	40.37
Long Beach	69.04	187,500	15.80	35.54
Los Angeles	**15.68**	**225,000**	**9.97**	**26.09**
Lynwood	98.81	137,500	50.57	64.82
Monrovia	40.40	187,500	9.15	53.63
Paramount	100.00	162,500	19.54	55.21
Pasadena	**26.53**	**275,000**	**14.68**	**39.47**
Pomona	67.13	137,500	48.16	68.11
Signal Hill	100.00	187,500	19.55	34.93
Others[a]	30.12	225,000	38.74	62.58
County [b]	32.64	187,500	26.00	43.06

[a]These data represent the aggregate total of the other seventy-four cities in the region.

[b]The aggregate total of all cities within Los Angeles County. Data for residents in unincorporated territory are not included.

Note: Boldfaced cities represent those with the largest black populations.

Source: Computed from data obtained from the U.S. Bureau of the Census, Census of Population and Housing, 1990 (computer file): Summary tape file 1A, 1990 (computer file): P.L. 94-171.

In one sense these declining neighborhoods represent what the literature describes as "invasion/succession" areas. Traditional black residential areas are witnessing rapid in-migration of Latinos, particularly in Los Angeles and Compton. Keep in mind that D1 tracts had black residential populations of more than 65 percent in 1970, but by 1990 the black population in these areas had declined, even though blacks continued to be the numerical majority (e.g. over 50 percent of the population).

Latinos form the next largest ethnic group in all D1 areas (Compton 41.64 percent, Los Angeles 42.79 percent, and Pasadena 32.31 percent). It should also be noted that approximately 40 percent of all blacks in Compton, Los Angeles, and Pasadena live in these declining neighborhoods.

EMERGING NEIGHBORHOODS

Table 5. 8 shows data on neighborhood quality for emerging neighborhoods. What is most noticeable about these data is that cities with the largest proportion of blacks (i.e., Los Angeles, Compton, and Pasadena) showed the lowest percentage of blacks residing in E1 neighborhoods. In ten of the other eleven cities, more than 50 percent of the black population resided within this type of area.

Median housing values are noticeably higher in E1 tracts compared to the declining tracts, with the exception of the city of Compton. From a price-range perspective, the data show that blacks in emerging areas within the region have a wide range of housing price options. The median prices ranged from a low of $112,500 in the cities of Compton and Lynwood to a high of $350,000 in Culver City.

Equally interesting is the distribution of home ownership among blacks within E1 neighborhoods. In the city of Carson, for example, 57.69 percent of the city's blacks live in emerging tracts, and it appears that a very high proportion of them are home owners (76.19 percent). This relatively high rate of home ownership among blacks in emerging neighborhoods also existed for the city of Compton where 9.17 percent of blacks live in this type of tract and 62.22 percent of them are homeowners. In Pomona, however, 67.13 percent of the blacks reside in E1 tracts but only 48.16 percent are home owners.

In the other cities with sizable African-American populations, many of the new residents are renting instead of becoming home owners. For example, in the city of Hawthorne, 88 percent of the black population reside in an E1 neighborhood but only 3.38 percent are home owners. In Monrovia, of the 40.40 percent of the blacks who live in emerging tracts, only 9.15 percent are home owners. Within the other cities, among the 30.12 percent of blacks residing in emerging neighborhoods, 38.74 percent are home owners. These findings suggest that in E1 neighborhoods, blacks in a majority of the fourteen cities are more likely to become renters than home owners. These findings are consistent with the literature

Table 5.9
Assessment of Neighborhood Quality in Emerging (E2) Neighborhoods

City	% Black Population	Median Home Value	% Black Owned	% Single-Family Units
Carson	31.84	187,500	89.16	75.50
Compton	**16.81**	**112,500**	**60.11**	**67.61**
Culver City	4.99	350,000	13.85	62.79
Gardena	3.28	225,000	16.52	50.98
Hawthorne	11.08	275,000	79.19	85.78
Inglewood	9.86	162,500	73.17	75.26
Long Beach	17.42	275,000	21.21	58.50
Los Angeles	**12.69**	**275,000**	**32.00**	**54.98**
Lynwood	1.19	112,500	62.86	78.95
Monrovia	7.64	275,000	32.00	86.10
Paramount	——	——	——	——
Pasadena	**26.42**	**275,000**	**37.82**	**72.98**
Pomona	3.61	225,000	58.97	69.45
Signal Hill	——	——	——	——
Others[a]	27.60	225,000	47.56	66.48
County[b]	16.38	275,000	41.82	61.98

[a]These data represent the aggregate total of the other 74 cities in the region.

[b]The aggregate total of all cities within Los Angeles County. Data for residents in unincorporated territory are not included.

Note: Boldfaced cities represent those with the largest black populations.

Source: Computed from data obtained from the U.S. Bureau of the Census, Census of Population and Housing, 1990 (computer file): Summary tape file 1A, 1990 (computer file): P.L. 94-171.

that suggests that even though blacks are suburbanizing they are becoming renters more often than owners (Grigsby and Hruby 1985).

Within these emerging areas the ethnic composition tends to be more diverse compared to declining areas. With the exception of Compton, Inglewood, and Lynwood, whites comprise at least 20 percent of the population of these areas. In Carson and Gardena, there is nearly an equal distribution

Table 5.10
Assessment of Neighborhood Quality in Stable (S1) Neighborhoods

City	% Black Population	Median Home Value	% Black Owned	% Single-Family Units
Compton	32.24	112,500	78.89	91.01
Los Angeles	28.78	112,500	44.62	58.41
Other[a]	13.56	137,500	63.49	74.18
County[b]	18.73	112,500	49.89	62.91

[a]These data represent the aggregate total of the other seventy-four cities in the region.

[b]The aggregate total of all cities within Los Angeles County. Data for residents in unincorporated territory are not included.

Source: Computed from data obtained from the U.S. Bureau of the Census, Census of population and Housing, 1990 (computer file): Summary tape file 1A, 1990 (computer file): P.L. 94-171.

of whites, blacks, Latinos, and Asians. There are also sizable Asian populations in Hawthorne, Long Beach, Los Angeles, Pasadena, and Signal Hill. Clearly, blacks moving into most emerging areas have the opportunity to live in racially diverse neighborhoods. This same pattern of racially diverse neighborhoods was also observed in E2 areas.

Table 9 presents the same information for the E2 neighborhood sub-type. The pattern of black concentration in these types of neighborhoods is somewhat different than that found in the E1 neighborhood sub-type. Fewer African Americans live in E2 neighborhoods compared to E1 areas. Two patterns emerge relative to median home values in E1 and E2 neighborhoods. The E2 neighborhoods either have the same median home values as E1 areas (Carson, Compton, Culver City, Inglewood, and Pasadena) or the values are higher (Gardena, Hawthorne, Long Beach, Los Angeles, Monrovia, and Pomona). Only Lynwood showed a decline in median home values.

The price range in E2 neighborhoods is identical to that found in the E1 neighborhood sub-type. There is also no consistent pattern of black home ownership or distribution of single family units between the two emerging neighborhood sub-types. However, it looks as if there is a much higher proportion of black home ownership in E2 compared to E1 neighborhoods. Perhaps most noteworthy is that after Carson, Pasadena has the largest number of blacks living in E2 neighborhoods; indeed, over 50 percent of blacks in Pasadena live in emerging areas. Given that Pasadena has a somewhat longer history as an area of black settlement, changes in the residential location of its black population indicate its continuing desirability and accessibility for black households.

STABLE NEIGHBORHOODS

Only Compton and Los Angeles had a sufficient number of S1 stable neighborhoods for analytic purposes. Median home values in the S1 neighborhoods are clearly more like home values in the declining areas rather than those in emerging neighborhoods. Interestingly, the percentage of black home ownership in Compton's S1 neighborhoods is higher than for stable neighborhoods in either Los Angeles or Pasadena. For example, only 32.24 percent of the blacks in Compton live in S1 neighborhoods, but the black home ownership rate within these neighborhoods is nearly 80 percent. In Los Angeles, 28.78 percent of the blacks live in S1 neighborhoods, but the black home ownership rate is 44.62 percent.

This pattern of relatively high black home ownership rates also exists among stable neighborhoods in the other cities. S1 neighborhoods in these cities housed 13.56 of the black population, and yet the home ownership rate was 63.49 percent (see table 10). These findings suggest that stable neighborhoods may have both greater numbers of single family homes as well as black residents—many of them elderly—who have owned homes for a long time. Opportunities for residential mobility for residents of these areas may be influenced more by personal preferences and/or income constraints than is true for younger households. Analysis of age data for each neighborhood type revealed that in Compton the highest proportion of elderly reside in S1 neighborhoods (10.07 percent). In Los Angeles, the proportion of elderly living in S1 neighborhoods is 11.09 percent. The percentage of elderly living in S1 neighborhoods in all other cities is 10.89 percent.

Given their defining criteria, there is very little racial diversity among the stable neighborhood types. blacks constitute over 75 percent of the residential population in Compton and Los Angeles as well as in the other cities and for the county. Latinos comprised virtually all of the other residents in this neighborhood type.

Table 5.11
Comparative Summary of Neighborhood Quality Measures

	D1	D2	E1	E2	S1
Black Home Ownership (%)					
Compton	51.20	46.71	62.22	60.11	78.89
Los Angeles	33.92	29.67	9.97	32.00	44.62
Pasadena	47.91	28.59	14.68	37.82	——
Other[a]	40.59	44.17	38.74	47.56	63.49
County[b]	36.39	32.15	26.00	41.82	49.89
Median Home Value ($000,000)					
Compton	112.5	87.5	112.5	112.5	112.5
Los Angeles	112.5	112.5	225.0	275.0	112.5
Pasadena	162.5	225.0	275.0	275.0	——
Other[a]	112.5	87.5	225.0	225.0	137.5
County[b]	112.5	112.5	187.5	275.0	112.5
Single-Family Homes (%)					
Compton	67.93	69.21	77.80	67.61	91.01
Los Angeles	55.39	50.03	26.09	54.98	58.41
Pasadena	74.38	47.82	39.47	72.98	——
Other[a]	68.92	73.38	62.58	66.48	74.18
County[b]	59.01	53.26	43.06	61.98	62.91

[a]These data represent the aggregate total of the other seventy-four cities in the region.

[b]The aggregate total of all cities within Los Angeles County. Data for residents in unincorporated territory are not included.

Source: Computed from data obtained from the U.S. Bureau of the Census, Census of population and Housing, 1990 (computer file): Summary tape file 1A, 1990 (computer file): P.L. 94–171.

SUMMARY

The preceding analysis indicates that some systematic differences in neighborhood quality exist between black residential neighborhoods within the Los Angeles metropolitan area. This is true for different types of neighborhoods within cities as well as between cities.

Among the largest cities with substantial African-American populations (Compton, Los Angeles, Pasadena) the percentage of black home owners declines when the proportion of blacks in a neighborhood falls below 50 percent of the area's residential base. This may be a direct result of out-migration of higher-income black residents (see table 11). Reflecting its long history as a suburban area of black residence, a greater proportion of blacks in Compton are home owners, irrespective of neighborhood type, compared to the other two cities.

Median housing values in Compton were lower in D2 compared to D1 neighborhoods. Compton also had the lowest median housing values of any of the emerging areas. Housing values stayed the same in declining areas for both Los Angeles and Pasadena but increased substantially in the emerging areas.

Compton also has a higher proportion of single family units in stable areas than does Los Angeles. We suspect this is because there has been relatively little new housing development in Compton, whereas stable areas in Los Angeles have often been the focus of city-sponsored re-development. These activities have created a higher value housing stock and, at the same time, reduced the number of single family units. Grigsby and Hruby (1992) using data from the Los Angeles Planning Department Building and Safety file have demonstrated that between 1980 and 1988, 17.7 percent of all residential units removed from the city were in black and Hispanic neighborhoods. Furthermore, they found that the units removed represented some of the most affordable dwellings in the city. Replacement units while generally affordable within the greater Los Angeles housing market, were not affordable for most blacks living in neighborhoods from which older, affordable units had been removed.

If little new housing has been constructed in Compton, given the relatively tight housing market throughout the region one would expect that housing prices would have risen based upon the conditions of supply and demand. In the case of Compton, we strongly suspect that other factors such as negative stereotypes about a predominantly black city and lower median household incomes have helped to keep housing prices in Compton artificially low. It should also be noted that the median housing values in the stable neighborhoods closely resemble those of the declining areas.

What is more interesting perhaps, is that in comparison to Compton, Pasadena and Los Angeles have fewer single family units in emerging neighborhoods. This suggests that while blacks moving to these areas may have more limited opportunities to become home owners, the supply of affordable rental units might be quite attractive. We believe that given the cost of housing in emerging neighborhoods and because virtually all new construction over the past decade has been in either multi-units or condominiums, many African-Americans moving into emerging areas may have a greater choice of rental units compared to single family units and, if cost is a significant factor, the new black residents may choose to become renters rather than owners.

CONCLUSION

Some blacks in the Los Angeles metropolitan area have experienced residential mobility over the past twenty years. Data presented in this paper indicate that blacks seeking to become home owners have a wider range of residential areas and prices from which to choose. They also have a variety of neighborhood types in which they can reside; however, these neighborhoods do not have the same degree of residential quality.

Blacks living in stable or declining areas are likely to occupy the oldest housing, and housing whose value and market demand may be limited. Blacks seeking to reside in emerging neighborhoods appear to be able to acquire better quality residential environments commensurate with their ability to pay. Only for the City of Compton do we find evidence that residential quality may be limited irrespective of the neighborhood type.

Looking at residential mobility patterns within the black population over a twenty-year period, many blacks within the Los Angeles metropolitan area have some modicum of residential "choice." Therefore race, *per se,* may not be as strong a barrier to housing access as it once was. In the Los Angeles metropolitan area, at least, it is more likely that constrained income (which is highly correlated with race) may be the largest inhibiting factor preventing blacks from gaining greater access to quality residential areas. However, there are still seventy-four cities within Los Angeles County which have very few African-American residents. Whether blacks are not moving to these cities by choice or because of the cost of housing, racial discrimination, the availability of employment or other factors needs to be determined. Thus, while greater mobility is evident, there is still room for progress.

IMPLICATIONS FOR POLICY

General consensus within the scholarly community is that racially segregated neighborhoods are the norm. However, no such consensus exists regarding just what should be done about this situation. At present, there does not appear to be a great deal of national political support to vigorously prosecute and/or sanction individuals or institutions whose actions and practices help perpetuate racially segregated neighborhoods. What then are some reasonable policy options which might be initiated at the local level that, if successful, will enhance residential choice for minority households?

Obviously, one could call for more rigorous legislation forbidding practices that perpetuate racial discrimination in housing. At the same time, rigorous monitoring mechanisms need to be in place to "catch the cheaters" and identified violators should be prosecuted to the fullest extent of the law. Undoubtedly, efforts along these lines should continue. But in the long run are these the most effective means of achieving the desired result?

Based upon the findings in this paper we doubt that aggressive efforts aimed at reducing barriers to racially segregated neighborhoods in and of themselves will ultimately have much impact. First of all, seventy-four cities within the Los Angeles area would likely resist such efforts; their minority populations are currently so small it simply is not very cost effective to try to find and subsequently prosecute wrong doers. Publicized cases of large punitive damages against discriminators are all too often seen as isolated incidents and are unlikely to significantly alter current discriminatory housing practices. Similarly, given that fourteen cities have substantial black populations, a rather strong argument could be mounted that black residential mobility over the past twenty years has demonstrated that, given the means and the desire, blacks can gain access to a variety of residential neighborhoods.

What is needed is for local officials to be more knowledgeable about what is and is not happening in regard to who is living in what units within their jurisdictions. California law mandates that every municipality produce a housing element as part of its general plan. This element is to be updated every five years. Municipalities are supposed to identify housing needs of various populations, including low-income households, the elderly, and the homeless. The law does not require that racial or ethnic characteristic be taken into account. Given California's growing ethnic diversity, we believe omission of this factor should be re-examined.

While most municipalities have in one form or another attempted to provide housing for the elderly and low-income populations, few cities can give any account of the ethnic characteristics of the elderly or low-income people occupying these units. Preliminary results of a survey we conducted among planning directors throughout the region indicate that white elderly have been one of the primary beneficiaries of most city-sponsored elderly housing programs. Whether this is the result of racial discrimination or happenstance we cannot say. Similarly, affordable housing produced as a result of redevelopment activities is seldom occupied by former minority residents from the areas in which this new housing has been produced. They simply cannot afford these new "affordable" units. What we do know, however, is that if cities would routinely identify who benefits from city-sponsored housing production, it would certainly be much easier to assess whether or not there is equity among different ethnic groups as a result of locally initiated housing policy.

In California both local officials and community-based housing advocates agree that an inadequate supply of affordable housing is a critical problem for minorities. Efforts to increase the rate of production of affordable units are dependent upon a number of different factors including the availability of developable land, the state of the economy, local land-use policies and administrative practices, as well as federal tax laws. At present, most California municipalities have decided that production of new units, often involving large subsidies up to $100,000 per unit, is the most prudent way to proceed.

An alternative strategy—albeit more short than long range—would be to utilize current construction subsidies to provide vouchers for low-income households to secure available rental units at a variety of price ranges. This strategy assumes that vacancy rates in the middle and upper-price range are significantly higher than those at the lowest end of the market (this assumption holds true for most California cities). Market-rate rental housing has been the predominant type of unit produced throughout the Los Angeles metropolitan area and these units have not required public subsidies. Thus, given an available supply of these units, a voucher system, much like the Gautreaux program in Chicago, would provide a larger number of individuals with the opportunity to gain access to housing located in a number of different geographic areas. This strategy could produce more positive residential choice and quality outcomes compared to those of current low-income housing production approaches which locate affordable units primarily in downtown areas or in existing low-income residential neighborhoods.

Given its size, ethnic diversity and jurisdictional heterogeneity, the Los Angeles metropolitan area provides a natural "laboratory" for creating, implementing, and assessing a variety of housing and housing-related policies that could affect residential choice and quality of life for those whose options are constrained by race, income, or other factors. Our next step is to examine local policy initiatives, or lack of them, in order to illustrate positive, innovative planning and development practices with respect to housing. At the same time, we will also be documenting the conditions and issues that lead to different levels of attention to such matters among cities within the region.

NOTES

1. By declining neighborhood we simply mean loss of black population. There is no implication of economic disinvestment and/or social pathology, attributes often associated with the term "declining neighborhood".

2. For D1, D2, D3 neighborhood types at least one hundred blacks had to reside in these census tracts in 1970 in order to be included in these neighborhood clusters.

3. Previous studies have indicated that when blacks reach some critical mass or tipping point within a designated area, wholesale exodus of whites begins, typically between 10 and 30 percent. We have assumed that two hundred blacks in a tract constitutes a minimum threshold and that increasing this number by 100 percent would become a "noticeable" factor. Taeuber and Taeuber (1965) assumed that all tracts must have at least two hundred and fifty non-white residents to be considered.

REFERENCES

Farley, Reynolds and Walter R. Allen. 1987. *The color line and the quality of life in America.* New York: Sage.

Goering, John. 1986. *Housing desegregation and federal policy.* Chapel Hill, NC: University of North Carolina Press.

———. 1978. Neighborhood tipping and racial transition: A review of socal science evidence. *Journal of the American Institute of Planners* 44: 68.

Grigsby, J. Eugene, III and Mary L. Hruby. 1992. Recent changes in housing status of blacks in Los Angeles. In *The housing status of black Americans* 211–240, Wilhelmina A. Leigh and James B. Stewart, eds., New Brunswick, NJ: Transaction Publishers.

———. 1985. A review of the status of black renters 1970–1980. *The Review of Black Political Economy* 13 (Spring):98–113.

Hacker, Andrew. 1992. *Two nations: Black and white, separate, hostile, and unequal.* New York: Ballantine.

Jaynes, Gerald D. and Robin Williams. 1989. *A common destiny: Blacks and American society.* Washington, DC: National Academy Press.

King, A. Thomas and Peter Mieskowski. 1973. Racial discrimination, segregation, and the price of housing. *Journal of Political Economy* 81 (May/June): 590–605.

Leigh, Wilhelmina A. (1992). Civil rights legislation and the housing status of black Americans: An overview. In *The housing status of black Americans* 5–28, W. A. Leigh and J.B. Stewart, eds., New Brunswick, NJ: Transaction Publishers.

Martinez, Gebe. 1991. Putting the squeeze on crowding. *Los Angeles Times,* 2 January 1991.

Massey, Douglas S. and Nancy A. Denton. 1993. *American apartheid: Segregation and the making of the underclass.* Cambridge, Mass.: Harvard University Press.

———. 1987. Trends in the residential segregation of blacks, Hispanics, and Asians. *American Sociological Review* 52: 802–825.

Schafer, Robert. 1979. Racial discrimination in the Boston housing market. *Journal of Urban Economics* 6 (April): 176–196.

Taeuber, Karl and Alma Taeuber. 1965. *Negroes in cities.* Chicago: Aldine.

Yinger, John. 1978. The black-white price differential in housing: Some Further Evidence. *Land Economics* 54 (May): 187–206.

CHAPTER 6

Taking It to the Bank:
Race, Credit, and Income in Los Angeles[1]

by Gary A. Dymski & John M. Veitch

The economic well-being of residents and businesses in any urban neighbor-hood depends in part on whether financial institutions choose to locate and lend there. Banks are often accused of systematically avoiding locating in and lending to neighborhoods solely on the basis of the area's racial composition. They are also accused of differential treatment of individual borrowers or customers solely on the basis of the individual's race. The first practice is termed racial redlining; the second practice constitutes racial discrimination.

Federal legislation over the past twenty-five years has made both practices illegal. The Fair Housing Act of 1968 and the Equal Credit Opportunity Act of 1975 made it illegal to discriminate against individuals or areas on the basis of race in credit transactions. The Community Reinvestment Act (CRA) of 1977, in turn, required that banks assess and meet credit needs of the entire community whose market they were chartered to service, including lower-income neighborhoods. The Home Mortgage Disclosure Act (HMDA) of 1975 required banks to release detailed public information about their residential lending practices and thus provided one way to assess bank performance.

A sustained community-based movement has tried to expose, and reverse, patterns of racial redlining and bank disinvestment since the mid-1970s. The links between race, income, and lending received renewed national attention with the highly publicized studies of Atlanta and Detroit in 1988, followed by two studies of Boston in 1989.[2] In every case, African American neighborhoods received a much lower share of residential and business credit than did other neighborhoods. Meanwhile, audit studies have consistently demonstrated that nonwhite individuals are subjected to discrimination in credit and housing markets.[3] The combination of community pressure, public disclosures of bank lending patterns, and urban decline led several states and localities to adopt "linked deposit" programs in the 1980s. These programs tried, with varying degrees of success, to award city and state banking business to those banks that performed best in inner-city lending and financial services.[4]

In mid-1989, the mayor and city council of Los Angeles commissioned a report examining the role of financial institutions in lower-income and high-minority areas in Los Angeles. Was there racial redlining? Which types of lenders were at fault for lending less in lower-income and high-minority areas? What was the impact of the unique multiethnic fabric in Los Angeles, not just the black-white patterns of other cities, on lending flows within the city? We conducted this study under the auspices of the Western Center on Law and Poverty; it was released on November 6, 1991, by Mayor Tom Bradley.[5] Less than six months later, racial tensions, fueled in part by the economic disparities documented in our study, had exploded, and the city was in flames.

This chapter sets out the main results of our study. Its highlights are readily summarized. Banks and savings and loan associations (thrifts) make fewer and smaller residential loans in low-income and high-minority neighborhoods in Los Angeles. One might guess that lower lending levels to minority neighborhoods are due to their relative poverty. This is not the case. Banks and thrifts make fewer and smaller loans to African American and to Latino American neighborhoods than to white neighborhoods with comparable income levels. Financial institutions operate fewer branches both in low-income and high-minority communities. They also provide little financing to small businesses in these neighborhoods. Problems exist in banks' financing for the construction of multifamily rental housing, particularly affordable housing developments in low-income or high-minority neighborhoods. Banks generally offer little in the way of affordable banking services to the nonelderly poor—94 percent of Los Angeles banks do not allow nondepositors to cash government benefits checks, and fewer than half offer low-cost checking accounts to the nonelderly poor.

The patterns of racially disparate lending and banking services indicate that banks in Los Angeles systematically contribute to, and over time deepen, economic inequality across neighborhoods. This uneven economic development arises from two related features of urban lending. The first is that credit markets are interlinked with past and future levels of income and wealth generated by a community's labor markets and businesses. Minority workers and small businesses have traditionally fared worse than whites in income-earning opportunities—they have been subject to a profound degree of racial segregation. If banks take the lesser economic prospects of minority applicants or areas as given, they will systematically supply less credit and fewer banking services to individuals in these areas. This credit starvation will, in turn, have adverse consequences for future income and wealth prospects in high-minority areas, feeding the downward economic spiral in these areas.

The second mechanism involves spillover effects from the location of bank branches in an area, effects that are not fully captured in the price of housing or credit market transactions. These spillovers can lead to the divergence of income and wealth across neighborhoods over time. The fewer bank branches located in an area, the more difficult the access to mortgage credit, resulting in fewer homes sold in the area. This makes homes in the area less liquid, lowering their worth as collateral, which makes it harder for small-business owners to secure bank financing. Thus the fewer bank branches in a neighborhood, the less economically viable the neighborhood for both businesses and residents, and in turn, the less viable the neighborhood as a bank branch site. Widespread discrimination against people of color in housing and credit markets can make it appear "economically rational" for banks to use the racial character of a neighborhood as a guide to lending decisions, even though it is banks' avoidance of these areas (redlining) that deepens racial economic disparities in income and wealth. The results of past racial discrimination thus become institutionalized in a "forward-looking" economic rationale for discriminatory lending practices.

THE DEMOGRAPHIC AND ECONOMIC TOPOGRAPHY OF LOS ANGELES

Exploring the links between banking, income, and race in Los Angeles required that two technical problems be overcome: The city of Los Angeles is vast and diverse, and the subject matter of our study is controversial. How could the data be presented in a way that is both clear and analytically neutral?

Our solution was to separate the city's 741 census tracts into five roughly equal groups, termed *quintiles*. Each quintile represents 20 percent (about 148) of the census tracts in the city of Los Angeles. We established groupings of census tracts for median income, percentage of residents who were African American, percentage Latino American, percentage Asian-Pacific, and total minority concentration (the percentage of residents who were either African American, Latino American, or Asian Pacific). The quintile grouping for each variable is independent of all other groupings. For example, the income rank groupings of census tracts have no necessary relationship to the racial concentration groupings of census tracts. Thus, the same census tract may appear in different quintiles for different variables. Any relationships that arise in the census tracts reflect the demographic and economic topography of Los Angeles.

INCOME QUINTILES

The use of quintiles avoids the need for ad hoc definitions for "high minority" areas or "lowest income" areas. The lowest-income census tracts in our study are those 20 percent of all census tracts in the city of Los Angeles with the lowest income fractions. The income fraction for a census tract equals its median income, as reported in the 1980 census, expressed as a percentage of the median 1980 income in the Los Angeles-Long Beach Metropolitan Statistical Area. These income fractions do not change significantly when using 1990 census data median income levels.

The income quintiles for Los Angeles are shown in table 6.1.[6] Each quintile represents 20 percent of Los Angeles' census tracts. Neither population nor the number of residential buildings need be uniformly distributed by income quintile. The disparities are greater across income quintiles for the distribution of residential structures than for population. The lowest 40 percent income census tracts have 40 percent of the city's population but only 28 percent of its residential structures. By comparison, the highest 40 percent income census tracts have 38 percent of the population but 52 percent of the residential structures. Population density is higher in the lower-income census tracts.

MINORITY POPULATION QUINTILES

Each minority quintile also represents approximately 20 percent of the census tracts in the city. The disparities in the distribution of residential structures are once again greater across minority quintiles than elsewhere. The lowest 40 percent minority census tracts in the city have 37 percent of the population but 48 percent of the city's residential structures. By comparison, the highest 40 percent minority census tracts, with 42 percent of the population, have only 32 percent of the residential structures. Density is higher in the higher-minority census tracts.

While total population may be spread out evenly across the total minority quintiles, the distribution of individual minority groups within the city of Los Angeles is highly segregated. Census tracts in the second-highest African American minority quintile have populations of between 5 percent and 29 percent of African Americans; but some 37 percent of these tracts are more than 70 percent minority overall, and more than 50 percent of census tracts in this quintile have populations that are at least 50 percent overall minority. Even tracts that are ethnically diverse—having some African American residents, but not an overwhelming proportion—are, in the main, populated by significant percentages of all three minority subgroupings. Census tracts with significant numbers of African American residents and a majority of white residents are extremely rare in the city of Los Angeles.

The quintile with the lowest proportion of Latino American residents encompasses census tracts with between 0 and 5 percent Latino Americans. The 5 percent figure was the breakpoint for the second-highest quintile of African Americans, so Latino Americans are not only a larger percentage of the population in Los Angeles but are also spread more widely throughout the city than African Americans are. The middle three Latino American quintiles all consist of census tracts in which most residents are non-Latino. These census tracts are also likely to have a majority of white residents. The highest Latino American quintile, by contrast, is composed entirely of census tracts having a majority of Latino American residents—51 percent to 100 percent.

The smaller Asian-Pacific population in Los Angeles is even more widely dispersed. The lowest two Asian-Pacific quintiles have 0 to 3 percent Asian-Pacific residents, while the next two quintiles have only 4 to 14 percent. Within the quintile containing the highest proportion of Asian-Pacific residents (between 15 percent and 97 percent Asian-Pacific) over three-quarters (75 percent) of the census tracts have overall minority populations in excess of 50 percent.

The overarching conclusion here is that once the members of any minority subgroup become significant in a census tract, that census tract is likely to be populated primarily by minority residents. There is a high degree of racial segregation in the city of Los Angeles. Minorities are more likely to live in an area populated primarily by minorities, while white residents are more likely to live in areas that are primarily white.

THE RELATIONSHIP OF RACE AND INCOME IN LOS ANGELES

Census tract median income and minority percentage are highly inversely related within the city of Los Angeles. There are 149 census tracts in the lowest income quintile. Of these, only four census tracts are low minority, while ninety census tracts (60 percent) are highest minority. In the highest income quintile there are 148 census tracts, of which ninety-one (61 percent) are low-minority and none are high-minority census tracts. Similar patterns appear between income levels and African American or Latino American populations. Almost 50 percent (73 of the 149 census tracts) of the highest African American-minority census tracts are found in the lowest income quintile; only 2 percent (three tracts) are in the highest income quintile. Similarly, almost 80 percent of the highest Latino American-minority census tracts appear in the bottom

Table 6.1
Quintile Breakpoints for Variables

Quintile	Income Fraction	Overall Minority Percent	African-American Percent	Latino-American Percent	Asian-Pacific Percent
1st	0–52	0–15	0	0–5	0–1
(Lowest 20% of census tracts)					
2nd	53–73	16–35	1	6–13	2–3
3rd	74–97	36–70	2–4	14–26	4–6
4th	98–127	71–93	5–29	27–50	7–14
5th	128–395	94–100	30–98	51–100	15–97
(Highest 20% of census tracts)					

Note: To interpret this table, consider the column entitled "Overall Minority Percent" as an example. Suppose all census tracts in Los Angeles are sorted from lowest to highest according to the percentage of minorities they contain. The 20% of Los Angeles census tracts with the lowest minority percentage have between 0 and 15% minority residents; the next 20% of Los Angeles census tracts contain 16 to 35% minority residents; and so on. Each column is independent of every other column.

two income quintiles. There are no census tracts from the highest 40 percent Latino American-minority census tracts in the highest income quintile.

The African American and Latino American populations tend to be systematically related within each income quintile. In the three lowest income quintiles, the majority of the census tracts have high overall minority populations. A low African American-minority census tract in these income quintiles is usually associated with a high Latino American population. Lower-income census tracts with few African Americans have a high proportion of Latino Americans; those with high proportions of African Americans have few Latino Americans. By contrast, most census tracts in the highest two income quintiles in the city have low minority populations; therefore, low African American or low Latino American populations typically are found in low-minority census tracts.

RESIDENTIAL LOAN FLOWS, 1981–89

Our study of residential lending in Los Angeles is based on data collected under the Home Mortgage Disclosure Act of 1975 (HMDA) for the period 1981–1989. Virtually all commercial banks, savings and loan associations (thrifts), credit unions, and other depository institutions report, by census tract, any loans secured by residential real estate.[7] Residence-based loans are reported in four distinct categories: (1) loans for single-family residences (SFRs) that are government-backed under the FHA, FmHA, and VA programs; (2) conventional SFR loans; (3) home improvement loans for SFRs; and (4) loans for multifamily residential units. Single-family residences (SFRs) are defined under HMDA as buildings with between one and four units, while multifamily dwellings are defined as those with five or more units.

The residential building stock of Los Angeles was estimated in 1989 at 616,899 buildings. Over the period of 1981 to 1989, a total of 323,723 residential loans were made in Los Angeles; the dollar volume of these loans was $50.1 billion. Residential loans in these nine years amounted to over 50 percent of the total number of residential buildings, a citywide turnover rate of 5.5 percent of residential properties per year. Most residential loans were conventional loans made for single-family residences—about 83 percent by number and 76 percent by dollar amount—in the period of 1981 to 1989. Next in frequency were home improvement loans, accounting for approximately 9 percent of the reported total. Least frequent were government-backed SFR loans (FHA, FmHA, and VA); the 6,289 loans in this category are only 2 percent of reported loans. Government-backed loans for first-time home buyers in 1989 were virtually nonexistent—138 loans out of 50,000 total for the city of Los Angeles.

Thrifts made the vast majority of 1981–1989 residential loans, over 88 percent by number and 82 percent by dollar volume. Other lenders formed a small part of the residential market, although certain institutions specialized in particular types of loans. National banks, for instance, specialized in home improvement loans. Credit unions are numerically unimportant in every loan category.

RACIALLY DISPARATE LENDING VERSUS REDLINING

The purpose of our study is to illuminate the relationship between lending, other banking activities, and the racial composition of Los Angeles. Our focal point is to demonstrate the existence of racially disparate lending—that is, to show that loan flows are lower to high-minority census tracts, even after corrections are for made for economic variables that might systematically influence lending decisions. Three such corrections are made in this study: We adjust for differing levels of median income between census tracts, for tracts' differing crime levels, and for differences in census tracts' "loan potential."

Both income and crime levels are relevant for lending decisions. Median income constitutes a measure of the debt service capacity of residents in an area, while crime level constitutes a measure of safety and desirability (that is, of risk). Establishing racial disparities in lending involves holding these other variables roughly constant and then measuring the relationship between loan levels and racial concentration. We report only results controlling for income levels here. Our results indicate that crime levels have no significant impact on the level of lending flows.

We also correct for differences in loan potential across census tracts. High-income, low-minority census tracts consist primarily of single-family residences. There are more potential residences on which loans can be made, and these census tracts' higher absolute levels of loans may reflect, in part, their larger housing stock. To adjust for this loan potential factor, we examine the number and dollar value of loan flows per 100 residential buildings across census tracts. These measures of loan flows filter out differences in the number of residential buildings across census tracts.

Demonstrating racially disparate lending does not prove that banks discriminate against certain populations or redline certain areas. Racially disparate lending is an aggregate phenomenon and discrimination an individual-level phenomenon. Racially disparate lending is consistent with discrimination but neither proves nor disproves its existence. Neither are the terms *racially disparate lending* and *redlining* identical. Redlining is appropriate after racial disparities in lending remain when all other economic factors that affect credit worthiness and/or housing demand have been taken into account. Our examination of lending disparities here adjusts for three important variables. Our study does not account for other significant variables, including individual borrowers' incomes, credit histories, and employment records. Since our study does not encompass data about individual borrowers' circumstances, the term racially disparate lending best describes the patterns we find.[8] The economic significance of racially disparate lending is discussed below.

LOAN FLOWS BY INCOME QUINTILE

Our main finding about the relationship between loan flows and income levels is simply stated: low- and moderate-income areas receive systematically lower levels of all types of residential lending by all types of financial institutions covered under HMDA. The patterns of loan flows across income classes are the same for national banks, thrifts, and state banks. Institutions in each category make more loans per building as income rises and have higher dollar flows per building as income rises. It appears that contrary to their obligations under CRA, the entire spectrum of financial institutions has concentrated its activities outside of the low- to moderate-income areas in the city of Los Angeles.

As discussed above, the number of residential buildings increases from the lowest to the highest income quintile. The ratio of residential structures between the highest and lowest income quintiles is 1 to 1.5. The ratio of loans in the highest income quintile to those in the lowest income quintile, however, is 4.8 to 1, more than twice the disparity in residential structures. The number of loans per 100 residential buildings illustrates the gap in loan flows. Twenty percent of the highest-income census tracts received 66 loans per 100 residential buildings between 1981 and 1989—an average annual turnover of more than 7 percent of residential structures there. In contrast, 20 percent of the lowest-income census tracts received only 31 loans per 100 residential buildings; an average annual turnover of just over 3 percent. Table 6.2 demonstrates that 40 percent of the highest-income census tracts received 60 percent of the residential loans made by number over the entire period 1981-89, while the bottom 40 percent received less than 20 percent of loans. Even after adjusting for residential building differentials, the pattern is clear: The higher the median income is in a census tract, the more loans are made, and there are more dollars loaned per residential structure.

In addition to a higher turnover rate, the highest income quintile has larger average loan sizes than the lowest income quintile: $197,150 versus $113,425. Significantly, the ratio between the two average loan sizes (1 to 7) is considerably less than the average income ratio of 1 to 2.5 between these two quintiles. This suggests a housing affordability problem, as residential real estate values decline less quickly than does average income across the income quintiles. The more modest the incomes of an area's residents, the smaller the proportion of residents able to afford residential real estate in that area. Data for the middle income quintiles provide further evidence of the uneven relationship between income and residential values. Across all financial institutions, the average loan falls from the second to the fourth income quintile; $142,500 in the second, $139,000 in the third, and $131,250 in the fourth income quintile. This suggests that perhaps the inability to find a down payment the greatest obstacle to home ownership for moderate-income households. FHA and VA loan programs are designed to address this specific problem, but they are rarely a solution in Los Angeles because the median house price ($192,000 in December 1990) exceeds the loan maximum of $124,000 available under these programs.

LOAN FLOWS AND RACIAL CONCENTRATION

This section compares financial institutions' performance in residential lending across areas of the city of Los Angeles with different degrees of racial concentration. We focus on the differential treatment received by high-minority census tracts. Our main finding is that all categories of financial institutions make systematically higher levels of loans to low-minority census tracts than to high-minority census tracts in the city. Loans per eligible residential building are significantly lower in the top 40 percent minority population census tracts than in the remainder of the city.

The higher the proportion of minority residents in a census tract, the fewer residential loans are made, even after adjusting for the number of loans per 100 residential buildings. Almost 2.5 loans per building were made in the lowest minority quintile for every loan in the highest minority quintile. This pattern is consistent across minority quintiles. The data present an unchanging pattern of lower loan flows to higher minority areas; the pattern in 1989 is roughly the same as over the period 1981–88. Table 6.2 demonstrates that the lowest 40 percent minority census tracts received more than half of all residential loans by number over the period 1981–89. By contrast the highest 40 percent minority census tracts—where minority residents are 73 percent or more of the population—received only 20 percent of residential loan flows, far lower than their share of the city's residential structures. The dollar flows of loans are even more heavily weighted toward tracts with few minority residents. Almost $5.70 in residential loans per building went to the lowest minority quintile for every $1 lent in the highest minority quintile.

The lowest 60 percent African American census tracts in Los Angeles have very few African American residents (1 in 25 or fewer). The second-highest African American quintile is somewhat diverse, primarily because of the presence of other minorities. The highest quintile is composed largely of census tracts with a majority of African American residents. Table 6.2 shows that residential lending flows—especially on a per-building basis—are essentially constant for census tracts in the lowest four African American-minority quintiles, but exhibit a precipitous decline for census tracts in the highest African American-minority quintile. Between 48 and 51 conventional SFR

Table 6.2
Distribution of HMDA Loan Flows by Quintile, 1981-1989

Quintile:	Income Fraction		Overall Minority Percent		African-American Percent		Latino-American Percent		Asian-Pacific Percent	
	#	$	#	$	#	$	#	$	#	$
1st (Lowest 20% of census tracts)	7%	5%	31%	41%	19%	20%	27%	35%	18%	17%
2nd	13%	12%	27%	25%	23%	23%	24%	24%	22%	26%
3rd	19%	17%	21%	18%	30%	32%	22%	19%	20%	18%
4th	27%	23%	13%	11%	17%	19%	17%	13%	23%	22%
5th (Highest 20% of census tracts)	34%	43%	9%	5%	12%	7%	11%	8%	17%	17%

Total number (#) of HMDA loans, 1981–1989 = 323,723

Total dollar value ($) of HMDA loans, 1981–1989 = $50,142,734,000

Notes: This table shows how HMDA-reported loans in Los Angeles, for years 1981-1989, are distributed for various census tract quintiles. The distribution of loans is shown by both the number and dollar value of loans for each quintile. For example, the 20% of Los Angeles census tracts with the highest percentage of African-American residents (the 5th African-American quintile) received 12% of all HMDA loans by number, and 7% by dollar value.

loans were made per 100 buildings in each of the lowest four African American quintiles, but only 24.5 in the highest African American quintile. In dollar-flow terms, the difference between the first four African American quintiles and the highest quintile is even more pronounced: $3.80 lent in the lowest African American quintile for each dollar lent in the highest African American quintile.

The Latino American population is spread more uniformly across the city. Tracts in which Latino Americans constitute only a small percent are likely to have a low percentage of overall minority residents. Reflecting this pattern, residential lending to Latino American quintiles contrasts with the precipitous decline in lending to the highest African American quintile census tracts. Instead, the number and dollar volume of residential loans in table 6.2 decline smoothly as the concentration of Latino Americans increases. The lowest Latino American quintile received 1.8 conventional SFR loans per building for every loan in the highest Latino American quintile, and $4.10 per building in the lowest Latino American quintile for every $1 in the highest Latino American quintile. The higher the percentage of Latino Americans in a census tract, the lower the level of loan flows, both in numbers and in dollars.

Table 6.2 provides little or no evidence of any systematic relationship between Asian-Pacific quintiles and residential lending flows. Conventional SFR loan flows are approximately equal across all Asian-Pacific quintiles. A qualitatively different pattern between loan flows and Asian-Pacific population exists in the city than for other minority populations. Heavily Asian-Pacific-minority areas do not appear to be treated much differently than predominantly white areas. One explanation might be the large number of Asian-Pacific banks in Los Angeles relative to other minority-owned lenders.

RESIDENTIAL LENDING, INCOME, AND RACIAL CONCENTRATION

This section analyzes the relationship between residential lending flows and race, controlling for the influence of median income. We have seen that lending flows decline when there is a large concentration of African American residents or an increasing percentage of Latino Americans in a census tract. This pattern suggests racially disparate lending but is not definitive proof. Are these differentials rooted in economic variables?

It is crucial to isolate the effects of economic and racial variables on the lending decision. This is accomplished here by investigating the relationship between loan flows and racial characteristics within income quintiles. Income is thus held approximately constant, so loan flow differentials reflect differences in census tracts' racial composition. If racially disparate lending is not an important feature of the data, loan flows per 100 buildings should be roughly constant as minority population changes across census tracts with similar median income levels.

The analysis is complicated by the excessive polarization of high-minority populations within the lowest-income census tracts and of low-minority populations within the highest-income census tracts. There are almost no lowest income/low minority census tracts and similarly almost no highest income/high minority census tracts. As a result it is impossible to examine how loan flows vary with race in the lowest and highest income quintile census tracts. The analysis is therefore largely confined to the relationship between loan flows and race in the middle three income quintiles, since only in these census tracts is there a diversity of racial composition.

We investigate the relationship of loan flows and minority populations across the middle three income quintiles. After controlling for income levels, loan flows are lower in both number and dollar volume per 100 residential structures, the higher the minority population percentage in a census tract. Within each of the three middle income quintiles, the lowest-minority census tracts receive almost twice the number of loans per building and almost five times the dollar amounts per 100 buildings as are received by the highest-minority tracts. For example, in the third (middle) income quintile, the loans per building in the lowest minority quintile were 45 per 100 residential buildings between 1981 and 1989, but only 25 per 100 residential buildings in the highest minority quintile—a ratio of 1.83 to 1. In dollar terms, the discrepancy is even greater. Dollars per building are $91,395 in the first minority quintile, but only $17,977 in the fifth—a ratio of $5.08 to $1.

Table 6.3 shows that loan flow disparities holding income constant are roughly similar for both the African American and Latino American populations. There is a precipitous decline in loan flows to census tracts with high African American or Latino American populations. In the third (middle) income quintile, lending flows fall from 43 loans per 100 residential buildings in the second-highest African American quintile to 28 per 100 residential buildings in the highest African American quintile. Dollars per building in the third income quintile fall from $73,540 per building in the second-highest African American quintile to $23,400 per building in the highest African American quintile. Table 6.3 illustrates a similar pattern for Latino American populations in the middle three income quintiles. In the third (middle) income quintile, the number of loans per 100 residential buildings is 38.5 in the second-highest Latino American quintile, but only 30.5 in the highest Latino American quintile. The disparity is once again greater for the flow of dollars per building in this income quintile—$63,000 in the second-highest Latino American areas versus $33,000 in the highest Latino American quintile.

Table 6.3 illustrates another pattern in loan flows that reflects the relationship of African American and Latino American populations within income quintiles. In the middle three income quintiles, the numbers and dollar volumes of loans are notably lower in the lowest and highest African American quintiles than in the middle African American quintiles. This tent-shaped pattern in lending also appears across Latino American minority quintiles for the middle three income quintiles. This pattern does not appear for either African American or Latino American percentages in the highest income quintile.

Recall that in the three lowest income quintiles there are considerably more high-minority census tracts than low-minority tracts. In particular, a low African American minority in these income quintiles implies a high Latino American minority population. Hence the tent-shaped low loan flows to the lowest and highest African American quintiles—but higher flows to the middle three African American quintiles—is a consequence of loan flows reacting to higher overall minority populations in both. Loan flows fall in the highest African American quintile in response to a high African American population; they fall in the lowest African American quintile in response to a high Latino American population. This pattern disappears in the highest income quintile simply because this quintile contains no high Latino American census tracts. When the minority population becomes too large as a proportion of census tract population, either African American or Latino American, residential lenders shun the area, regardless of the area's income characteristics. This is racially disparate lending at its most transparent, and it is a pronounced pattern for both African American and Latino American-minority areas. This "racial tipping" is based on overall minority population rather than on any individual minority's presence.

Loan flows to the Asian-Pacific population in table 6.3 show little or no evidence that lending flows across Asian-Pacific quintiles are uneven after holding income quintiles constant. This conclusion is consistent for all five income quintiles. Loan flows actually increase as the percentage of Asian-Pacific population increases. These data do not prove that individual Asian-Pacific loan applicants face no discrimination in residential credit markets; as discussed above, the analysis here pertains only to aggregate geographic patterns. The data, however, disclose no explanation for the systematic difference between the Asian-Pacific population and African Americans or Latino Americans. Perhaps there are sufficient Asian-Pacific-controlled financial institutions to

Table 6.3
HMDA Loan Flows within the 3rd (Middle) Income Quintile: Distribution across Minority Quintiles

Quintile	Overall Minority		African-American		Latino-American		Asian-Pacific	
	# loans per 100 buildings	*$ loans per building*	*# loans per 100 buildings*	*$ loans per building*	*# loans per 100 buildings*	*$ loans per building*	*# loans per 100 buildings*	*$ loans per building*
1st	45.1	$91,395	34.4	$33,337	27.4	$27,560	26.4	$23,490
(Lowest 20% of census tracts)								
2nd	42.8	$65,305	37.7	$45,089	43.7	$74,647	35.9	$51,640
3rd	41.5	$56,391	40.1	$57,715	43.7	$68,352	37.9	$50,371
4th	30.2	$33,997	42.7	$73,536	38.5	$48,544	37.9	$52,652
5th	24.6	$17,977	27.8	$23,406	30.6	$29,621	46.1	$66,534
(Highest 20% of census tracts)								

Notes: Census tracts in the 3rd income quintile have income fractions between 74% and 97% of the 1980 median income for the Los Angeles-Long Beach metropolitan statistical area.

service the community, while there are few African American or Latino American-controlled financial institutions in Los Angeles. In any event, racially disparate lending is not significant in the Asian-Pacific community, when measured by the quintile method.

TITLE TRANSFER DATA ON RESIDENTIAL LENDING IN 1989

To complement our HMDA data, we obtained title transfer data on properties changing ownership in Los Angeles during 1989. An important limitation of HMDA lending data is that it excludes lending by small mortgage and finance companies, many of which are active in high-minority areas. The attraction of title transfer data is that it reports all residential lending flows, including those for small mortgage and finance companies.

We assembled a title transfer data set for the City for 1989. The median transaction was a sale price of $216,000 financed with a 20 percent down payment and a loan of $168,300. According to this data set, loan terms vary little across financial institutions; a 20 percent down payment is close to the median for every type of lender. Small mortgage and finance companies, exempt from HMDA reporting, finance the low end of the market with the lower sale prices and loan amounts, but they charge interest rates comparable to the rest of the industry.

With respect to income quintiles, the title transfer data suggest the same pattern as do the 1981–89 HMDA data: more loans are made in larger dollar amounts to higher-income census tracts. More than twice (2.3 times) as many loans were made in the highest income quintile as in the lowest income quintile in 1989. Median sale price and median loan amount increase uniformly with higher income quintiles. The median sale price in the highest income quintile is $380,000, roughly 3.3 times the $114,250 median sale price in the lowest income quintile. Similarly, the median loan amount in the highest income quintile is $285,000, roughly 2.8 times the $100,700 median loan in the lowest income quintile.

As these data suggest, median down payments are larger in higher income quintiles, in both dollar and percentage terms—$23,168 and 20%, respectively, in the lowest income quintile versus $133,796 and 39 percent in the highest income quintile. This pattern suggests that in higher income quintiles, home sales are more likely to reflect trading up, wherein existing home owners use equity in previously acquired homes for their down payment on more expensive residences. First-time buyers are thus largely confined to lower income quintiles. The median interest rate on loans is similar across all income quintiles.

The patterns of residential lending in the 1989 title transfer data across minority areas are also similar to those found in the HMDA data. The higher the minority population of a census tract, the lower the number and dollar volume of loans going to that tract. The highest overall minority quintile census tracts received 8 percent of loans by dollar volume and 18 percent of loans by number in 1989. In contrast, the lowest 40 percent minority census tracts within the city received 46 percent of the loans by number and 61 percent of dollar volume in the 1989 title transfer data.

The decline in lending as minority population percentage increases—which is also found for African American and Latino American quintiles—is not as dramatic as the decline found using HMDA data. This is primarily because small mortgage and finance companies make a higher percentage of their loans to high-minority areas than to low-minority areas. But overall, racially disparate lending stands out clearly in these data, too. A larger decline in dollar volume occurs from low-minority to high-minority areas, due largely to lower average sale prices and consequently smaller loan amounts in the highest-minority census tracts.

Increases in minority populations are associated with lower median sale prices and loan amounts. There is a particularly sharp drop-off in both sale price and loan amount when one moves to the highest-minority population quintile. This drop in sale price is associated with a corresponding dramatic decline in the median down payment percentage and a noticeable increase in the median interest rate (from 8.87 percent to 9.25 percent) in the highest minority quintile.

RESIDENTIAL LENDING DISPARITIES IN LOS ANGELES

Our quintile approach to stratifying census tracts by income and race demonstrates that racially disparate lending—defined here as significantly lower loan flows into high-minority areas than low-minority areas, holding area income approximately constant—occurs in Los Angeles. No method of determining racial biases in lending can claim to be definitive; but the quintile method is analytically neutral, and hence findings based upon it are very suggestive. The differentials across median income levels and minority populations are striking over the entire 1981–88 period and are even more acute in the data for 1989. While some financial institutions target special-needs populations, the industry as a whole stands accused of systematically making fewer loans to low-income and high-minority areas. These systematically divergent loan flows have diverse and damaging consequences. In particular, they increase wealth differentials by denying minority and low-income populations access to the single most important form of household wealth formation. In addition, divergent loan flows impede opportunities for integration in the city of Los Angeles.

When minorities are considered together, there is strong evidence of racially differentiated lending flows across all income quintiles (except perhaps the highest). When any minority group becomes a numerically significant proportion in any tract, that tract is likely to be inhabited by significant numbers of other minority groups. So there is an important interaction between the location of the different categories of minority population. Evidence that looks just to the distribution of each minority subgrouping, considered on its own, ignores this interaction and hence does not reflect a phenomenon that is apparently at work for minorities as a whole. Racially disparate lending is a phenomenon that jointly affects the African American, Latino American, and Asian-Pacific communities; its locus is the minority population taken as a whole.

BANK BRANCHES, BANKING SERVICES, AND NONRESIDENTIAL LENDING

Residents and businesses in urban communities have other financial needs besides residential credit. To gain insight into lenders' provision of nonresidential credit and banking services, we collected information from several additional sources besides those used so far. These sources included data on the branch locations of financial institutions in 1988; CRA statements from 175 Los Angeles financial institutions; surveys we distributed to these lenders, seventy-five of which were completed and returned; a survey we sent to experienced developers of affordable housing in Los Angeles, thirty-five of which were completed and returned; and finally surveys and meetings we conducted with business owners in Los Angeles' enterprise zones. This section summarizes our insights from this supplemental information.

THE LOCATION OF BANK BRANCHES IN LOS ANGELES

Banking institutions within the city of Los Angeles display remarkable diversity in their size and market scope. Some 26 percent have market areas at least as large as Los Angeles County, yet 62 percent have market areas smaller than the Los Angeles city limits. Despite this diversity in size and market scope, however, the overall pattern of bank branch locations in Los Angeles closely resembles that identified above for residential lending.

Banks' branch locations demonstrate a bias toward suburban locations. Just over one-third of Los Angeles County bank branches and automated teller machines (ATMs) are located within the city itself, versus about half the population of the county. Of the seventy-five institutions returning our bank survey, forty-one institutions operate Los Angeles county branches both inside and outside the city boundaries; but seventeen have Los Angeles county branches without any inside the city itself, while only four operate in the city but not elsewhere in the county. There has been a net loss of branches since 1980 in both the city and the county of Los Angeles; but the relative loss has been greater in the city than in the surrounding county.

BRANCH LOCATION WITHIN THE CITY OF LOS ANGELES

Commercial banks, thrifts, and all other institutions that reported loan activity under HMDA operated 810 branches within the city of Los Angeles at year's end 1988. Some 41 percent of bank branches were located in low-income areas, which composed about 45 percent of all tracts.[9] This suggests only a slight bias in the pattern of branch location by income, but this result is misleading; Los Angeles's central business district (CBD) and mid-Wilshire area are in these census tracts. When CBD and mid-Wilshire branches are excluded, only 33 percent of branches are located in low-income areas. By contrast, 53 percent of all branches are in the top 40 percent income quintiles in Los Angeles census tracts by median income; this branch percentage climbs to 60 percent if CBD and mid-Wilshire branches are excluded from lower-income tract totals.

This pattern of branch location indicates an underrepresentation of bank branches in lower-income and minority areas. There were almost three bank branches per 10,000 residents in the highest two income quintiles. This contrasts with roughly two branches per 10,000 residents in the two lowest income quintiles. If CBD and mid-Wilshire branches are dropped, the disparity is even greater: there are two bank branches for every 10,000 residents in high-income areas for every one in low-income areas.

Turning to racial concentration, disturbing patterns again appear. Counting all branches, the quintile of census tracts with the fewest minority residents had 4.69 branches per 10,000 persons in 1988. By contrast, the 20 percent of all census tracts with the highest proportion of minority residents had only 0.83 branches per 10,000 residents. When the CBD and mid-Wilshire branches are excluded, these disparities become more dramatic: 4.51 branches per 10,000 residents in tracts with the lowest minority concentrations compared to 0.79 branches in tracts with the most minority residents.

Businesses also need access to banking services. We measured the availability of banking services for businesses by computing the number of bank branches per 100 business (commercial and industrial) buildings in each census tract. This measure of the availability of bank branches also indicates systematic biases. There were 5.76 branches per 100 business buildings in the highest income quintile versus only 0.61 branches in the lowest income quintile. The same pattern was observed for racial concentration: the lowest minority quintile had 5.33 branches per 100 business buildings, versus 0.42 for the highest minority quintile. Excluding CBD and mid-Wilshire branches simply makes these disparities more dramatic.

Data on deposit levels by bank branch were also available. These deposit data provide another indicator of bank performance in upper and lower-income census tracts. There are more deposits per residence in higher-income areas than in lower-income areas: ignoring CBD and mid-Wilshire branches, there are $8.74 in per-capita deposits in low-income areas, versus $21.40 in deposits per person elsewhere in Los Angeles. Loans made to an area per dollar of deposit within that area provide a measure of credit uses (loans) versus credit sources (deposits). Thus dollars of loans per dollar of deposits provides a crude measure of whether an area is experiencing credit inflows or outflows through banks.

No direct measure of the total volume of loans by census tract in 1988 was available. A simple summation of residential loans over the 1981–88 period, however, serves as a convenient substitute. This procedure produced a total of $36 billion in 1981–88 residential loans, versus $50 billion in 1988 deposits. We indexed the loan/deposit ratio for Los Angeles as a whole to 1.0. In low-income areas, however, the adjusted loan/deposit ratio was less than one (0.81); elsewhere in Los Angeles, it exceeded one (1.08).[10] These differential ratios indicate lower loan flows in lower-income areas than would be expected, even given the paucity of bank branches there. They also support the contention that banks located in low-income (and high-minority) areas tend to disinvest from these areas, channeling deposits outside the community.

BANKING SERVICES FOR SPECIAL-NEEDS CUSTOMERS

Banks often make special provisions for the banking needs of their elderly low-income customers but seldom for the banking needs of the nonelderly poor. All institutions allow direct deposit of government checks for elderly recipients; but only 44 percent provide this service for nonelderly welfare recipients. Most institutions (94 percent, according to CRA statements) do not allow nondepositors to cash government benefit checks in their branches. This, together with the paucity of bank branches in lower-income neighborhoods, pushes government-benefits recipients into check-cashing stores, whose rates may be as high as 10 percent of the check's face value. In addition, having to take an entire check in cash makes these recipients particularly vulnerable to robbery and physical abuse.

Most institutions offer special accounts for elderly low-income deposi-tors, usually with no monthly service fee. The deposit accounts available to the nonelderly poor have much less attractive terms, including monthly service fees and larger minimum amounts (usually $500 to $1,500) to open and maintain an account.

BEHAVIOR AND OUTCOMES IN NONRESIDENTIAL CREDIT MARKETS

According to the CRA reports we collected, Los Angeles appears to be amply supplied with financial institutions. At least 121 institutions (69 percent) provide credit in each of the four lending categories of single-family residential (SFR), multifamily residential, business, and individual. Most institutions specialize in credit markets: 55 percent make loans in just two or three of these four categories.

Evidently, institutions specialize in market niches, and there are numerous institutions within each market niche. But how well are credit needs being met in nonresidential credit markets? Our surveys of banks, small businesses, and affordable-housing developers probed this question. We did not obtain comprehensive statistics on credit flows from returned surveys, but we did learn about how these nonresidential credit markets operate.

FINDINGS ON LENDING TO SMALL BUSINESSES

Perhaps the most telling of our findings about lending to small businesses is how little is known. Federal regulators do not collect comprehensive information about small-business loans. Some patterns did emerge in our survey of financial institutions. Many banks offer working capital arrange-ments for businesses, but only seventeen institutions provide start-up financing. Lenders reported that 85 percent of business loan applications that are not withdrawn are funded; those funded receive about 75 percent of the credit they request, on average. Loans to businesses require average collateral of 90 percent of the loan amount. Lenders reported their reasons for denying credit to businesses, in order of importance, as debt/income ratio, inadequate capitalization, insufficient collateral, and business's credit history.

FINDINGS ON LENDING FOR AFFORDABLE-HOUSING DEVELOPMENT

In their survey responses, both financial institutions and low-income housing developers agree that there are formidable obstacles to financing the construction of multifamily rental housing in Los Angeles.

Developers overwhelmingly report that it is harder to get financing for affordable housing projects planned for minority or lower-income communities than for projects planned for upper-income or low-minority neighborhoods. The reluctance of many affluent communities to accept these projects is well known. Development of these projects thus becomes doubly difficult, squeezed between lender and community preferences.

Construction projects for affordable housing move through three stages of financing: predevelopment and site acquisition, construction, and permanent financing. Only six lenders provide predevelopment financing; so almost all affordable housing developers have to rely on internal funds or on monies from specialized external sources for the predevelopment stage. Further, developers report that land acquisition, their most expensive cost item, is the most difficult area for which to obtain credit from conventional lenders.

Financial institutions are much more likely to make construction loans: 95.5 percent of the eighty-six institutions financing multifamily housing indicate they make such loans. However, very few Los Angeles banks and thrifts will provide permanent financing for these projects. The vast majority—all but six, according to CRA statements—will not provide long-term mortgages for multifamily projects.

Does the paucity of financing—"financing constraints"—slow the pace of housing development? Developers were asked whether they would begin projects without prior financing arrangements. Most developers (58.5 percent) responded that they cannot initiate a project until they have secured financing for construction and/or permanent financing. Developers also indicated that banks are frequently reluctant to finance land acquisition costs, a cost item singled out as the largest and fastest-growing.

Developers also indicated that low-income housing projects would be more viable if they were located in a high-minority community. And developers overwhelmingly replied—by 14 or 15 to 1 in both cases—that it is harder to get financing for low/moderate-income projects both in high-minority areas and in low-income areas.

We asked both banks and developers some questions about why developers' applications are denied or underfunded. Banks and developers agreed that banks' stated reasons for denying or underfunding developers' applications are, in order of importance, inadequate capitalization, insufficient collateral, and high debt-to-income ratio. Developers were also asked about several other reasons that lenders might deny credit. No respondents selected either the race or gender of the company's members as a reason for credit denial. However, almost all cited the area of project location as among lenders' unstated rationales; and many mentioned lenders' reluctance to be involved with low/moderate-income housing.

LENDING, ECONOMIC DEVELOPMENT, AND INSTITUTIONAL RACISM

Racially disparate lending occurred across Los Angeles throughout the 1980s, even after correcting for differing income levels and different levels of residential housing across areas. Neighborhoods with high concentrations of African American and/or Latino American populations received less than half the number of residential loans issued in white areas with comparable incomes. Disparities were not confined simply to residential lending. Access to financial services for minorities was constrained by a lack of bank branches in minority neighborhoods and by an absence of services geared toward their needs. This was not the case for primarily white areas with comparable incomes.[11]

As disturbing as these results are, they understate the true extent of the disparities in access to credit and the effects of this restricted access on the economic well-being of minority neighborhoods. There is no necessary reason that high-minority neighborhoods need to be those with lower incomes or with a far lower number of residential structures. The uncorrected figures bear stark testimony to the unequal access to financial services across the city of Los Angeles. Between 1981 and 1989, areas in the lowest minority quintile for the Los Angeles received $8.30 in residential loans for every $1 received by areas in the highest minority quintile. These lowest-minority areas received 3.3 times as many loans as the highest-minority areas. Areas in the highest income quintile received $8.30 in loans for every $1 received by the lowest-income areas. Almost five times as many residential loans were made to the highest-income areas in Los Angeles as to the lowest-income areas.

Racially disparate lending and differential access to bank services in these communities perpetuate and deepen historic inequities arising from past discrimination practices, such as Jim Crow laws or racist assessor practices.[12] Financial institutions are thus an important nexus in the institutionalization of racism through the workings of the "free" market system. Minority workers and small businesses, historically subject to a profound degree of racial segregation in labor and credit markets, have traditionally fared worse than whites in income and wealth measures. If banks take the lesser economic prospects of minority applicants or areas as given, they will systematically supply less credit and fewer banking services to individuals in these areas. This credit starvation will, in turn, have adverse consequences for future income and wealth prospects in high-minority areas—the consequences of past discrimination continue to feed a downward economic spiral into the future. Credit markets, with their links to past and future levels of income and wealth, institutionalize past racial discrimination in an economic rationale for disparate lending practices.

Spillover effects from the location of bank branches in an area can also lead to the divergence of income and wealth across neighborhoods over time. There is a "chicken or the egg"-type of dilemma in the provision of financial services to urban communities. Economically viable communities have bank branches, unviable communities do not. Or is it that communities with bank branches are economically viable, while those without bank branches are not? The fewer the bank branches located in an area, the more difficult the access to mortgage credit, resulting in fewer homes sold in the area. This makes homes in the area less liquid, lowering their worth as collateral, which makes it harder for small-business owners to secure bank financing. Thus the fewer bank branches in a neighborhood, the less economically viable is the neighborhood for both business and residents, and in turn, the less viable is the neighborhood as a bank branch site. Widespread discrimination against people of color in housing and credit markets can make it appear "economically rational" for banks to use the racial character of a neighborhood as a guide to lending decisions, even though it is bank avoidance of these areas which deepens racial economic disparities in income and wealth. Once again the results of past racial discrimination form the economic basis for not providing financial services to minority areas.

ARE SMALL LENDERS BETTER LENDERS?

Our results indicate that financial institutions generally avoid providing loans or services to high-minority or low-income areas. Advocates of community-based banking have suggested that larger banks and thrifts are more guilty of this than are smaller lenders. We examined this claim by dividing the 220 residential lenders we examined into four groups based on their 1989 HMDA dollar lending volume. We identified four distinct groups—large, medium, small, and smallest—by identifying clear "breaks" in the scale of lending.[13]

Institutions in the large group made 81 percent of the 50,000 residential loans in 1989, accounting for 83 percent of the almost $11 billion loaned. A further 15 percent of the market, both in numbers and dollars, is attributable to institutions in the medium group. The remaining 156 institutions in the small and smallest cohorts have small, almost insignificant, market shares. The large market share of the large and medium groups together means their lending records, on average, closely follow the aggregate lending patterns discussed earlier. It is interesting then to compare this group's performance with those of small lenders. Much has been made of the value of smaller financial institutions to "special-needs" communities because they provide services that larger institutions do not. In fact, the majority of smallest institutions by our definition made no loans to either low-income or high-minority areas in 1989. It is difficult to judge if this reflects a systematic avoidance of these areas or the fact that the smallest lenders operate on a scale so small that they have no substantial lending presence in these areas.

The main results for these lending-size groups are somewhat surprising. Table 6.4 illustrates that the performance of the median lender in the large, medium, and small groups is approximately the same. However, the best lenders in the large group have lower lending percentages to high-minority and low-income areas than do the best lenders in the medium group. Similarly, the best lenders in the small group supply a higher percentage of loans to low-income and high-minority areas than do the best lenders in the medium group. The dispersion of lender performance within a group increases as the average size of financial institutions decreases. This is consistent with increasing lender specialization, both in the type of area and the type of loan, as the size of the institution decreases. Smaller institutions secure market niches while only the largest institutions have the ability to be all things to all customers in all places. Therefore, this specialization on the part of smaller lenders may contribute to further disparities in lending by avoiding low-income and/or high-minority areas.

Banking Industry Shrinkage and Banking Services in Los Angeles. The national market structure of financial institutions has changed drastically over the period of our analysis, 1981–1989. For example, the number of insured commercial banks decreased by about 16 percent nationally during this period. We attempted to estimate the impact of this shrinkage on the Los Angeles residential lending market. Our estimate is that between 1981 and 1988, approximately 12 percent of residential lenders by loan dollar volume dropped out of the Los Angeles market. Some of these lenders were closed by regulators, while others were merged into other financial institutions, hence it is difficult to measure the true impact on the availability of residential loans. We estimate that between 1988 and 1991, an additional 14 percent of Los Angeles' residential lenders were closed, merged, or taken over.

Table 6.4:
Lending Patterns by Scale of Bank Residential Lending

Lending as a Percentage of Total Loans in:	Large Lenders:		Medium lenders:		Small Lenders:	
	Best	Median	Best	Median	Best	Median
Lowest income quintile						
Number of loans:	22%	4%	48%	3%	60%	5%
Dollar value of loans:	14%	3%	42%	1%	59%	4%
Two highest minority quintiles						
Number of loans:	56%	14%	89%	15%	100%	21%
Dollar value of loans:	41%	9%	83%	11%	100%	15%

Notes: Large lenders are those with HMDA loans in 1989 of more than $100 million in the City of Los Angeles; medium lenders are those with $10–$100 million in 1989 HMDA loans; and small lenders are those with $1–10 million in 1989 HMDA loans.

These failed, merged, or taken-over lenders do not appear to have concentrated their lending activities in low-income quintiles. Therefore, market adjustments in recent years have not significantly affected the distribution of loans between income quintiles across the city. Indeed, loans by these now inactive lenders are skewed toward higher-income census tracts. For example, in the lowest income quintile, inactive institutions account for only 1,335 loans worth $10.4 million, adding just 1.83 loans per 100 residential buildings over the eight years. By contrast, in the highest income quintile, these institutions account for 9,480 loans worth $1.41 billion, adding 4.64 loans per 100 buildings. Almost this entire difference—7,614 loans worth $1.21 billion—is due to inactive thrifts.

POLICY IMPLICATIONS

Our empirical results highlight the enormity of the scale of racially disparate lending in Los Angeles. Racially disparate lending is one aspect of a systematic pattern of institutionalized racism whereby inherited discrepancies in economic opportunity are amplified by racial segregation, leading to still greater racial differentials—and a wider gulf between the resources of Los Angeles's have and have-not communities—in the future. The role of the city's financial system is akin to that of a heart in a bifurcated body that pumps blood several times faster into some limbs than into others.

The recent strengthening of federal reinvestment and lending-disclosure policies under the CRA and HMDA represents progress in lessening the differential flow of blood through the urban body. So, too, does the passage of a linked-deposit program in Los Angeles. But these steps, taken on their own, are not sufficient; given the increasing importance of nonbank lenders in residential finance, the CRA's reinvestment requirement should be extended to all financial intermediaries.[14]

In the area of banking services, reversing institutionalized racism means reducing significantly the scale of racially disparate lending and bank branch disparities. The demise of much of the thrift industry and the downsizing of commercial bank operations only make the challenge more profound. The crisis of the U.S. financial system must be seen as a dual crisis, which involves not only the solvency of the country's financial institutions but also the health of the communities in which those institutions are based.

Efforts are needed to preserve and expand the bank branch network in low-income and high-minority areas. Further contraction of this network will only make these areas even more economically disadvantageous places to live and do business. And lending volume must be increased significantly in low-income and high-minority communities. Increased residential lending could have significant spillover benefits for entrepreneurship, because it will increase the collateral in owner-occupied homes. Innovative programs aimed at improved business planning, at business start-ups, and at expanding capitalization could significantly enhance economic development in needy areas. There is substantial room for improvement: only one in ten lenders we surveyed have special credit programs for businesses in lower-income areas; one in five have such programs for minority- or women-owned businesses.

There has been substantial recent interest in creating community development banks to solve inner-city banking problems. The enormity of the racial lending disparities we have identified suggests that the potential impact of establishing community development banks will be profoundly limited unless already-existing financial institutions can be induced to make significant changes in their lending and location policies. Small lenders account for an insignificant share of the residential lending market in Los Angeles; the addition of more small community-based banks, on its own, will not change this picture.

We observed above all that the city's minority groups—African American, Latino American, and Asian-Pacific—are jointly affected by racially disparate lending; we might conclude by observing that racially disparate lending and its consequences can be reversed only by the joint action of lenders of all sizes. Failure to move in this direction today will only make the challenge we face tomorrow seem the more intractable.

NOTES

1. The authors acknowledge the support of the city of Los Angeles, the Western Center on Law and Poverty, and their respective academic institutions in conducting this research. They also thank Nicole Rivas for her research assistance.

2. The four studies are: The color of money, *Atlanta Constitution,* May 1–4, 1988; The race for money, *Detroit Free Press,* August, 1988; Geographic patterns of mortgage lending in Boston, 1982–87, Katherine Bradbury, Karl Case, and Constance Dunham, Federal Reserve Bank of Boston, August, 1988; and Mortgage lending in Boston's neighborhoods, 1981–87, Charles Finn, December, 1989. Hula (1991) reviews pro and con redlining studies.

3. Galster (1990) reviews recent audit studies of discrimination in credit and housing markets.

4. The essays in Squires (1993) describe the emergence of the reinvestment movement and governmental policy responses to bank disinvestment.

5. The full report, "Taking It to The Bank: Poverty, Race, and Credit in Los Angeles," contains 212 pages of text, plus numerous figures and over one thousand pages of appendices. The full report had a third author, Michelle White, executive director of the Fair Housing Congress of Southern California.

6. The two lower income quintiles correspond closely to the definitions of low and moderate-income areas used by various government agencies.

7. Nondepository mortgage companies owned by depository institutions were also subject to HMDA reporting requirements. Certain exemptions were allowed; institutions with assets of $10 million or less were exempt, and refinancing loans were not reported. Legislation passed in 1989 and 1991 have changed some of these reporting requirements.

8. Our subsequent research into residential lending in Los Angeles, using individual mortgage applications for 1990 and 1991, does find patterns that are more clearly redlining. This later research has benefited from improvements in the HMDA data collected after 1989.

9. *Low-income areas* in Los Angeles are defined here to equal all census tracts that are "block-grant eligible" by virtue of having median incomes less than 80 percent of the overall Los Angeles-Long Beach median income.

10. Ratios of loans to deposits should be interpreted with caution for two reasons: first, they compare "flow" and "stock" variables; second, they are artificially skewed because there are already fewer branches in lower-income and minority areas than elsewhere.

11. For example, the Melrose area in Los Angeles, a primarily white neighborhood, has fifteen bank branches to serve 20,000 residents. In stark contrast, the neighborhood of Watts, which has roughly similar income levels and residential composition, but is primarily African American and Latino, has only one bank branch to serve 32,000 residents.

12. For example, Homer Hoyt, an early authority hired by the Federal Housing Adminstration to develop its underwriting standards, ranked residents of English and German extraction as the most desirable neighbors, and "Negroes" and "Mexicans" as the least desirable (Hoyt 1933, 136). Many of these "principles" survived through to the end of the 1960s. McWilliams (1973) traces the growth of the Watts neighborhood as a response to Jim Crow renter laws enforced by the city of Los Angeles in the 1920s. Our own ideas about the relationship between financial dynamics and community development are set out more fully in Dymski and Veitch (1992).

13. The *large* group contains twenty-four thrifts and banks that made more than $100 million in 1989 HMDA loans. The forty *medium* lenders made 1989 HMDA loans between $10 and $100 million, while seventy-three lenders with between $1 million and $100 million in 1989 loans were in the *small* group. The *smallest* group consisted of eighty banks and thrifts making less than $1 million in 1989 HMDA loans.

14. This and other ideas for transforming the U.S. financial system are discussed at length in Dymski, Epstein, and Pollin (1993).

References

Dymski, Gary, Gerald Epstein, and Robert Pollin, eds. 1993. *Transforming the U.S. financial system: An equitable and efficient structure for the 21st century.* Armonk, N.Y.: M. E. Sharpe.

Dymski, Gary, and John Veitch. 1992. Race and the financial dynamics of urban growth: L.A. as Fay Wray. In *City of angels,* edited by Gerry Riposa and Carolyn Dersch. Los Angeles: Kendall Hunt.

Galster, George. 1990. Racial discrimination in housing markets during the 1980s: A review of audit evidence. *Journal of Planning and Educational Research* 9 (3): 183–202.

Hoyt, Homer. 1933. *The hundred years of land values in Chicago.* Chicago: University of Chicago Press.

Hula, Richard. 1991. Neighborhood development and local credit markets. *Urban Affairs Quarterly* 27 (2): 249–67.

McWilliams, Carey. 1973. *An island upon the land.* Santa Barbara, Calif.: Peregrine Smith.

Squires, Gregory. 1992. Community reinvestment: An emerging social movement. In *From redlining to reinvestment,* edited by Gregory Squires. Philadelphia: Temple University Press.

CHAPTER 7

Race and Housing in a "New South" City: Houston

by Robert D. Bullard

Much has been written about the rise of the "New South." The South has been defined in different ways by a host of journalists, social scientists, and government bureaucrats. For example, the Census Bureau has defined the South as a statistical entity comprising sixteen states and the District of Columbia. This is the definition that will be used in this analysis. The South has the largest population of any region in the country: One-third of the nation's population live in this region (Bullard 1991).

The South has always been home for a large share of the African American population. More than 90 percent of African Americans lived in southern states at the turn of the century. In 1990, over 53 percent of all African Americans lived in the South—the same percentage as in 1980 and 1970. Today, African Americans make up about one-fifth of the region's population.

This chapter examines the changing housing patterns and opportunity structure in Houston, the South's largest city and the region's largest African American community.

POPULATION SHIFT SOUTHWARD

The 1970s saw the South become a human magnet attracting people from all over the nation. Beginning in the mid-1970s, the number of African Americans moving into the South exceeded the number departing for other regions of the country. This trend led some to conclude that the "black exodus" had ended, and a "new" South was at hand (Bullard 1991).

The "Go South" theme became a potent message in African American communities outside the region. This message continued into the 1980s as African Americans searched for improved economic opportunities and improved quality of life. The region attracted the skilled and unskilled, educated

180

and uneducated, as well as low-income and middle-income African Americans who sought to make their fortunes.

Where did these individuals settle? Most of the migrants settled in the central cities during a period when jobs were moving to the suburbs. The city's traditional function as an "economic launching pad" for upwardly mobile African Americans was diminished by the disinvestment process taking place in central cities and the relocation of new industries to distant suburbs. More than 57 percent of African Americans live in central cities, the highest concentration of any racial and ethnic group. By comparison, 26.8 percent of African Americans live in the suburbs, and 16.2 percent live in rural areas.

Even affluent African American families—those with household incomes of $50,000 or more—are more likely to live in central cities than their white counterparts. For example, 56 percent of affluent African Americans live in central cities, and 40 percent live in the suburbs. By comparison, 25 percent of affluent whites live in central cities, and 61 percent live in the suburbs.

Five of the six cities that have the largest percentage of African Americans are located in the South. In 1990, African Americans made up 75.7 percent of the population in Atlanta, 65.8 percent in Washington, D.C., 61.9 percent in New Orleans, 59.2 in Baltimore, and 54.8 percent in Memphis.

The data in table 7.1 show the population change in the seven southern cities that had the largest black population in 1990. Three of these cities experienced a drop in black population during the 1980s: Washington, D.C.; Atlanta, and New Orleans. On the other hand, black Houston grew by 4 percent between 1980 and 1990 (from 440,257 to 457,990).

Houston's black population grew by more than 39 percent during the 1970s, making it one of the fastest-growing black communities in the South (Shelton et al. 1989). Blacks made up just under 27.6 percent of the city's total population—a figure that is nearly unchanged since 1980. Still, Houston's black population is the largest black community in the South.

THE ELUSIVE AMERICAN DREAM

Black Houstonians and their counterparts in other southern cities struggled to get a piece of the American Dream and reap the benefits of the new and improved South. African Americans wanted and expected what all Americans want and expect, an opportunity to buy houses and live in quality neighborhoods of their choice. Institutionial barriers still limit housing options available to millions of African Americans.

Table 7.1
Population Change in Seven Southern Cities

City	% Black 1990	Black Population 1990	Black Population 1980	%Gain/Loss
Houston	27.6	457,990	440,257	+4.0
Baltimore	54.8	435,768	431,151	+1.1
Washington	65.8	399,604	448,229	-10.8
Memphis	54.8	334,737	307,702	+8.8
New Orleans	59.2	307,728	308,136	-0.13
Dallas	30.0	296,262	265,594	+11.5
Atlanta	67.1	264,262	282,912	-6.6

Source: Data from U.S. Bureau of the Census. 1990. *Summary population and housing characteristics.* Washington, D.C.: U.S. Government Printing Office.

Nevertheless, home ownership continues to be an integral part of the American Dream. Home ownership rates among African Americans have increased over the past four decades. Nationally, 44 percent of African Americans own their home. The home ownership rate is highest in the South, where more than half (51.1 percent) of all African Americans own their homes. Nearly one out of every two (48 percent) black Houstonians own their homes.

There can be little doubt that the opportunity structure in Houston did change during the 1980s. However, many social, economic, and political barriers have gone unabated. Ownership of property, land, and private businesses remains a central part of the dream of success, a dream that has eluded many black Houstonians.

The housing owned and occupied by Houston's African American residents continues to be of lower value than that of other Houstonians. Homes owned by blacks often have more deficiencies than those owned by their white counterparts. Home ownership options are often limited to older central city areas. Many of the city's older minority neighborhoods now mirror the physical decay of their northern counterparts. Generally, homes in these older minority areas do not yield the same return on investment as homes in other parts of the city or surrounding suburbs. Housing inadequacy has been increasing in the region's large urban centers.

Most of the single-family homes built in Houston during the 1980s were constructed in the suburbs and in targeted developments outside central city neighborhoods. Construction priorities of developers increased housing opportunities primarily for whites, higher-income households, and former home owners who had accumulated capital to finance down payments. Specifically, Houston has not escaped the national trend of a dwindling supply of low- and moderate-income housing.

Houston's African American housing patterns can be traced directly to the long-established segregated and often isolated wards and the segregated enclaves on the suburban fringe. The city's African American population expanded outward from the Third, Fourth, and Fifth wards. Many of these older neighborhoods suffered during the city's rapid expansion through the aggressive annexation of surrounding areas.

African Americans in Houston's wards experienced hardships not unlike those faced by northern ghetto residents. Houston's ghettos have been as difficult to eliminate as those in the Northeast and Midwest. The city's black ghettos are well on a course of experiencing the social and fiscal problems common to urban centers in other regions of the country, that is, unemployment, dependency, limited education, crowded housing, and poverty (Feagin 1988; Bullard 1987, 1991). Houston's Third, Fourth and Fifth Wards are classic case studies of urban decay and abandonment.

The Fourth Ward is home to the city's oldest black neighborhood, Freedmen's Town. Following the Civil War, thousands of newly freed slaves found their way into the Fourth Ward. Fueled by Jim Crow laws, the neighborhood became a center of black life in Houston. For decades, it was the only neighborhood where blacks could own homes and businesses. By the 1880s, black settlers had acquired most of the land in Freedmen's Town.

Blacks steadily lost control of the land in Freedmen's Town during the years of the Great Depression and subsequent decades. In 1990, less than 5 percent of the housing in the neighborhood was owner-occupied. The neighborhood has been redlined by lending institutions and denied public infrastructure improvements by the city under its community development block grant (CDBG) program (Aprea et al. 1983). Row after row of houses are boarded up, shops are abandoned, and churches have moved, leaving behind elderly black renters and low-income families (Aprea et al. 1983; Bullard 1987, 1991; Feagin 1988; Shelton et al. 1989).

The Fourth Ward's prime location adjacent to the sprawling central business district makes it ripe for speculation and displacement of incumbent residents. The neighborhood has been under siege for more than two decades. This black neighborhood and the other Houston wards stand as landmarks to the city's failed neighborhood revitalization efforts.

SEPARATE AND UNEQUAL NEIGHBORHOODS

Urban housing continues to be segregated along racial lines. Federal housing policies subsidized white flight to the suburbs and accelerated the abandonment of central cities (Kushner 1980, 130). As a region, the South was not as segregated in 1990 as the Midwest and Northeast. However, blacks and whites in southern cities continue to live apart. A case in point is Birmingham, Alabama, a city tagged the "Johannesburg of the South" in the 1960s. In 1990, Birmingham, Memphis, and Baltimore were the most segregated southern metropolitan areas (Usdansky 1991).

Birmingham is the sixth most segregated metropolitan area in the United States. Birmingham was the only southern metropolitan area ranked in the top ten most segregated metropolitan areas in 1990 (see table 7.2). The Birmingham metropolitan area had a segregation index of .77, which means that 77 percent of either blacks or whites would have to move from segregated neighborhoods to achieve integration. Blacks make up 27.1 percent of the five-county Birmingham metropolitan area. White flight has left the central city with a 63 percent black population and a suburban ring that is 89 percent white (Usdansky 1991).

The Houston metropolitan area is made up of five counties (Brazoria, Fort Bend, Harris, Montgomery, and Waller). The 1990 population of the Houston metropolitan area was 3.3 million. The Houston metropolitan area is 56.4 percent white, 20.8 percent Hispanic, 18.6 percent black, 3.8 percent Asian, and 4 percent other races. The Houston metropolitan area gained over 100,000 African Americans—a 20 percent increase—but lost about 0.3 percentage points of African American population, dropping from 18.2 to 17.9 percent from 1980 to 1990. (University of Houston 1991).

The bulk of the area's black population is clustered in Harris County. Black concentrations are also found in Fort Bend County (Missouri City and Kendleton) and Waller County (Prairie View and Waller). The African American population remained virtually constant in most counties in the Houston area. However, the African American population in Fort Bend County increased from 15.6 percent in 1980 to 20.7 percent in 1990. On other

Table 7.2

Segregation in Southern Metropolitan Areas with Highest Percentage of
Blacks

Metropolitan Area	% Black 1980	% Black 1990	1990 Segregation Index
Memphis	39.9	40.6	75
Richmond-Petersburg, Virginia	32.6	34.7	63
Norfolk, Virginia	29.1	28.5	55
Birmingham, Alabama	27.2	27.1	77
Washington, D.C.	26.9	26.6	67
Atlanta	24.6	26.0	71
Baltimore	25.5	25.9	75
Charlotte, NC	20.0	19.9	62
Houston	18.2	18.6	71
Miami-Fort Lauderdale	15.1	18.5	72

Source: Data from Margaret L. Usdansky, "By the numbers, tracking segregation in 219 metro areas," *USA Today,* 11 November 1991.

other hand, the African American share of Waller County's population dropped from 42 to 37.6 percent (University of Houston 1991).

Houston's African American population has continued to expand beyond the traditional black neighborhoods away from the central core (see figure 7.1). However, Black Houstonians remain segregated from their white counterparts. The 1990 segregation index for the Houston metropolitan area was .71. Overall, the city's black population was less segregated in 1990 than it was in 1980 and 1970 (Taeuber 1983; Usdansky 1991).

Although blacks moved into Houston's suburbs during the 1970s, their numbers there remain relatively small given the size of the central city black population. In 1980, there were just 80,000 blacks living in Houston's suburbs. The black share of Houston's suburbs has actually dropped—from 12.9 percent in 1960 to 8.8 percent in 1970 to 6.2 percent in 1980 (Long and DeAre 1981, 20).

This decrease continued in the eighties. Nevertheless, the area's black suburbanization trend has meant a successive spillover from mostly black neighborhoods and an extension of the segregated housing pattern typical of the central city (Feagin 1988, Shelton et al. 1989; Bullard 1991). During the 1980s, Houston's African American residential concentrations extended northeast to southwest.

Several formerly majority white neighborhoods (areas that were adjacent to majority black tracts) during the 1970s and 1980s have "tipped" toward majority black during the 1990s. Examples of these neighborhoods include Fondren Southwest, Almeda Genoa, and Briar Ridge to the south-southwest and Northline, Melrose, and Gulf Bank to the north. Similarly, a number of other neighborhoods (that is, Alief, Gulton, and Greenspoint) that were not adjacent to majority black areas have seen a significant increase in African American residents (Purser 1992).

HOUSING AND SCHOOL DESEGREGATION

Houston's residential housing pattern has complicated efforts to desegregate public schools in the central city. The Houston Independent School District (HISD) experienced a dramatic demographic shift from a majority Anglo district in the late 1960s to a predominately minority (African American, Latino, and Asian) district in 1990 (Houston Independent School District 1991). For example, the Houston school district experienced a 62.8 percent decline in its Anglo pupil enrollment between 1968 and 1980, followed by a 43 percent decline between 1980 and 1990.

In 1970, 49.9 percent of the district's students were Anglo, 35.7 percent were black, and 14.4 percent were Latino. By the fall of 1990, only 14.3 percent of the district's students were Anglo, 38.2 percent were black, 44.9 percent were Latino, and 2.6 percent were of other races (see table 7.3).

The most significant enrollment change occurred among Latino students. The Latino pupil share skyrocketed from 14.4 percent in 1970 to nearly 45 percent in 1990. Latino students now make up the largest share of students enrolled in the Houston Independent School District.

Suburban housing patterns have affected the ethnic composition of Houston's surrounding school districts. The twenty-one Houston area suburban districts were highly segregated in 1980 (see table 7.4). Nine of the twenty-one suburban districts had enrollments in which Anglos made up 90 percent or more of the student population (Texas Educational Agency 1991). Only one of the Houston suburban school districts was a minority district in 1980. African American students made up 85.2 percent of the North Forest Independent School District in 1980 and 88.4 percent in 1990.

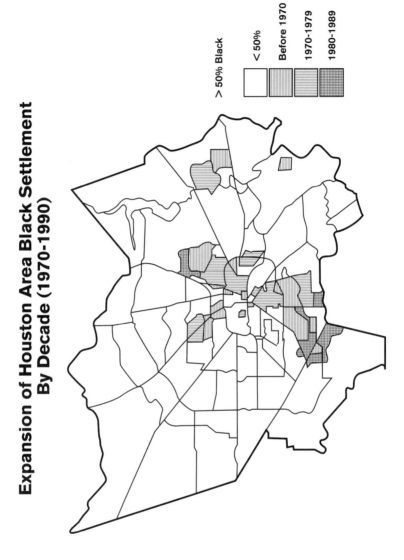

Expansion of Houston Area Black Settlement By Decade (1970-1990)

> 50% Black

< 50%

Before 1970

1970-1979

1980-1989

Source: 1970, 1980, 1990 U.S. Census

Figure 7.1

The decade of the 1980s saw a dramatic increase in minority students enrolled in Houston-area suburban school districts. In 1990, African Americans, Latinos, Asians, and Native Americans made up a majority of students in six Houston area suburban school districts. Minority students made up at least one-third of the students in another five surrounding school districts (Texas Educational Agency 1991).

Some Houston suburbs were especially attractive to minorities during the 1980s. The Alief School District (located in southwest Houston) typified this pattern. In 1980, the district was 82.5 percent Anglo, 2.7 percent black, 7.8 percent Latino, and 7.0 percent Asian. By 1990, the white share of the district had fallen to 38.2 percent. The minority share in the Alief School District increased to 23.3 percent black, 19.1 percent Latino, and 19.4 percent Asian.

On the other hand, four Houston suburbs that experienced only minimal change in minority pupil enrollment during the 1980s—the Huffman, Tomball, Deer Park, and Katy school districts—remained largely Anglo districts. These Houston area suburbs are not generally thought of as places where minorities are welcomed with open arms. Generally, minority families have refused to place their children in what they see as hostile living and school environments.

HOUSING DISCRIMINATION HOUSTON STYLE

It has been nearly twenty-five years since the federal Fair Housing Act of 1968 banned racial discrimination in housing. Barriers to free choice remain, even after the passage of the Fair Housing Amendment in 1988. Housing discrimination contributes to the physical decay of inner-city neighborhoods and denies a substantial segment of society a basic form of wealth accumulation and investment through home ownership. The number of African American home owners would probably be higher in the absence of discrimination by lending institutions (Darden 1987; Bullard and Feagin 1991). Only about 59 percent of middle-class African Americans own their homes, compared with 74 percent of whites.

Affluent and poor African Americans are confronted with the same harsh realities of housing discrimination. Race is still an important factor that influences housing options and residential choices. No matter what their educational or occupational achievement or income level, all blacks are exposed to higher crime rates, less effective educational systems, higher mortality risks, and more dilapidated surroundings because of their race (Darden 1987; Denton and Massey 1988; Bullard and Feagin 1991).

Table 7.3
Pupil Enrollment in the Houston Independent School District,
1970–1990

		Race of Students (in %)			
Year	*Total Enrollment*	*Black*	*Latino*	*Anglo*	*Other*
1970	241,138	35.7	14.4	49.9	—
1971	231,922	37.5	15.6	46.9	—
1972	225,397	39.4	16.6	44.0	—
1973	216,981	41.2	17.9	40.4	0.5
1974	211,547	41.9	19.0	38.6	0.5
1975	210,408	42.6	20.3	36.5	0.6
1976	210,025	43.1	21.8	34.2	0.9
1977	206,998	44.0	22.8	32.1	1.1
1978	201,960	45.0	24.2	29.4	1.4
1979	193,906	45.3	25.6	27.3	1.8
1980	194,043	44.9	27.8	25.1	2.2
1981	193,702	44.3	29.7	23.3	2.7
1982	194,439	44.1	30.9	21.7	3.3
1983	194,467	44.1	32.4	20.3	3.2
1984	187,031	43.6	34.2	19.0	3.2
1985	193,899	43.0	36.0	17.6	3.4
1986	193,855	42.6	37.4	16.9	3.1
1987	191,831	41.9	38.9	16.3	2.9
1988	190,381	40.9	40.8	15.5	2.8
1989	191,284	39.6	42.6	15.2	2.6
1990	194,548	38.2	44.9	14.3	2.7

Source: Data from Houston Independent School District, "Pupil enrollment data 1970–1990," (Houston: Pupil Enrollment Division, 1991).

Table 7.4
Ethnic Composition of Houston's Suburban School Districts,
1980 and 1990

	Ethnic Composition (in %)			
	1980		1990	
School District	White	Minority	White	Minority
Aldine	68.0	32.0	33.1	66.9
Alief	82.5	17.5	38.2	61.8
Channelview	90.0	10.0	65.0	35.0
Clear Creek	92.2	7.8	77.8	22.2
Crosby	55.0	45.0	65.7	34.3
Cyprus-Fairbanks	86.9	13.1	73.0	27.0
Deer Park	91.4	8.6	81.6	18.4
Galena Park	74.0	26.0	41.0	59.0
Goose Creek	71.0	29.0	55.3	44.7
Huffman	98.0	2.0	95.5	4.5
Humble	94.5	5.5	85.0	15.0
Katy	90.0	10.0	81.6	18.4
Klein	92.0	8.0	74.2	25.8
LaPorte	82.2	7.8	72.1	27.9
North Forest	14.8	85.2	2.3	97.7
Pasadena	74.8	24.2	50.7	49.3
Pearland	83.9	16.1	74.3	25.7
Spring	91.7	8.3	66.9	33.1
Spring Branch	86.1	14.9	48.8	51.2
Fort Bend	64.0	36.0	46.9	53.1
Tomball	91.0	9.0	89.8	10.2

Source: Data from Texas Educational Agency, "Texas public school membership by sex and ethnic group" (District/County Report, Austin, Texas, 1991).

Institutional barriers make it difficult for minority families to buy their way out of segregated neighborhoods. Generally, African American home seekers must expend more time, effort, and resources than other Americans for the same end. Real estate brokers and lending institutions often serve as "gatekeepers" in distributing housing and residential areas.

The development of spatially differentiated metropolitan areas where African Americans are segregated from other Americans have resulted from governmental policies and marketing practices of the housing industry and lending institutions (Logan and Molotch 1987). At the rate the nation is going, it will take more than six decades for African Americans to achieve even the minimal level of integration with whites that Asians and Hispanics have now (Jaynes and Williams 1989).

The Houston city government passed its Fair Housing Ordinance in 1975, seven years after the federal Fair Housing Act. The city ordinance created the Fair Housing Division. This division was charged with monitoring housing discrimination complaints that originate within the Houston city limits.

A total of 1,662 housing discrimination complaints were received by the Fair Housing Division between 1975 and 1991 (see table 7.5). Complaint activity fluctuated from year to year, with the greatest number of complaints coming in the early years. Renters made up the overwhelming majority of Houstonians filing housing discrimination complaints. Nearly three-fourths of those filing housing discrimination complaints were African Americans.

More than 66 percent of the complaints based on race/color and 56 percent of complaints based on national origin came from individuals who were seeking housing in areas where African Americans and Latinos made up less than 25 percent of the census tract population.

Complaints based on sex were nearly evenly divided between tracts that contained small minority populations and tracts where African Americans and Latinos were in the majority. Over 45 percent of the sex discrimination complaints originated from tracts where minorities made up 50 percent or more of the tract population. Similarly, 41 percent of the complaints charging sex discrimination originated from persons in tracts where minorities were less than 25 percent of the tract population. These data support other findings that women of color are hit especially hard by the "triple whammy" of race, sex, and family status (e.g., single-parent status) discrimination (Leigh 1989).

Fair housing enforcement has not been a top priority in Houston. The biggest setback to fair housing came in the form of the city's weak commitment to enforcing its own ordinance and the diminished support over the years. The Fair Housing Division has experienced a roller-coaster existence. In 1977, just

Table 7.5
Housing Discrimination Complaints in Houston 1975–1982

Year of Complaint	*Number*
1975[a]	73
1976	478
1977	233
1978	316
1979	175
1980	120
1981	117
1982	105
1991	45
Total	1,662

[a] Only includes the period July 9, 1975, through December 31, 1975.
Source: Data from Houston Fair Housing Authority, *Houston fair housing division annual report* (Houston: City of Houston, 1992), and from City of Houston, "Housing Discrimination Complaints in Houston" (Houston: Affirmative Action Division, March, 1992).

two years after the program got off the ground, the Fair Housing Agency was staffed with nine full-time employees. Four of these employees were compliance officers who did testing.

By 1984, the city agency was allowed to dwindle to only three staff persons—an "acting" director, a secretary, and one compliance officer. In 1985, the severely crippled Houston Fair Housing Division was merged with the city's Affirmative Action Division. This action, part of the mayor's reorganization plan, all but killed the city's role in fair housing enforcement.

In October 1989, after the passage of the federal Fair Housing Amendment Act of 1988, Houston's fair housing program was reestablished under the city's Housing and Community Development Department. The program operates with three staff persons, who receive 100 percent of their funds from the Houston's Community Development Block Grant (CDBG) program. In 1992, for example, the fair housing office identified forty-five instances of discriminatory treatment. The majority of these complaints were negotiated locally, while seventeen of the complaints were transmitted to the U.S. Department of Housing and Urban Development (HUD) for legal action (Hill 1992).

REDLINING THE NEIGHBORHOODS

Discrimination by real estate brokers is not the only barrier that has persisted over the years. Redlining by banks, savings and loans, and insurance companies all diminish housing options for minorities. Studies over the past twenty-five years have clearly documented the impact of redlining on neighborhood decline (Feins and Bratt 1983; Bradbury, Case, and Dunham 1989; Feagin 1990; Jaynes and Williams 1989; Dedman 1988). The pattern is clear in cities all across the nation: African Americans still do not have full access to lending by banks and saving institutions. Institutional racism is alive and well in the financial community.

The problem of redlining was highlighted in the *Atlanta Journal and Constitution's* "Color of Money" series (Dedman 1988). This study found that four of the ten metropolitan areas with the highest ratio of black-to-white loan rejection were located in the South. They include: Norfolk-Virginia Beach-Newport News, Virginia; Charlotte-Gastonia, North Carolina; Baltimore, Maryland, and Memphis, Tennesee, metropolitan areas. Although the national black-white loan rejection ratio was 2 to 1, the ratio in the four southern metropolitan areas was more than 3 to 1 in 1988 (Dedman 1988).

The Federal Financial Institutions Examination Council (1991) found that for southern cities, loan denial rates for African Americans were greatest in Houston, Atlanta, and Dallas (see table 7.6). For example, 33 percent of the African American loan applicants were rejected in the Houston metropolitan area. The loan rejection rates were 26.5 percent in Atlanta and 25.6 percent in Dallas.

Discriminatory lending practices subsidize the physical destruction of African American communities. Today, residents of Houston's black wards must share in paying the hundreds of billions of dollars to bail out the failed savings and loan institutions, some of which engaged in redlining African American communities (Bullard and Feagin 1991).

THE POLITICS OF PUBLIC HOUSING

Houston is a classic example of recent history: African American neighborhoods were passed over during the height of the boom period of the 1970s and

Table 7.6
Black and White Disparities in Mortgage Rejection Rates

Metropolitan Area	Black Rejection Rate (%)	White Rejection Rate (%)	Black-White Rejection Ratio
Minneapolis	19.9	6.1	3.26:1
Chicago	23.6	7.3	3.23:1
Boston	34.9	11.0	3.17:1
Philadelphia	25.0	8.3	3.01:1
St. Louis	31.8	12.1	2.62:1
Houston	33.0	12.6	2.61:1
Pittsburgh	31.0	12.0	2.58:1
Atlanta	26.5	10.5	2.52:1
Detroit	23.7	9.7	2.44:1
Dallas	25.6	10.7	2.39:1
Phoenix	30.0	14.4	2.08:1
Baltimore	15.6	7.5	2.08:1
New York	29.4	15.0	1.96:1
San Diego	17.8	9.8	1.81:1
Oakland	16.5	9.6	1.72:1
Seattle	18.3	10.7	1.71:1
Washington, D.C.	14.4	6.3	1.61:1
Los Angeles	19.8	12.8	1.54:1
Miami	22.9	16.0	1.43:1

Source: Data from Federal Financial Institutions Examination Council, "Home Mortgage Disclosure Act: Expanded data on residential lending," *Federal Reserve Bulletin,* November, 1991: 859–81.

allowed to deteriorate during the bust period of the 1980s (Bullard 1987; Feagin 1988; Shelton et al. 1989). In the 1990s, the city is struggling to recover from a deep economic recession that has driven many to seek jobs and economic security elsewhere. The recessions of the early 1980s and 1990s hit Houston's low-income and minority neighborhoods especially hard.

The city's poor have few advocates. Public attitudes have made it difficult to build subsidized family housing. Public housing has become a political football. Dwindling public resources have created massive headaches for the Houston Housing Authority (HHA), the largest of the forty public housing authorities in the Houston-Galveston area.

The Houston Housing Authority had a budget of $50 million in 1990. The city was able to increase its supply of assisted housing between 1983 and 1990. For example, the housing authority provided 9,893 units in 1983. By 1990, the number had increase to 12,808 units of subsidized housing, of which 4,443 were located in fifteen developments. The agency provided a total of 7,999 units of Section 8 assisted housing.

The need for additional units of low-rent and assisted housing in Houston far exceeds the current supply. About one-fifth of the city's 600,000 households are inadequately housed and could qualify for some type of housing assistance. More than 13,000 persons were on the city's waiting list for assisted housing in 1987 (Bullard 1991a).

African Americans make up the bulk of the tenants in Houston's family developments. In 1990, black Houstonians made up a majority of tenants in all twelve of the city's family developments (see table 7.7). On the other hand, African Americans made up a smaller share of the residents in the housing authority's elderly high-rise developments.

Both African Americans and Latinos have increased their share of Houston's elderly developments during the 1980s. In 1984, for example, Anglos made up 64.1 percent of the population in the Lyerly elderly development, 72.9 percent in the Bellerive development, and 70.9 percent in the Telephone Road development. By 1990, over half of the tenants in both the Lyerly and Bellerive development were African American or Latino tenants.

Although gains were made in expanding the supply of assisted housing available to elderly Houstonians, the city experienced repeated setbacks in its attempts to build family developments during the 1980s. Citizen opposition to public housing sites made it difficult for the local housing authority to build new developments in most white areas.

In addition, the housing authority allowed one of its largest family developments, the one thousand-unit Allen Parkway Village, to fall into

Table 7.7

Ethnic Composition of Houston Housing Authority Developments, 1990

Development	No. of Units	Ethnic Composition (%)			
		Black	Latino	Anglo	Other
Family					
Allen Parkway Village	1,000	62.2	4.5	11.1	22.2
Clayton Homes	348	60.0	19.5	0.5	20.0
Cuney Homes	564	98.1	1.3	0.4	0.2
Ewing	42	88.9	2.8	8.3	0.0
Forest Green	100	97.8	1.1	1.1	0.0
Irvington Village	318	53.9	38.8	4.7	0.0
Kelly Village	333	95.7	0.8	1.5	2.0
Lincoln Park	264	98.5	1.0	0.5	0.0
Oxford Place	230	93.9	1.5	3.8	0.8
Kennedy Place	60	88.3	5.0	0.0	6.7
Wilmington House	108	89.1	0.0	0.0	10.9
Long Drive	100	87.3	8.0	3.4	1.3
Elderly					
Lyerly	200	35.6	20.1	43.8	0.5
Bellerive	210	12.6	24.8	46.6	16.0
Telephone Road	200	12.6	24.8	46.6	1.5

Source: Housing Authority of the City of Houston, *Annual Report* (Houston: City of Houston), 1990.

disrepair and go largely unoccupied. Houston's Allen Parkway Village is located in the Fourth Ward, the city's oldest black neighborhood. The project sits on prime real estate just west of the central business district and just across from the Buffalo Bayou Park and the planned Riverwalk.

Allen Parkway Village was allowed to deteriorate over the years. The majority of the apartments have remained boarded up and unoccupied. African American tenants were replaced with Indochinese refugees. In 1976 African American tenants made up 66 percent of the Allen Parkway Village population, and Asians (mostly Indochinese refugees) made up just 5 percent of the project population. By 1983, the African American tenant share had decreased to 33 percent, and the Indochinese share had risen to 58 percent. In 1990, most of the units were boarded up: Only forty-five of the one thousand units in Allen Parkway Village were occupied.

The Houston Housing Authority plans called for demolishing the dilapidated project and selling the thirty-seven-acre site. Its plan also included replacement housing units that would be scattered throughout the city and not concentrated in the low-income Fourth Ward. After lengthy public hearings and lawsuits brought by tenants, the housing authority was able to unload the project. Renovations, however, have been slow in coming. Many people still tie the fate of the Fourth Ward to what will happen to Allen Parkway Village: "As goes Allen Parkway Village, so goes the Fourth Ward" (Aprea et al. 1983).

CONCLUSION

Houston was the boom capital of the Sun Belt during the 1970s, leading the nation in housing construction and creation of new jobs. However, this new growth was not distributed equitably across different segments of the community. Houston's African American community, the largest in the region, was passed over during the boom period of the 1970s and the bust period of the 1980s.

Economic recessions of the early 1980s and 1990s exacted a heavy toll on the city's low-income and minority neighborhoods. Talk of a New South was only an illusion to the many Houstonians who lived in economically depressed neighborhoods. Housing construction and home ownership opportunities were extended largely to those outside the central city. The older inner-city neighborhoods were left to decay.

Housing discrimination played an essential role in creating separate and unequal neighborhoods for Houston's black and white residents. Although the city was less segregated in 1990 than in 1970, black and white Houstonians still lived in two separate worlds. The segregated housing patterns were reinforced by lending practices and lingering racial stereotypes.

Attempts to dismantle barriers to free housing choice have fallen short. Houston was late in adopting a formal open-housing plan. The local government created a Fair Housing Division in 1975, seven years after the federal Fair Housing Act of 1968. However, the city's Fair Housing Division was dismantled after less than ten years of operation.

The bulk of Houston's African American population is still concentrated in the wards and older areas of the city. The 1980s did witness some movement of minorities into selected suburban areas, but much of the black suburbanization occurred along predictable corridors that extended the boundaries of traditional black neighborhoods. The movement of minority families into the surrounding suburbs has resulted in a dramatic increase in minority enrollment in most of the outlying districts. On the other hand, some Houston suburban school districts have remained largely white.

Finally, it is clear that racial discrimination continues to play an important part in limiting housing options available to Houston's African American and other minority communities. Discrimination not only complicates the efforts to desegregate public schools, it also limits access of low-income households to decent and affordable housing. Despite the efforts by government to level the playing field with legislative mandates, housing inequities persist. New initiatives are needed to combat this age-old problem.

REFERENCES

Aprea, Robert, Robert D. Bullard, Jeff Baloutine, and Jacquline Alford 1983. *Allen Parkway Village/Fourth Ward Technical Report.* Houston: Houston Housing Authority.

Bradbury, Katherine L., Karl E. Case, and Constance R. Dunham. 1989. Geographic patterns of mortgage lending in Boston, 1982–1987. *New England Economic Review* (September/October): 3–30.

Bullard, Robert D., ed. 1991a. "Blacks in heavenly Houston." In *In search of the new South: The black urban experience in the 1970s and 1980s.* Tuscaloosa, Ala.: University of Alabama Press.

———. 1991b. Housing problems and prospects for blacks in Houston. *The Review of Black Political Economy* 20 (Fall): 175–94.

———. 1987. Invisible Houston: The black experience in boom and bust. College Station: Texas A&M University Press.

Bullard, R. D., and Joe R. Feagin. 1991. Racism and the city. In *Urban life in transition,* edited by Mark Gottdiener and C. V. Pickvance. Newbury Park, Calif.: Sage.

Darden, Joe T. 1987. Choosing neighbors and neighborhoods: The role of race in changing patterns of racial segregation. In *Divided neighborhoods: Changing patterns of racial segregation,* edited by Gary Tobin. Newbury Park, Calif.: Sage.

Dedman, Bill. 1988. The color of money. *The Atlanta Journal/Constitution,* 1–16 May.

Denton, Nancy A., and Douglas S. Massey. 1988. Residential segregation of blacks, Hispanics, and Asians by socioeconomic status and generation. *Social Science Quarterly* 69 (December): 797–817.

Feagin, Joe R. 1990. *Building American cities: The urban real estate game.* Englewood Cliffs, N.J.: Prentice Hall.

———. 1988. *Free enterprise city: Houston in political and economic perspective.* New Brunswick, N.J.: Rutgers University Press.

Federal Financial Institution Examination Council. 1991. Home Mortgage Disclosure Act: Expanded data on residential lending. *Federal Reserve Bulletin* (November): 859–81.

Feins, Judith D., and R. G. Bratt 1983. Barred in Boston: Racial discrimination in housing. *Journal of the American Planning Association* 49 (summer): 344–55.

Hill, Annie R. 1992. Memorandum from the Fair Housing Manager to the author, entitled, Status of the Fair Housing Program, City of Houston, Texas, 13 July.

Houston Independent School District. 1991. *Pupil enrollment data, 1970–1990.* Houston: Pupil Enrollment Division.

James, Franklin, Betty I. McCummings, and E.A. Tynan. 1984. *Minorities in the Sunbelt.* New Brunswick, N.J.: Rutgers University Center for Urban Policy Research.

Kushner, James A. 1988. An unfinished agenda: The federal fair housing enforcement effort. *Yale Law & Policy Review* 6 (2): 348–60.

———. 1980. Apartheid in America: An historical and legal analysis of contemporary racial segregation in the United States. Frederick, Md.: Associated Faculty Press.

Leigh, Wilhelmina. 1989. Barriers to fair housing for black women. *Sex Roles* 21 (1/2): 69–84.

Logan, John H., and Harvey Molotch. 1987. *Urban fortunes: The political economy of place.* Berkeley: University of California.

Long, Larry, and D. DeAre. 1981. The suburbanization of blacks. *American Demographics* 3 (September): 16–22.

Massey, Douglas S., and Nancy A. Denton. 1993. *American apartheid: Segregation and the making of the underclass.* Cambridge, Mass.: Harvard University Press.

———. 1987. Trends in the residential segregation of blacks, Hispanics, and Asians: 1970–1980. *American Sociological Review* 52 (December): 802–25.

Purser, Peg. 1992. *Minority settlement patterns in the Houston area.* Houston: University of Houston Center for Public Policy.

Shelton, Beth Ann, Nestor Rodriguez, Joe R. Feagin, Robert D. Bullard, and Robert Thomas. 1989. *Houston: Growth and decline in a Sunbelt boomtown.* Philadelphia: Temple University Press.

Taeuber, Karl. 1983. Racial residential segregation, 28 cities, 1970–1980. Working paper, Center for Demography and Ecology, University of Wisconsin, Madison.

Texas Educational Agency. 1991. *Texas public school membership by sex and ethnic group.* District/County Report, Austin, Texas (fall).

University of Houston. 1991. *Metropolitan population trends: 1970–1990 Harris and suburban trends.* Houston: University of Houston Center for Public Policy.

U.S. Bureau of the Census. 1990. *Summary population and housing characteristics.* Washington, D.C.: U.S. Government Printing Office.

Usdansky, Margaret L. 1991. By the numbers, tracking segregation in 219 metro areas. *USA Today,* 11 November.

CHAPTER 8

Latino Settlement Patterns in "The Free Enterprise City"

by Nestor Rodriguez

Prominent analysts and institutes have heralded Houston as a model of urban development in the free enterprise system (Johnson 1982; Jones 1982). Houston's robust economic development, its oil-industrial specialization in the world economy, and its dynamic and prosperous real estate industry have been cited as examples of economic growth and prosperity that result from a *laissez-faire* economic philosophy, in which market forces, not social planning, determine growth. The city's economic configuration of a skyscraper-dotted downtown, an oil- and petrochemical-industrial hinterland, an expanding port area, and a sprawling business sector in inner-city neighborhoods attest to Houston's fame as "the free-enterprise city," a premier capitalist city. Often overlooked in this extollment of Houston, however, is the growth of its working-class settlements, the living areas of workers and their families. Of the three largest groups (white, African American, and Latino) that have provided labor power for Houston's economic development, Latinos have experienced the most dynamic growth. From 1970 to 1990 the number of Latinos in the city has grown by 201 percent (see table 8.1). Along with the dramatic growth rate, an increasing ethnic and residential differentiation characterizes the development of Houston's Latino settlements in the late twentieth century.

In this chapter I will discusses Latino growth in Houston from the perspective of Latino settlement patterns in the central city and from the perspective of the relationship of these patterns to the area's housing market.[1] First, for background purposes I will briefly describe Houston's recession in the 1980s and how it affected the city's housing market. Second, I will describe the settlement patterns of different Latino groups and how these patterns interact with housing market conditions, producing different social and economic outcomes. Finally, I will address the future of Houston's Latino settlements.

Table 8.1
White, African American, Latino,
and Other Populations in the City of Houston, 1970–1990

	1970	*1980*	*1990*
City of Houston	1,232,802	1,595,138	1,630,553
White	755,162	837,285	650,841
African American	316,551	440,346	457,990
Latino	149,727	281,331	450,483
Asian & Other	11,362	36,176	71,239

Source: U.S. Bureau of the Census (1972, 1983, 1992a, 1992b).

HOUSTON'S CHANGING ECONOMIC CONDITIONS AND HOUSING MARKET

The early 1980s saw the beginning of a dramatic downturn in Houston's economy, which did not bottom out until 1987. This downturn ended a pattern of economic growth and business prosperity in the Houston area that had lasted since the 1920s. So robust was this economic development that in 1939 *Fortune* magazine called Houston the city that the Depression missed. Houston's early economic prosperity was overshadowed by even greater prosperity in the post–World War II years, reaching a Golden Age in the 1970s. The decade of the 1970s witnessed Houston's maturation as an industrial power in the world economy and, much related to this, its growth as a major industrial center in the United States (Rodriguez and Feagin 1986). At home, Houston companies manufactured oil and petrochemical machinery and refined domestic and foreign petroleum; abroad, Houston companies explored for oil and built petrochemical plants in many world regions.

Becoming well-established in international business, for several years in the 1970s Houston ranked first in foreign-trade port tonnage and in the number of foreign banks outside New York City (Rodriguez and Feagin 1986). The rise of oil prices, which caused economic hardships in the United States and severe economic problems in less developed countries, only brought more prosperity to Houston's economy. Higher-priced oil translated into higher oil profits, increasing capitalization and production in Houston's oil-and petrochemical-related manufacturing sector and creating growth in ancillary construction and service industries.

Houston's dramatic economic expansion in the 1970s thrust the area's real estate industry into hypergrowth, generating an office construction momentum that continued past the 1982/1983 start of the area's economic downturn. As sociologist Joe R. Feagin's (1988) study of Houston shows, 33 percent of Houston's 485 office buildings and towers of 100,000 square feet or more in 1987 were built in 1971–1980 and 52 percent in 1981–1987, mainly before 1985. Feagin shows a definite parallel between the movement of crude oil prices and the rise (and later decline) of office building construction in Houston. The construction of apartments and single-family homes also continued in the early 1980s.

Public housing was the only segment of the city's housing sector that did not expand during the boom years. In the late 1980s Houston had the fourth largest population in the country but fewer public housing units than other cities of much smaller size.

FROM BOOM TO BUST

The city's dramatic economic growth in the 1970s and early 1980s was followed by an equally dramatic downturn in the 1982–1987 period. Simply put, the Houston area economy entered cardiac arrest in late 1982. A large oversupply of oil when world market demand was dropping lowered the spot oil price by 10 percent and, more importantly, the oil price expectation by 50 percent. This reduced oil exploration by half and created an immediate oversupply of oil-related equipment (Smith 1989). Strongly tied to international commerce, the Houston economy suffered an additional setback when the U.S. trade dollar gained strength (a 56 percent value increase) against other currencies in 1983–1987 (Feagin 1988). The strong U.S. trade dollar reduced foreign demand for Houston's industrial products.

In the first phase of the downturn (1982–1984), Houston's energy-related manufacturing sector lost 43 percent of its jobs. This accounted for many of the nearly 160,000 jobs lost in the Houston area within the first year of the recession (Smith 1989). In the second phase of the recession (1985–1987) many business services closed down or reduced their operations, and the construction industry practically disappeared. This contributed to tens of thousands of additional job losses and an unemployment rate of 13 percent in the summer of 1986.

IMPACT ON THE REAL ESTATE SECTOR AND THE HOUSING MARKET

The boom period of Houston's growth strongly energized the area's real estate sector. Foreign, domestic, and local capital flooded the Houston real estate sector. Insurance companies, banks, and savings and loan associations heavily financed the area's construction industry, increasing the construction workforce by 73 percent between 1975 and 1982 (Smith 1986). In less than five years, builders in Houston doubled the amount of office space in the city and added over 200,000 units to the housing market (Smith 1986). Many of these units were built as large apartment complexes in the western half of the city and were settled mainly by middle-income white residents.

The population growth accompanying the Houston area's economic development kept the housing market prosperous. An estimated 1,023,000 units in 1981 had a vacancy rate of less than 10 percent (see table 8.2). Even after the start of the downturn, builders continued to construct new units, over 97,000 more by the time the recession bottomed out in 1987.

Heavily financed by debt, Houston's real estate sector suffered large numbers of bankruptcies and foreclosures in the second half of the recession. In 1986 alone, 485 real estate firms went bankrupt, and foreclosures averaged about 3,000 per month (Rodriguez and Hagan 1992). By 1987 real estate values had dropped by over 30 percent. Needless to say, the real estate sector became moribund.

In the housing market the number of vacant units grew by 154 percent from 1981 to 1985 (see table 8.2). Many of the vacancies occurred in the city's West Side, where builders had constructed many of the 3,067 apartment projects in the Houston area. The massive number of West Side apartments were built mainly for a growing white middle-income population. While the recession also affected the housing market in the city's eastern half, where the established African American and Latino communities are located, the effect was less severe for the landlords in this part of the city. In the West Side, the out-migration of unemployed office workers and subsequent vacancies placed the value of multimillion-dollar apartment projects in jeopardy, while in the East Side the out-migration of low-income workers pressured mainly small landlords of working-class frame houses and garage apartments.

As I will describe in the next section, Houston's economic downturn coincided with a massive immigration of Latino immigrants, which enabled West Side apartment landlords to implement apartment restructuring strategies to survive the area's economic crisis. The strategies, which involved drastically reducing rent prices to attract arriving low-income Latino immi-

Table 8.2
Houston's Housing Market, 1979–1988

Year	Total Housing Units	Vacancy Rate (%)
1979	937,927	10.4
1980	983,730	11.4
1981	1,023,066	8.5
1982	1,084,145	9.9
1983	1,147,304	15.8
1984	1,186,641	17.7
1985	1,199,507	18.4
1986	1,192,932	18.3
1987	1,181,252	17.7
1988	1,171,132	16.2

Source: Smith (1989).

grants, changed the course of social and cultural development in the West Side and the course of Latino settlement in the city.

LATINO SETTLEMENT IN HOUSTON

Latino population growth in Houston has paralleled the city's dynamic economic growth. On the average Latino growth rates have been 2.0 times higher than the city's total population growth rates in the decades from 1900 to 1990. High Latino growth rates were easy to achieve in the pre-World War II years because of the relatively small (base) number of Latinos. In the 1960s and 1970s, however, when Latinos already numbered in the hundreds of thousands, they continued to score high growth rates in the city. In the 1980s the Latino population in Houston grew by 60.1 percent, while the total city population grew by less than 1 percent. Immigration accounts for a large part of the high Latino growth rate.

High population growth has raised the Latino renter rate in the Houston housing market. From 1970 to 1980, when the city's Latino population grew by 87.9 percent, the renter rate among Latino households in the city increased from 55.5 percent to 64.0 percent (U.S. Bureau of the Census 1972, 1983). In the same time interval the city's overall renter rate increased from 47.3 percent to 52.6 percent. The black renter rate increased only slightly between 1970 and 1980, from 55.3 percent to 56.5 percent.

Immigration contributes to the growth of the Latino renter rate. A 1992 random survey of Houston-area Latinos found a renter rate of 44.0 percent among the U.S.-born respondents and a renter rate of 56.9 percent among the foreign-born respondents (Romo and Rodriguez 1993). The median monthly rental payments of the U.S.-born and foreign-born respondents were $400 and $325, respectively.

Immigration also contributes to the growing ethnic diversity of the Houston Latino population. Presently this diversity includes Mexican Americans, Mexican immigrants, Central Americans, and Latinos from the Caribbean and South America. The first three Latino populations constitute identifiable settlement areas in the city.

MEXICAN AMERICANS

Of 450,483 Latinos counted by the 1990 census in the city of Houston, 80 percent were of Mexican descent (U.S. Bureau of the Census 1992b). About half of this number can be considered Mexican American through birth in the United States. The origin of Mexican Americans in Houston in the 1800s has two sources, in-migration from other Texas localities and immigration from Mexico. A common but not well-documented belief maintains that the first Mexicans in Houston were prisoners taken from Santa Anna's defeated army and forced to help clear the swampland in the site where the city of Houston was founded.

Through most of the twentieth century, Mexican American settlement in Houston was located in the eastern half of the city, east of Main Street and adjacent to African American communities. In the pre-World War II era, Mexican Americans and Mexican immigrants established several sizable settlements *(colonias* and *barrios)* east, southeast, and just north of the central business district. Eventually moving into neighborhoods and a housing market occupied by European and Middle Eastern (Lebanese) settlers, the growing Latino population in the East End clustered around emerging port, railroad, and manufacturing industries. Along with black and white workers, Mexican Americans became an

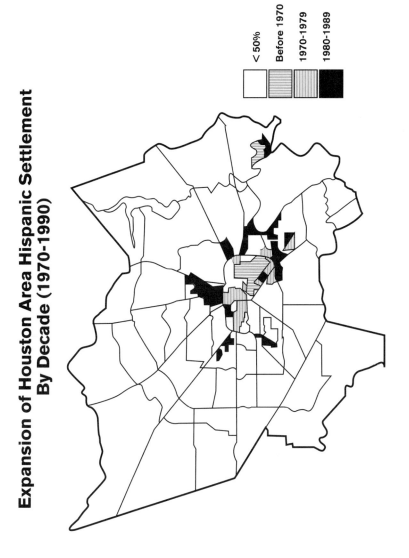

Expansion of Houston Area Hispanic Settlement
By Decade (1970-1990)

< 50%

Before 1970

1970-1979

1980-1989

Source: 1970, 1980, 1990 U.S. Census

Figure 8.1

important labor resource for the city's industrial growth. Occupying the housing market closest to East Side industries gave Mexican Americans a labor market advantage. Moreover, a vibrant ethnic economy in the colonias and barrios provided an additional employment source (De Leon 1989).

The post–World War II years saw the settlement of Mexican American families in neighborhoods farther north of downtown and in the Heights, a large district a couple of miles northwest of downtown. In these neighborhoods the housing market consisted mainly of homes formerly occupied by white, working-class families. The Heights, for example, originated in the late 1800s as a settlement of working- and middle-class white families residing in Victorian and California bungalow-style homes. Mexican American and other Latino in-migration, as well as gentrification by arriving white middle-income couples, transformed the Heights into a social patchwork of white, black, Latino, middle-income, poor, straight, and gay households. By the late 1980s, Latino families, churches, restaurants, bars, gangs, and so on substantially turned sections of the Heights into zones of Latino transition (Shelton et al. 1989).

The 1950s through the 1980s also saw the migration of Mexican Americans from the central city to surrounding blue-collar suburbs. While these suburbs provided new housing, they still contrasted sharply with the growing number of middle-class and upper middle-class suburbs of white families in areas to the north, west, and south of the central city. A massive freeway system gave Latinos living outside the inner city easier access to jobs, in some cases, than Latinos in the East Side barrios, with inferior freeway connections, experienced.

Houston's boom in the 1970s brought the prosperity that enabled some Mexican American families to resettle in other parts of the Houston area. While the boom did not elevate the work status of Latinos by more than 4 percentage points in any occupational category, it did create an abundance of jobs, with wages usually running higher than in other Texas cities; it also brought an expanding housing supply in a social climate of decreasing, but not completely dissipated, de facto residential restrictions. The growth of port and manufacturing industries located near, or actually inside, the East Side barrios created a major economic advantage (but environmental disadvantages) for the Mexican American residents. In some of the forty-nine manufacturing plants located inside the East Side barrios, Latinos from the surrounding neighborhoods reached union leadership positions and negotiated wages as high as $8 an hour for starting laborers (W. R. Morris, personal communication, January 21, 1991).

The downturn eroded the economic achievements of many Mexican Americans in the East Side and in other parts of Houston. Heavily involved in manufacturing industries, East Side Mexican American workers took the "first hit" of the recession. The large manufacturing plants in the barrios, which had employed thousands of workers, quickly reduced their workforces to skeleton crews that handle the surplus equipment inventory. Some plants closed down completely, creating acres of industrial ghost towns in the barrios.

For Rent and For Sale signs (in English and Spanish) throughout the barrios told the story of the out-migration of unemployed residents. In the commercial areas, closed-down restaurants, *taquerias,* bars, barber and beauty shops, Spanish theaters, and so on, also indicated the blow dealt to the ethnic economy. Large numbers of Mexican Americans joined the lines of immigrants and white homeless men who sought food and shelter at local relief agencies.

After the downturn bottomed out in 1987, it became clear that the future would not include a swift return to the prosperity of the prerecession years. Many of the unemployed Mexican American workers who stayed in Houston, or returned to the city, found low-wage service jobs, for example, in health care, security, and maintenance services. With an enormous oversupply of housing, the construction sector also failed to generate the abundance of jobs, which formerly offered high wages and long work weeks with hefty overtime wages. For many Mexican American workers the new "good jobs" now offered $4 or $5 an hour and a 40-hour or shorter workweek.

From the standpoint of the housing market, however, the recession produced a significant advantage for Mexican Americans, as well as for Latinos in general. At least until home prices and apartment rents started rising in late 1989, the large oversupply of apartment housing created an opportunity for Mexican American renters to relocate closer to the more dynamic centers of job growth in the city. An optimal location was the city's West Side, an area dotted by large apartment projects. In the late 1980s the West Side became the center of gravity for new job growth in the city's service sector. Mexican Americans, however, did not move in large numbers to the West Side. Perhaps Mexican Americans living elsewhere viewed the new service jobs in the West Side as unattractive, or perhaps they viewed apartment-complex housing as too different from their family dwellings in the established Mexican American settlements. The sense of community—that is, Mexican American community—no doubt also kept Mexican Americans in their established settlements.

MEXICAN IMMIGRANTS

As in other areas of the Southwest, the Mexican American experience in Houston is intertwined with the growth of the Mexican immigrant population. More than their common Mexican origin unites the two populations; yet, social and cultural boundaries run between the two groups (Rodriguez and Nunez 1986). In Houston, Mexican immigrants played as important a role as Mexican Americans in the development of the traditional Latino settlement zones. Coming mostly from peasant and working-class backgrounds, Mexican immigrants settled in the East Side areas of industrial growth in the early part of the century. The immigrants' families, foods, music, Catholicism, and social clubs, and organizations played a major role in the emergence of the city's first Mexican-origin settlements (De Leon 1989).

Many of the early Mexican immigrants in Houston came as undocumented workers. While some came as sojourners, others stayed and later brought their families from Mexico. Undocumented Mexican immigrant men and women created an optimal labor supply for Houston's capitalistic growth: They worked for low wages, had no union protection, and expanded their numbers through self-recruitment of kin and other compatriots. In the boom years of the 1970s and early 1980s, Mexican immigrant workers became a central labor resource for the low-skill sectors of the area's labor market, such as the construction and service industries. The sign *Ofecina De Empleo* (Employment Office) outside the hiring hall of a huge rice storage complex near downtown illustrated the prominence of Mexican immigrant labor in the city.

In the Houston area's boom period of the 1970s and early 1980s, Mexican immigrants swelled the housing market in Latino neighborhoods in the city's East Side and near North Side and in neighborhoods north and northwest of downtown undergoing Latino growth (Shelton et al. 1989). The vigorous growth of Mexican immigrant enclaves promoted the buying of homes by Mexican immigrants, especially business families who had developed binational households. In contrast to a small segment of socially elite Mexican families who settled in condominiums and high-priced homes in white, affluent West Side neighborhoods, many Mexican immigrants bought homes in traditional and transitional Latino settlement zones in the city and in a few surrounding working-class suburbs (Shelton et al. 1989).

Poor Mexican immigrants reacted in several ways to the Houston recession. Facing layoffs and a severe shrinkage of the job market, many Mexican immigrants left Houston for more prosperous labor markets in other parts of the country, especially in the eastern seaboard. Other Mexican immigrants returned to Mexico. The Mexican immigrants who stayed faced a depressed job market of fewer jobs, lower wages, and shorter workweeks. Among the undocumented immigrants, the lack of unemployment compensation and other public assistance created havoc.

Out-migration, return migration, and depressed incomes in the Mexican immigrant population led to excess housing in the city's barrios. Even when landlords reduced rents, by as much as 50 percent in some cases, the oversupply of barrio housing remained substantial. The presence of excess housing alongside growing numbers of native and immigrant homeless persons revealed the capitalistic nature of the city's housing market: Housing existed primarily to create profit, not to shelter people.

The end of the downturn in 1987 brought mixed outcomes for Houston's Mexican immigrant population. With sharply reduced manufacturing and construction activities and with the shift of job growth to the lower-paying service sector, the postrecession economy in Houston offered moderate opportunities, at best, for Mexican immigrant residents. Since Mexican immigration had continued during the recession, the moderate opportunities had to be divided up among a growing number of Mexican immigrant workers and shared with an increasing number of Central American immigrants.

But 1987 also brought the implementation of the Immigration Reform and Control Act (IRCA), a federal measure that gave undocumented Mexican immigrants and other undocumented newcomers a more secure position in the labor market. Over 90,000 undocumented Mexican immigrants applied at the Houston office of the Immigration and Naturalization Service (INS) for amnesty and legalization under the provisions of IRCA, which also contained employer sanctions as a means to deter "unauthorized" immigrant workers (U.S. Immigration and Naturalization Service n.d.).

Among the Mexican immigrants who settled in the large, West Side apartment projects after 1985 were many who were going through the IRCA legalization process. Applying for legalization provided a work authorization card, which helped locate a job in the service industries surrounding the apartment complexes. From these housing settings, Mexican immigrant women also found jobs as domestics in the large West Side sections of white, affluent, and middle-class homes.

CENTRAL AMERICAN IMMIGRANTS

The arrival of an estimated 100,000 Central Americans in Houston in the 1980s created a new pattern of Latino settlement in the city. Several conditions distinguished this development as a new settlement experience, that is, as an experience significantly different from earlier Latino settlement in the city.

First, Central Americans brought backgrounds of other Latino nations (El Salvador, Guatemala, Honduras, and so on), backgrounds that contrasted with the city's predominant Mexican origin population. Second, the Central American immigrants brought a much higher degree of internal social differentiation, including racial distinctions (Black Carib and Mayan), than existed among the city's Mexican origin groups (Rodriguez 1987).

Third, the Central Americans came from political circumstances not normally characteristic of Mexican origin settlers and which necessitated resources (such as refugee centers) to aid their settlement. Finally, the Central Americans, especially Salvadorans, brought community-mobilizing skills that helped materialize political-legal support from U.S. residents to help stabilize the new Central American settlements in the city.

Central Americans arrived in Houston at about the same time that the area's economy started to decline. To be sure, a small number of Central Americans had immigrated during the boom in the 1970s and located employment in the West Side. A group of Salvadorans located apartment construction jobs about four miles southwest of downtown and settled in small nearby apartment projects. When Central American turmoil sent massive waves of refugees and other migrants to the United States, this initial Salvadoran presence became the cornerstone of a Central American settlement that by the mid-1980s stretched for miles into the southwest section of the city and contained tens of thousands of new immigrants. Apartment owners and managers played an active and deliberate role in this development.

When thousands of unemployed office workers left the area during the recession, creating massive apartment vacancies, many West Side apartment owners and managers turned to the new Central American immigrants to rebuild their tenant populations. Built originally for white middle-income office workers, the West Side apartments were an economic and cultural mismatch for the undocumented Central Americans who were arriving in the city. Undoubtedly planning only a temporary survival strategy, West Side apartment landlords drastically reduced monthly rental prices, by more than half in some projects, gave a month of free rent, and did away with move-in deposits. To further entice new Central American renters, some apartment landlords changed apartment names to Spanish ones and offered conveniences such as free English classes and Latino nightclubs on apartment grounds. Moreover, bilingual personnel were placed in apartment management offices. The landlords' apartment restructuring strategies worked.

While numbers of Central American newcomers also settled in the East Side barrios, the West Side apartment projects of several hundred to over a thousand units became the densest Central American settlements in the city. Crowding into apartment units in multifamily households, many Central American immigrants were able to survive in the West Side to look for work mainly in service jobs in surrounding industries. In many apartment complexes, the Central Americans formed household clusters, developing a sense of community and accumulating social resources to survive in their new social and cultural environment. High unemployment, changing household survival strategies, and INS raids kept many Central Americans at a high level of transiency in their West Side apartment neighborhoods.

The West Side settlement experience of the Central American immigrants has had mixed outcomes. On the positive side, the Central Americans found more housing in the vicinity of the dynamic West Side job market than any other Latino group in the city. While many of the jobs that Central Americans find in the West Side are in low-paying service industries, employment—any employment—is crucial for immigrants to establish some initial residential success. This is no small factor, given that Central Americans and other newcomers continue to arrive daily in the West Side. Some of the Central Americans who obtained legal status through IRCA achieved some employment mobility, creating job openings for more recent arrivals.

On the negative side, the housing situation of Central Americans in the West Side is not secure. With improving economic conditions, many apartment owners and managers have implemented a second apartment restructuring process that involves upgrading apartment units and facilities to attract white middle-income office workers, who are returning with the economic upswing. Part of this restructuring process involves raising rental rates to levels beyond the capacity of many Central Americans and other new immigrants.

The large apartment projects in the West Side have served as an important resource in the settlement of many new Latino immigrants in Houston. The resource goes beyond providing a place to dwell. It is a social resource: the ability to use residential clusters as a base for the social reproduction of family households and community structures. Once initiated, the benefits of this social reproduction may reach as far as the immigrants' communities of origin.

In the section that follows I use the case of Guatemalan Mayan tenants in one large apartment complex to illustrate this housing-related process of social reproduction from the perspective of the two apartment restructuring phases in Houston's West Side.

MAYAN SETTLEMENT IN THE WEST SIDE

In several U.S. cities the streams of Central American immigration contain significant numbers of Mayan-origin people (Burns 1993). Political unrest, a crushing counterinsurgency program, and economic decline drove thousands of Mayans from Guatemala, especially from the western highlands, in the early 1980s. Large numbers of Mayans resettled in refugee camps in southern Mexico, but many others migrated to the United States as undocumented migrants. Houston became a destination point for Mayans from the Guatemalan highland provinces of El Quiché and Totonicapán.

The trickle of Mayan immigration from Totonicapán in 1980 and 1981 became a flood of several hundred migrants and families in 1982–1985. Their immigration coincided with the decline of the massive apartment industry in the city's West Side. After a few of the migrant men found jobs as floor cleaners and sackers in West Side supermarkets, the Totonicapán immigrants settled in nearby apartment projects. One apartment complex, Arboleda (fictitious name), housed a large number of the Totonicapán migrant families. With over eight hundred apartment units (divided into five buildings), manicured lawns, three large swimming pools and Jacuzzis, tennis courts, and wall-to-wall carpeting in the apartments, Arboleda had no resemblance to the highland adobe housing the Mayan newcomers left behind in Guatemala.

Eager to rebuild its renter population during the downturn, Arboleda management lowered monthly rental rates, by over $200 for some units, as an initial restructuring strategy. With a growing Latino tenant population, management introduced bilingual staff to help operate the apartments. When Mayan families arrived with children, management looked the other way, disregarding its own policy against families with children (a policy that had been implemented for the previous white middle-income tenants). In the apartment parking areas where earlier tenants had kept their German-built cars, Mayan and other Latino renters now washed, and worked on, their small Japanese-built trucks. By the mid-1980s, management printed apartment bulletins in English and Spanish (Hagan and Rodriguez 1992).

In Arboleda, Mayans reestablished families or created new ones and undertook several community-building activities. These activities included celebrating baptisms, birthdays, and weddings, cooking a variety of Guatemalan *tamales* to raise funds for their church group, and organizing soccer teams that played in the many new Latino-immigrant soccer leagues in the city. The community-building activities also included the formation of social networks that linked households to the supermarket workplaces and to white neighborhoods, in the case of the Mayan women who worked as domestics (Hagan and Rodriguez 1992).

The settlement success accomplished by the Mayans in Arboleda and other nearby apartments enabled the accumulation of monetary resources that were periodically remitted to family households in Guatemala. Within a short time of their initial settlement, the Totonicapán Mayans in Houston developed an informal courier system that on a regular basis transported televisions, radios, appliances, and other merchandise bought in Houston to families in Totonicapán. By the mid-1980s Mayans in Arboleda and other apartments had evolved a stable transnational support system for families back home.

In 1987, when the Houston recession bottomed out, the implementation of IRCA and the initiation of a second apartment restructuring process caused serious problems for the Mayan settlers in the West Side. Employers fearful of employer sanctions terminated or threatened to terminate the employment of their undocumented workers. Moreover, rumors among immigrants told of massive pending INS sweeps to rid the country of undocumented immigrants. Sixty of the Totonicapán migrants returned home, and a handful left for Canada hoping to find a more generous government policy toward immigrants.

Anticipating the return of higher-income tenants with the economic upswing, many apartment landlords in the West Side upgraded apartment projects and raised rents. Upgrading was necessary because the high transiency of Latino immigrant renters and the lessening of maintenance services to this population led to apartment deterioration. In Arboleda, as in many other West Side apartments, the second apartment restructuring process involved an attempt to rid apartments of immigrant tenants. In 1988, for the first time, Arboleda management made strong efforts to identify and evict families with children. Management also stopped printing tenant bulletins in Spanish and did not replace the bilingual staff who left the front office. Furthermore, a security fence was built around the apartment project and extended to enclose the large parking area of the apartment building that housed many of the Mayan and other Latino tenants (Hagan and Rodriguez 1992).

Some Mayan tenants in Arboleda responded to the rent increase by leaving the apartment complex. Others doubled up in apartment units to share rents, and others survived by taking in new household members to increase household income. These survival strategies continued until late 1992, when the apartment project closed down to be rebuilt as a stylish, high-price apartment complex, beyond the financial means of most Latino immigrants.

DIVERSE LATINO SETTLEMENT IN HOUSTON

The different Latino groups in the city of Houston have evolved different settlement patterns. As described, Mexican Americans initially settled predominantly in the East Side but have also moved in significant numbers to other city areas and to working-class suburbs. Mexican immigrants also established large communities in the East Side and in the North Side near downtown, and more recently they have spread farther north of downtown and into apartment projects in the West Side. Central Americans, on the other hand, have primarily settled in the West Side and in smaller numbers in the North and East Side barrios. Finally, members of all three Latino groups share a common settlement area, but not necessarily a common settlement experience, in the Heights neighborhoods northwest of downtown. Hence, while the history of Houston Latino settlement followed half (the eastern half) of a concentric pattern in the pre-World War II period, by the late 1980s this settlement was characterized more by a interspersed segmented growth.

In contrast to the widely dispersed white settlement patterns, Latinos in the Houston area have settled mainly in the housing market of the central city. According to the 1990 census, 63.6 percent of Latinos in the Houston metropolitan area live in the central city, while only 35.2 percent of the area's whites reside in the city (U.S. Bureau of the Census 1993; Sallee 1991). Given the large number of undocumented Latinos who were not counted in the city, the actual percentage of Latinos in the Houston area who reside in the central city is probably closer to 70 percent.

A comparison with African Americans shows that the latter have a slightly higher residential concentration in the central city than Latinos. According to the 1990 census, 74.9 percent of blacks in the Houston metropolitan area reside in the central city (Sallee 1991). Within the central city, African Americans have a higher concentration in black neighborhoods than do Latinos in Latino neighborhoods, and they have a less developed pattern of interspersed segmented growth in the city.

The Latino settlement experience in Houston also shows that immigrant survival strategies for adapting to a new environment significantly affect Latino involvement in the Houston housing market. In past decades immigrants have accounted for about half of the Latino growth in Houston. But more than just increasing the Latino population's size and, hence, housing demand, immigrants undertake settlement efforts that make them the most dynamic and flexible Latino group in the housing market. For the majority of Latino immigrants, the attachment to the housing market does not go beyond a renter relation. Moreover, for many it is a loose renter relation, as many immigrants shift through housing and job opportunities in the various Latino settlements of the city. This observation has not escaped Houston school officials, who are trying to reduce immigrant-student transiency (over 50 percent in some schools) by convincing apartment landlords to offer nine-month apartment leases that coincide with the school year.

In contrast to new immigrants, long-term Latino residents in Houston's inner-city barrios have a stronger attachment to their housing market. In these Latino areas of the city the housing market is synonymous with a well-established community structure, an *ethnic* community structure. It is safe to hypothesize that established ethnic communities, with a host of traditional institutions, have a greater hold on their residents than heterogeneous neighborhoods (such as the West Side apartments) where cultural attachments are less extensive. If true, this would help to explain why large numbers of Latino renters did not leave the North and East Side barrios for the higher quality apartment housing made accessible in the West Side during the city's recession.

The diversity of Latino groups and their experiences makes it risky, if not impossible, to generalize about Latino housing in Houston beyond the fact that presently it is predominantly a central city experience in the rental housing market. The recent arrival of the Central American group makes it difficult to predict what the long-term settlement patterns of these new Latinos will be. As the recent economic downturn made clear, even the settlement of long-term resident Latinos in the established barrios is not secure.

CONCLUSION:
FUTURE LATINO SETTLEMENT TRENDS IN HOUSTON

Given the momentum of current trends, Latino settlement in the Houston area will remain heavily concentrated in the central city and will continue to involve mostly renter households. These trends should continue as a high birthrate and immigration keep the Latino population growing at rates higher than those of the other major groups in the city. Latino immigration is certain to continue as the large number of Latinos who obtained legal status through IRCA become eligible to sponsor the legal immigration of their relatives. Undocumented immigration is also sure to continue, having become institutionalized as a support system for many communities in Mexico and Central America.

Within the diverse settlement experience of Houston's Latinos, we can project several developments. It is probable that the established East Side

Latino settlements will develop a greater immigrant presence. Already large residential and commercial sections in the East Side barrios are considered to be immigrant zones. The momentum of the ethnic economy in these zones, coupled with continuing Mexican immigration and a moderate manufacturing resurgence, should keep the East Side Latino barrios on a steady course towards greater Latino immigrant growth. More out-migration of Mexican Americans from the East Side barrios will also increase the Latino immigrant presence in these neighborhoods.

In the West Side, we can expect that the new Latino settlement zones will survive but with housing limitations imposed by the attempts of apartment landlords to recompose their tenant populations with higher-income renters. What probably will develop is a segmented housing market in which Latino immigrants, blacks, and other low-income groups will be concentrated in the lower-quality apartment projects in the area. While a number of new apartment projects have been built in the West Side, and several more are planned for the near future, they are clearly located in the housing market affordable mainly to professional middle-income tenants (Bivins 1991). There is no reason to expect that real estate capital will become interested in building affordable housing for the lower-paid minority working class in the West Side. Unless the Houston economy experiences an era of economic growth that promotes Latino occupational mobility, most of the West Side housing market will remain beyond the reach of a vast majority of the city's Latinos.

An additional housing restriction facing Latinos in the city's West Side is the movement in several white neighborhoods to close down and demolish apartment complexes that endanger the residential environment. While the intention is to target apartment projects that become crime-infested, inevitably Latinos will be affected as large numbers of apartment units are removed from the low-income housing market. The closing down of one apartment project in the summer of 1993 removed hundreds of apartment units from a Latino housing market in the city West Side. In times of tense intergroup relations, it is not difficult to imagine attempts to close down apartment complexes merely for having low-income immigrant tenants.

Latinos, especially Mexican Americans, who locate housing as home owners will more than likely settle in central city neighborhoods—such as the Heights—that are converting from mainly white settlements to mixed communities. But even in this scenario Latinos may face limitations as real estate investors and developers target these neighborhoods for redevelop-ment into more expensive housing areas. Already real estate firms have made inroads into neighborhoods just west of downtown and are set to rebuild in a public housing project at the western edge of downtown. It will remain to be seen whether the passage of zoning ordinances will equip Latinos and other low-income groups with the means to compete against big real estate capital for housing space in the city.

Obviously, for high-income Latinos these scenarios do not present problems. For low- and moderate-income Latinos who cannot afford to buy housing beyond that found in the established barrios, the choices may be limited. One choice could be to search for housing in the mixed working-class suburbs that exist at the edge of the city. Another choice could be to overextend their housing budget at the expense of other necessities.

Recently the proposal to convert a large West Side apartment complex into co-op housing offers an attractive alternative. The plan is to convert a 550-unit complex, obtained by the U.S. Department of Housing and Urban Development (HUD) through a foreclosure, into a housing cooperative for Mexican and Central American immigrants (Robinson 1993). Using HUD funds to repair the complex and plan social programs for the low-income tenants, the cooperative project would become the city's first tenant-owned apartment project if it succeeds. The involvement of federal sources and Latino immigrants will make it a difficult challenge in the free enterprise city, which has traditionally opposed federal aid for the poor and power to renter groups, especially in a period of growing anti-immigrant sentiments.

Houston's growth as a premier capitalist city in the world economy has involved the growth of a large Latino working class to work in the city's productive and supportive industries. In the late twentieth century, Latino immigrants have played a large role in the growth of this working class, especially in the lower echelons of the labor market. The doubling of the city's Latino population in recent decades, however, raises questions concerning the population's housing market for the future. While in the 1980s market forces provided substantial housing resources during the city's economic downturn, in the 1990s market and nonmarket factors—such as, intergroup tensions—threaten to restrict the Latinos' housing market outside the established barrios. Already in the city's West Side, Latinos face an apartment housing market that is moving beyond their economic means and that is affected by growing anti-immigrant opposition.

NOTE

1. I am grateful for the comments of professors Janet Chafetz and Michael Olivas on an earlier version of this chapter.

REFERENCES

Bivins, R. 1991. Apartments to spring up. *Houston Chronicle,* 31 March.

Burns, A. 1993. *Maya in exile.* Philadelphia: Temple University Press.

De Leon, A. 1989. *Ethnicity in the Sunbelt: A history of Mexican Americans in Houston.* Houston: Mexican American Studies Program, University of Houston.

Feagin, J. R. 1988. *Free enterprise city: Houston in political and economic perspective.* New Brunswick, N.J.: Rutgers University Press.

Fortune. 1939. Texas. *Fortune,* December.

Hagan, J. M., and N. P. Rodriguez. 1992. Recent economic restructuring and evolving intergroup relations in Houston. In *Structuring diversity: Ethnographic perspectives on the new immigration,* edited by Louise Lamphere. Chicago: University of Chicago Press.

Johnson, M. B. 1982. *Resolving the housing crisis.* San Francisco: Pacific Institute for Public Policy Research.

Jones. R. 1982. *Town and country chaos.* London: Adam Smith Institute.

Robinson, J. 1993. Complex shaping up for co-op. *Houston Chronicle,* 23 August.

Rodriguez, N. 1987. Undocumented Central Americans in Houston: Diverse populations. *International Migration Review* 21 (1): 4–26.

Rodriguez, N. P., and J. R. Feagin. 1986. Urban specialization in the world-system: An investigation of historical cases. *Urban Affairs Quarterly* 22 (2): 187–220.

Rodriguez, N. P., and J. M. Hagan. 1992. Apartment restructuring and Latino immigrant tenant struggles: A case study of human agency. *Comparative Urban and Community Research* 4:164–80.

Rodriguez, N., and R. T. Nunez. 1986. An exploration of factors that contribute to differentiation between Chicanos and indocumentados. In *Mexican immigrants and Mexican Americans: An evolving relation,* edited by H. L. Browning and R. de la Garza. Austin: Mexican American Studies, The University of Texas at Austin.

Romo, R., and N. Rodriguez. 1993. Houston Evaluation of Community Priorities Project. Unpublished raw data, the Tomas Rivera Center.

Sallee, R. 1991. Minority now majority in Houston. *Houston Chronicle,* 8 February.

Shelton, B. A., N. P. Rodriguez, J. R. Feagin, R. D. Bullard, and R. D. Thomas. 1989. *Houston: Growth and decline in a Sunbelt boomtown.* Philadelphia: Temple University Press.

Smith, B. A. 1989. *Handbook on the Houston economy.* Houston: Center for Public Policy, University of Houston.

————. 1986. *Handbook on the Houston economy.* Houston: Center for Public Policy, University of Houston.

U.S. Bureau of the Census. 1993. *1990 Census of population and housing.* Summary Tape File 3A; machine readable data file.

————. 1992a. *1990 census of population and housing, summary social, economic, and housing characteristics, Texas.* CPH-5-45. Washington, D.C.: U.S. Government Printing Office.

————. 1992b. *1990 census of population, general population characteristics, Texas.* CP-1-45. Washington, D.C.: U.S. Government Printing Office.

————. 1983. *Census of population and housing: 1980.* Census Tracts, PHC80-2-184, Houston, Texas, SMSA. Washington, D.C.: U.S. Government Printing Office.

————. 1972. *Census of population and housing: 1970.* Census Tracts, Final Report PHC (1)-89 Houston, Texas, SMSA. Washington, D.C.: U.S. Government Printing Office.

U.S. Immigration and Naturalization Service. (n.d.). Applications for legalization in the Houston INS office: Frequencies by nationalities. Unpublished raw data.

CHAPTER 9

Fair Housing Enforcement:
Is the Current System Adequate?

by Veronica M. Reed

This chapter examines housing discrimination and the value of fair housing tests and audits in monitoring compliance with the Fair Housing Act. In addition, it reviews the current system of federal fair housing enforcement, which includes: enforcement in the form of prohibitive laws and administrative and judicial remedies, audit studies to monitor compliance, and financial support to local fair housing initiatives.

The first section discusses the Fair Housing Act in its original and amended forms and summarizes its enforcement mechanisms. The Fair Housing Act, which was originally passed by Congress in 1968, was amended in 1988 in response to concern about continued discrimination and segregation. The Fair Housing amendments expanded the Act's protections and strengthened its enforcement mechanisms.

The second section discusses testing and auditing methodology (Reid 1984; Wienk and Simon 1984). It distinguishes between tests to gather evidence in support of fair housing complaints and audits to evaluate the extent of racial discrimination in a housing market. It also reviews two national audit studies, the Housing Market Practices Survey and the Housing Discrimination Study, sponsored by the U.S. Department of Housing and Urban Development (HUD).

The final section reviews HUD's financial support of local fair housing initiatives. The Fair Housing Assistance Program (FHAP) provides funds, training, and technical assistance to state and local fair housing agencies to improve local fair housing enforcement capacities. The Fair Housing Initiatives Program (FHIP) provides funding to public fair housing agencies and public and private fair housing organizations to prevent or eliminate housing discrimination.

Housing discrimination limits the housing choices of black households. With strengthened enforcement mechanisms, national audit studies, FHAP, and FHIP, HUD has taken proactive steps to lift the barriers that keep minorities from complete access to the housing market. Unfortunately, there is little evidence that these steps have had a widespread impact on behavior. The system is largely reactive; its enforcement mechanisms are triggered when individuals file complaints against alleged offenders. At the same time, there is much evidence that discriminatory treatment in housing transactions has become more subtle and more difficult to detect.

Audit studies show that auditors rarely encounter blatant discrimination; access is more commonly denied when information is withheld or units are falsely described as unavailable. With no control experience, minority home seekers have no way of knowing that they are being denied access to housing units. Fair housing tests and audits allow subtle differences in treatment to be detected. The lack of trends in the level of housing discrimination, as measured by national fair housing audits, stands as evidence of the limited effectiveness of the current system of enforcing the Fair Housing Act. Only an institutionalized system of industrywide random tests, to enforce compliance by increasing the probability of detection and prosecution of alleged offenders, will create enough of a deterrent to prevent discriminatory behavior.

FAIR HOUSING

For almost a quarter century, it has been the policy of the United States to provide for fair housing throughout the country, within constitutional limitations (Reed 1991). Title VIII of the Civil Rights Act of 1968 made discrimination in the rental or sale of housing on the basis of race, color, religion, or national origin a violation of federal law. The Civil Rights Act was the culmination of a long struggle against discriminatory practices that effectively barred minority access to certain segments of the housing market. Women became a protected class under the law in 1974, and in 1988, the Fair Housing Amendments Act extended protection to include persons with disabilities and families with children (*Congressional Quarterly* 1988). Together Title VIII of the Civil Rights Act of 1968 and the Fair Housing Amendments Act of 1988 (the Amendments) make up the Fair Housing Act (the Act).

Discriminatory housing practices that are prohibited in the Act include discrimination in terms and conditions, refusal to deal, discriminatory advertising, falsely representing availability, denying use of or participation in real estate services, and making representations regarding the entry or prospective entry of persons of a protected class into a neighborhood. These prohibitions apply to: (1) federally owned or operated dwellings; (2) dwellings supported in whole or part with the aid of federal loans, advances, grants, or contributions; (3) dwellings supported in whole or part by federally secured financing; and (4) dwellings purchased, rented, or otherwise obtained from public agencies receiving federal financial assistance. Exempted are single-family, privately owned dwellings and multifamily dwellings of five units or fewer where the owner resides in one of the units, but these exemptions do not apply if the dwellings are sold or rented through an agent or if discriminatory advertising is used.

In addition to expanding the protected classes under Title VIII, the Amendments strengthened the Act's enforcement mechanisms and increased the penalties against parties found guilty of discrimination. The legislation responded to widespread belief that discriminatory housing practices remained commonplace in most U.S. cities and that only increasing the cost of discriminating would change behavior. The American Civil Liberties Union wrote that the Amendments gave the Act "teeth" (*Congressional Digest* 1988).

Title VIII gave HUD the authority to enforce fair housing laws. Where state or local fair housing laws and remedies are certified "substantially equivalent" by HUD, the complaint is referred to the appropriate state or local agency for investigation. The state or local agency has the authority to investigate complaints and seek the elimination and correction of allegations through conciliation. Complaints may be filed in writing or over the telephone to HUD headquarters or at any HUD regional or field office.

If a complaint is filed over the telephone, the complaint is mailed to the complainant to sign and return. Under the original Act, if a pattern or practice of discrimination was found, HUD referred the case to the Justice Department, which has the authority to enforce the law through judicial action. A complainant could elect to bring private suit, in which a court could grant an injunction and restraining order and award actual damages, as well as up to $1,000 and attorney fees in punitive damages.

Many civil suits were brought by individuals and fair housing groups in response to complaints or as a result of fair housing tests for litigation purposes. While courts awarded damages that grew increasingly larger, most fair housing advocates felt the 1968 Act was not an effective deterrent. The Fair Housing Council of Greater Washington, which supported passage of the Amendments, said "the worst way to enforce the Fair Housing Act is to leave it to private plaintiffs, which is precisely what the existing law does" (*Congressional Digest* 1988, 180).

The Fair Housing Amendments Act of 1988 strengthened HUD's enforcement authority. Now, in addition to the authority to investigate and attempt to conciliate complaints, if upon completion of the investigation there is "reasonable cause" to believe discrimination occurred and no conciliation agreement can be reached, HUD can bring charges before an administrative law judge (ALJ) on behalf of the complainant. HUD can hold administrative hearings and issue subpoenas, unless one of the parties elects to have the case heard in U.S. District Court.

The ALJ has the authority to order a guilty party to cease discriminatory activities, compensate the complainant, and pay civil penalties. If either party elects to have the case heard in court, the Department of Justice represents the complainant. The Justice Department can seek compensation, civil penalties, and punitive damages.

The Amendments also increased the penalties against those found guilty of discriminatory housing practices. An ALJ can impose penalties to be paid to the federal government ranging from up to $10,000 for a first offense to up to $50,000 for third and subsequent violations. The Justice Department can obtain penalties up to $50,000 for a first-time violation and a maximum of $100,000 for any other. Also, the $1,000 limit on punitive damages in a civil suit was removed.

The Fair Housing Amendments Act has been in effect since March 1989. There is little evidence that the strengthened enforcement mechanisms and increased penalties have had widespread impact on the extent of housing market discrimination. The system continues to rely on individuals to file complaints against suspected violators to trigger its enforcement mechanisms. Higher damage amounts awarded to bona fide home seekers—some as high as $300,000 to $400,000—have generated much attention and created an atmosphere of change. But unless the discriminatory act is overt or blatant, home seekers are not likely to realize they have been discriminated against, thus limiting the probability that a complaint will be filed against an agent who discriminates. Tests and audits that provide the capability to identify subtle differences in treatment during a housing transaction can increase the effectiveness of the Act, allowing for enforcing and monitoring compliance, respectively.

FAIR HOUSING TESTS AND AUDITS

The terms *fair housing tests* and *fair housing audits* are often used interchangeably. For the purpose of this chapter, fair housing tests gather evidence in support of fair housing complaints and are used primarily for enforcement purposes. Fair housing audits objectively evaluate the extent of racial discrimination in a housing market and are used primarily for research purposes. Although there are clear differences between tests and audits as defined, they share a common methodology and purpose. Testing and auditing methodologies do differ. Tests to gather evidence in support of fair housing complaints differ from audits for research purposes in that tests require much more attention to details in recording what transpired during the housing transaction. Both use carefully paired individuals, who are alike in all characteristics relevant to the housing search process (i.e., sex, age, income, and family size) except race. These paired individuals enter into housing transactions and record all treatment for the purpose of identifying differences. Any differential treatment is then attributed to discrimination, because the matched pairs differ only by race. The value of tests and audits is that they allow subtle differences in treatment to be detected. Together, testing and auditing have contributed greatly to a wealth of information on the existence, extent, and nature of housing discrimination.

Fair Housing Tests. A fair housing test is a targeted method of gathering evidence in support of a fair housing compliant or for the specific purpose of litigation for compliance enforcement. The evolution of the use of testing in the enforcement of fair housing laws began in the late 1960s. By the early 1970s, the courts began accepting testing evidence in housing discrimination cases (Reid 1984). The courts generally concluded that evidence gathered during a test was reliable proof of racial discrimination. During that same time, private fair housing organizations across the country made testing a central part of their enforcement strategies, because of the effectiveness of testing evidence in resolving cases. Thousands of tests have been conducted by fair housing agencies and organizations during the past twenty years. And in 1982, the Supreme Court upheld, in a unanimous decision *(Havens Realty Corporation v. Coleman),* the standing of testers and fair housing organizations to bring suit under the Fair Housing Act. To date, use of fair housing tests alone or to substantiate the claim of a bona fide applicant remains the single most effective method of identifying, substantiating, and prosecuting noncompliance with fair housing laws.

Fair Housing Audits. Fair housing audits are different from fair housing tests for the purpose of litigation or in support of a fair housing complaint in that they produce an objective evaluation of the extent or prevalence of racial discrimination in a housing market. A fair housing audit is a controlled social science experiment. It is a method of monitoring the housing industry's compliance with fair housing laws. In addition to producing an objective evaluation of the extent of racial discrimination in a housing market, an audit also allows for clearer insights into the nature of housing discrimination. HUD has sponsored two national audit studies—the Housing Markets Practices Survey (HMPS) and the Housing Discrimination Study (HDS)—which provide national measures of the level of housing discrimination experienced by minority home seekers.

The National Committee Against Discrimination in Housing conducted the HMPS evaluation in forty metropolitan areas in 1977 (Appendix A). The principal focus of the study was the availability of housing units to black home seekers in comparison to white home seekers, because differential treatment with regard to access is a clear violation of fair housing laws and the most frequently employed discriminatory housing practice (Wienk et al. 1979).

A total of 1,609 rental audits and 1,655 sales audits were completed. Audited properties and real estate agencies, both rental and sales, were selected through a random sample of the real estate classified advertisements in each metropolitan area's major newspapers at the beginning of the audit process. Audit partners were paired in all relevant aspects. Individually, each followed identical procedures when conducting an audit and reporting their experience on report forms.

Audits results were summarized, white auditor and black auditor responses were compared, and the net difference of "white favored" and "black favored" treatment was attributed to racial discrimination. The HMPS researchers found that nationally blacks encountered discriminatory treatment with regard to availability in 27 percent of the rental audits and 15 percent of the sales audits. Researchers concluded that the study provided "definitive evidence that blacks are discriminated against in the sale and rental of housing."

During the summer of 1989, the Urban Institute carried out approximately 3,800 rental and sales audits in twenty-five metropolitan areas (Appendix A). Using the same paired audit team methodology, HDS anchored its audits to weekly random samples of rental and sales classified advertisements for the metropolitan area's major newspaper (Turner, Struyk, and Yinger 1991). Unlike HMPS, the proportion of audits where the white auditor was favored was used as a gross measure of the unfavorable treatment.

HDS researchers estimate that the overall incidence of discrimination against black home seekers is 53 percent for renters and 59 percent for home buyers. Researchers also found that black auditors encountered unfavorable treatment with regard to availability, the principal focus of HMPS, in 39 percent of rental audits and 36 percent of sales audits.

As reported above, the HMPS and HDS results are not comparable. There are four key differences in the methodologies employed. First, HMPS and HDS did not conduct audits in the same cities, although both samples were representative of the U.S. housing market (Appendix A).

Second, the HMPS audit was anchored to properties or real estate agencies, while the HDS audit was anchored to advertised units. HDS researchers expected unit anchoring to yield a more conservative estimate of unit availability than HMPS. It did.

Third, the HMPS rental audit responses were summarized into five categories: availability, courtesy, terms and conditions, information requested, and information volunteered. Sales audit responses were summarized to four categories: availability, courtesy, service, and household information requested. HDS refined this part of the methodology to reflect a three-stage housing-search process: (1) housing availability; (2) contributions to the transaction, that is, sales effort, terms and conditions, and financing assistance; and (3) steering to other units.

Finally, HMPS researchers calculated the percentage of discriminatory treatment as the net difference between "white-favored" and "black-favored" audits, while HDS used the proportion of "white-favored" audits as a gross measure of the incidence of discrimination.

In an attempt to arrive at some conclusion about trends in the extent of housing discrimination, HDS researchers replicated HMPS's measures so that HMPS and HDS results could be compared. Table 9.1 summarizes HMPS and HDS results for unit availability, the number of units shown, a housing availability index, and a rental terms and conditions index. HDS results were lower than HMPS with regard to unit availability and the number of units shown and recommended. But, as is shown, the sales housing availability indices are approximately the same, and the HMPS rental terms and conditions index is larger than the HDS index. Overall, HDS researchers conclude that the replication "presents a mixed picture, and provides no solid basis for concluding that the incidence of unfavorable treatment experienced by black home seekers has either risen or declined since the 1970s" (Turner, Struyk, and Yinger 1991).

Although the replication of HMPS measures with HDS results does not allow for any conclusions with regard to trends in the extent of housing discrimination, fair housing enforcement does have the ability to positively affect the level of discrimination in a metropolitan area. A coordinated system

Table 9.1
Replication of HMPS Using HDS Data

Share of Audits with Unfavorable Treatment of Blacks for:	Rentals		Sales	
	HMPS	HDS	HMPS	HDS
Unit availability	30	14	21	8
Numbers of units shown and recommended	42	35	54	42
Housing Availability Index[a]	—	—	39	42
Rental Terms and Conditions Index[b]	13	29	—	—

Source: Turner, Struyk, and Yinger (1991).

Note: All values reflect the gross incidence of unfavorable treatment, using weighted data. All reported estimates are statistically significant at a 95% confidence level.

[a]Includes: unit availability, number of units shown or recommended, whether a multiple listing directory was offered, and the number of houses inspected.

[b]Includes: average rent, lease requirements, security deposit, application fee, and credit check, and the number of units shown.

of fair housing education, tests for enforcement, and audits to measure compliance can result in downward trends in discriminatory behavior. In a study of audit evidence from the 1980s, Galster (1990) reviews five housing markets where audit studies reveal changes in the overall incidence of discrimination. Table 9.2 lists the audit results. Galster concludes that waning prejudice and increasing professionalism within the real estate industry, coupled with fair housing education and training and intensified enforcement efforts, contributed to the downward trends in the incidence of housing market discrimination in these metropolitan areas.

The racial prejudices of real estate agents and white home owners translate into discriminatory housing market practices. Researching sales-market housing discrimination within the context of the real estate industry's profit motive, Harriet Newburger (1989) found that in addition to their own prejudices, real estate agents may discriminate against black home seekers to avoid losing white

Table 9.2
Changes in the Percent of the
Overall Incidence of Housing Discrimination

Housing	*Years Audits Conducted*							
Market	72	78	82	83	84	85	86	88
Sales								
Cleveland		67		21		23		
Rental								
Baltimore	72	39	46					
South Bend						30	10	
Washington, D.C.							48	28

Source: Galster (1990).

customers and the potential income source they represent. If this is the case, fair housing enforcement must combine stiff financial penalties with the probability of detection. The Fair Housing Amendments Act provided for increased penalties against those found guilty of discriminatory housing practices. Since fair housing tests allow subtle differences in treatment to be detected, making testing a mandatory part of compliance enforcement would increase the chances that offenders would be identified and prosecuted.

Critics of testing and auditing question whether the practice is ethical and whether testers are reliable. Testing wastes the time of real estate and leasing agents and involves deception; testers may be predisposed to identifying discrimination. Some critics have even said that testing constitutes entrapment. Advocates respond that the value of testing far outweighs the minimal time and deception involved and that testers in no way encourage or entice discriminatory behavior. A tester or auditor enters into a housing transaction to observe and record the behavior of a real estate or leasing agent. If differential behavior is observed and a complaint filed, the alleged offender then has the right to defend his or her actions in an administrative hearing or a civil suit. Instituting a system of random testing would create an atmosphere where discriminating could never be in the economic interest of an agent because of the probability of detection and prosection.

FEDERAL SUPPORT FOR FAIR HOUSING

In addition to enforcing fair housing laws and conducting audit studies to measure the level of housing discrimination, HUD provides financial support for state and local fair housing initiatives. FHAP provides funds, training, and technical assistance to state and local fair housing agencies to improve local fair housing enforcement capacities. FHIP provides funding to public fair housing agencies and private fair housing organizations to prevent or eliminate housing discrimination. Together FHAP and FHIP contribute to an increased capability at the local level to identify discriminatory housing practices and enforce fair housing laws.

THE FAIR HOUSING ASSISTANCE PROGRAM

FHAP provides grants to state and local fair housing enforcement agencies that are certified substantially equivalent (HUD 1989). The goal of the program is to build a coordinated intergovernmental enforcement effort and to encourage states and localities to assume a greater share of the responsibility for administering their fair housing laws. The funding is targeted to support complaint processing, training, technical assistance, data and information systems, and other fair housing projects.

For funding purposes, HUD separates all eligible agencies into two categories: capacity-building agencies and contributions agencies. During the first two years of participation in FHAP an agency is considered a capacity-building agency. A capacity-building agency can only receive capacity-building funds. A fixed amount of funds is granted over the two-year period to support training, complaint monitoring and reporting systems, case processing, and any other fair housing activity proposed by the agency.

Contributions agencies have participated in FHAP for at least two years. They are eligible to receive training, complaint processing, and incentive funds. Training funds are available at the same level for all agencies. Complaint processing funding is based on the number of dual-filed housing discrimination complaints processed the preceding year. Agencies can also apply for incentive funding on an annual basis to implement special projects that would benefit their jurisdiction.

In a 1985 evaluation, Abt Associates found that FHAP had enhanced the complaint-processing capacity of state and local agencies (Wallace et al. 1985). The funding allowed fair housing agencies to grow and enhance their activities, handle a larger number of complaints and cases more efficiently, and resolve a larger number of cases.

FHIP was authorized under the Housing and Community Development Act of 1987. The program funds state and local agencies, public and private nonprofit organizations, and other public and private entities formulating or carrying out programs to prevent or eliminate discriminatory housing practices (HUD 1989). There are three categories of funding: the Administrative Enforcement Initiative, the Education and Outreach Initiative, and the Private Enforcement Initiative.

Like FHAP, the Administrative Enforcement Initiative provides funds to substantially equivalent state and local fair housing enforcement agencies. This initiative is designed to broaden the range of enforcement and compliance activities of agencies. Eligible activities include but are not limited to technical assistance, fair housing testing, and investigating systematic discrimination.

Under the Education and Outreach Initiative, funding can be used to develop, implement, carry out, or coordinate education and outreach programs to inform the public of their rights and obligations under the Fair Housing Act. Education projects eligible for funding are the development of materials on fair housing rights and responsibilities, the development of fair housing and affirmative marketing instructional materials, educational seminars and working sessions, and education materials specifically targeted at persons in need of specific information on their rights. Outreach activities can include media campaigns, educating fair housing practitioners, designing specialized informational outreach projects, responding to new or more sophisticated discriminatory housing practices, and responding to housing discrimination cases involving the threat of physical harm. All FHIP-eligible agencies and organizations can apply for funding under the Education and Outreach Initiative.

The Private Enforcement Initiative provides funding to nonprofit organizations to implement programs that prevent or eliminate housing discrimination. Eligible activities include investigation, testing, and enforcement. Testing programs are an integral part of this initiative. Evidence collected by testers can be used to prosecute alleged offenders. And funds can be used to establish means to meet legal expenses in support of litigation of fair housing cases.

Research has shown that education, training, and intensive enforcement can contribute to decreases in the incidence of housing discrimination. Testing is the most effective method of identifying housing discrimination and enforcing compliance with fair housing laws. Private fair housing organizations have made it an integral part of their successful enforcement efforts. HUD's system of fair housing enforcement includes financial support to public fair housing agencies and private fair housing groups to carry out testing programs. This support began the same year the last national audit study was conducted, and its impact is currently being evaluated.

While federal funding of local testing initiatives has no doubt increased the testing capacity of local fair housing organizations, it cannot and will not have a widespread impact on behavior. The current system of fair housing enforcement is largely reactive; enforcement mechanisms are triggered when discrimination is identified and a complaint is filed by an individual or fair housing group. But individuals, private fair housing groups, and local governments cannot change behavior alone.

To increase the level of compliance with fair housing laws and decrease the incidence of discriminatory housing practices, the most effective enforcement tool must become a mandatory component of fair housing enforcement across the country. The system must become prohibitive. In addition to continued education initiatives and training and financial support to increase the capacity of state and local agencies and private fair housing organizations, random fair housing testing to identify and prosecute offenders must become an institutionalized component of federal fair housing enforcement efforts.

This is not a new concept in fair housing enforcement or other publicly regulated activities. Inspecting or testing for compliance with industry quality standards, whether it be the Food and Drug Administration, the Environmental Protection Agency, or the Nuclear Regulatory Commission, is a responsibility the federal government has taken upon itself to protect the health and well-being of all citizens, because of the social value associated with preventing potentially harmful situations that could result from these activities. The question is whether our government sees the effects of housing market discrimination as harmful enough to warrant the same type of preventive measures. If the greater social good is improved by preventing housing market discrimination to the greatest extent possible, then it is imperative that there be a system of fair housing enforcement where discriminators are likely to be identified. The value of equal housing opportunity must be upheld with diligence.

Random testing could (1) be carried out by HUD, (2) be contracted to state and local fair housing agencies or private fair housing organizations, or (3) be conducted under a dual system with HUD carrying out testing where there is no qualified local agency or organization. But only when there is an ever-present threat of prosecution and the cost of discriminating outweighs any perceived benefit will equal housing opportunity become a reality in the United States. If the Fair Housing Amendments Act gave the Fair Housing Act teeth, it is now time to give the Act its eyes and ears.

SUMMARY AND CONCLUSION

Over twenty years ago, the Fair Housing Act made discrimination against minorities in the sale or rental of housing illegal. Today, black households can still expect to encounter discriminatory housing practices when looking for a home. In 1989, the Housing Discrimination Study (HDS) found that the overall incidence of discrimination against black home seekers is 53 percent for renters and 59 percent for home buyers. When HDS results were compared to the results of the Housing Market Practices Survey, no conclusion could be drawn about a rise or decline in the incidence of housing market discrimination during the 12 years separating the two audit studies.

Amendments to the Fair Housing Act strengthened its enforcement mechanisms and increased penalties against offenders, but the system still continues to rely largely on private individuals to file complaints. Complaints filed by individuals will never be a sufficient deterrent against discrimination. Today very little discrimination is blatant, and many individuals have no idea they are being treated differently than someone of another race. They have no point of comparison. Tests and audits allow comparisons to be made. In addition to continued and intensified national education campaigns, industry training and education, and federal support of local fair housing initiatives, nationwide random testing with the specific purpose of identifying and prosecuting offenders must become a component of federal fair housing enforcement.

REFERENCES

Congressional Digest. 1988. Should Congress approve the Fair Housing Amendment Act of 1987? Pros & Cons. *Congressional Digest,* 67 (June/July): 6–7.

Congressional Quarterly. 1988. Major provisions of fair housing legislation. *Congressional Quarterly,* 46 (August): 2348–50.

Galster, George. 1990. Racial discrimination in housing markets during the 1980s: A review of the audit evidence. *Journal of Planning Education and Research* 9:165–75.

Newburger, Harriet. 1989. Discrimination by a profit-maximizing real estate broker in response to white prejudice. *Journal of Urban Economics* 26:1–19.

Reed, Veronica. 1991. Civil rights legislation and the housing status of black Americans: Evidence from fair housing audits and segregation indices. *The Review of Black Political Economy* 19 (Winter/Spring).

Reid, Clifford E. 1984. The reliability of fair housing audits to detect racial discrimination in rental housing markets. *Journal of the American Real Estate and Urban Economics Association* 12 (Spring): 86–96.

Turner, M. R., R. J. Struyk, and J. Yinger. 1991. *Housing discrimination study: Synthesis.* Washington, D.C.: U.S. Department of Housing and Urban Development.

U.S. Congress. 1967. *The Fair Housing Act: Hearings before the Subcommittee on Housing and Urban Affairs, the Committee on Banking and Currency.* U.S. Senate, 90th Congress, 1st Session.

U.S. Department of Housing and Urban Development. 1989. *Fair Housing Assistance Program.* 24 CFR part 111, Office of the Assistant Secretary for Fair Housing and Equal Opportunity. Washington, D.C.

Wallace, J., W. L. Holshouser, T. Lane, and J. Williams. 1985. *The Fair Housing Assistance Program evaluation.* Washington, D.C.: U.S. Department of Housing and Urban Development.

Wienk, R., C. Reid, J. C. Simon, and F. J. Eggers. 1979. *Measuring racial discrimination in American housing markets: The housing market practice survey.* Washington, D.C.: U.S. Department of Housing and Urban Development.

Wienk, Ronald, and John C. Simon. 1984. Everything you ever wanted to know about auditing but didn't bother to ask. Background paper prepared for a research colloquium on Discrimination and the Audit: State of the Art, Washington, D.C.

Appendix A

Metropolitan Areas Audited in HMPS, 1977

Akron, Ohio
Albany-Schenectady-Troy, N.Y.
Asheville, N.C.
Atlanta
Boston, Mass.
Canton, Ohio
Cincinnati
Columbus, Ohio
Dallas
Dayton, Ohio
Detroit
Fort Lauderdale-Hollywood, Fla.
Fort Wayne, Ind.
Fort Worth, Texas
Greenville, S.C.
Harrisburg, Pa.
Hartford, Conn.
Indianapolis, Ind.
Lawton, Okla.
Lexington, Ky.

Los Angeles-Long Beach
Louisville, Ky.
Macon, Ga.
Milwaukee
Monroe, La.
Nashville, Davidson, Tenn.
New York
Oklahoma City, Okla.
Paterson-Clifton-Passaic, N.J.
Peoria, Ill.
Sacramento, Calif.
Saginaw, Mich.
San Bernardino-Riverside-Ontario, Calif.
Savannah, Ga.
Springfield-Chicopee-Holyoke, Mass.-Conn.
Stockton, Calif.
Tampa-St. Petersburg, Fla.
Tulsa, Okla.
Vallejo-Napa, Calif.
York, Pa.

Metropolitan Areas Audited in HDS, 1989

Atlanta
Austin, Texas
Bergen County, N.J.
Birmingham, Ala.
Chicago
Cincinnati
Dayton, Ohio
Denver
Detroit
Houston
Lansing, Mich.
Los Angeles

Macon, Ga.
Miami
New Orleans
New York
Orlando, Fla.
Philadelphia
Phoenix
Pittsburgh
Pueblo, Colo.
Tucson, Ariz.
San Antonio, Texas
San Diego
Washington, D.C.

CHAPTER 10

The National Fair Housing Alliance at Work

by Shanna L. Smith

The goal of fair housing for all Americans has not been acheived. Many of us would agree that government can only do so much in this effort. Much of the antidiscrimination work has fallen on private agencies (Wallace et al. 1985; U.S. Senate 1990; Rockefeller Foundation and The Urban Institute 1991). Federal footdragging and budgetary pressures in the 1980s resulted in many local agencies backing away from fair housing initiatives. Nevertheless, housing discrimination persists in all regions of the country (Dedman 1989; Dane 1991; Quint 1991).

This chapter explores the dual roles of the private fair housing movement for enforcement and education programs to ensure compliance with the federal fair housing laws and regulations by the housing, banking, and insurance industries. It also discusses how this movement uses enforcement and education to uncover the newest forms of housing, lending, and insurance discrimination and how this information is conveyed to the industry to prevent future violations and translated to home seekers to help them identify housing discrimination.

THE NATIONAL FAIR HOUSING ALLIANCE

The National Fair Housing Alliance was founded in 1988. Its mission is to promote the achievement of the policy of the United States to provide, within constitutional limitations, for fair housing throughout the United States. Alliance members believe that through vigorous, positive, and focused action, they can work together to achieve fair housing through outreach, education, litigation, conciliation, and research into the nature, extent, and effects of housing discrimination.

The alliance is dedicated to continuing the development and implementation of strategies designed to reduce, and eventually eliminate, racially and ethnically segregated housing patterns and to make all housing, financing, and insurance available regardless of race, color, religion, sex, family status, disability, or national origin.

Each operating member of the alliance specializes in fair housing education, outreach, and enforcement. The agencies with more financial resources also include research and mobility components. Research components document the nature, extent, and effects of housing discrimination within their communities. These agencies use this information to challenge the institutionalized practices of housing, lending, and insurance discrimination. Mobility components are used to increase housing opportunities for low- and moderate-income people through public housing desegregation programs and the use of state bond issue programs that provide incentives for pro-integration moves by all potential home buyers, regardless of income. Member agencies share their fair housing skills and investigative techniques with other members at quarterly training sessions.

The alliance established two short-term priorities in March 1991 designed to foster fair housing enforcement:

> 1. To increase the ability of private fair housing agencies to investigate, conciliate, and litigate the more complex and sophisticated acts of discrimination used in rental, sales, lending, and insurance practices in order to challenge the systemic nature of housing discrimination.

> 2. To target cities in the South and other communities where there is virtually no enforcement of the fair housing laws, recognizing how critical *local* education and enforcement efforts are in identifying and eliminating discriminatory housing practices.

The alliance will identify community groups interested in creating a private fair housing program and provide technical, legal, and, where possible, financial assistance to help in establishing a nonprofit, full-service fair housing program.

In 1992, the alliance was selected by the U.S. Department of Housing and Urban Development (HUD) to receive a Fair Housing Initiatives Program (FHIP) grant to assist in establishing a fair housing agency in Birmingham, Alabama. The alliance conducted testing for the National Lawyers' Committee in a housing discrimination case in Houma, Louisiana, a small community just outside of New Orleans. A lawsuit was filed in the case on behalf of minority apartment seekers denied apartments and past managers who were allegedly instructed to discriminate against African American applicants.

Community groups, interested civil rights attorneys, and individuals have contacted the alliance for assistance in establishing fair housing programs. Requests for assistance have come from North Carolina; South Carolina; Jackson, Mississippi; New Orleans; Tucson, Arizona; El Paso, Texas; Kansas City, Kansas; and Omaha, Nebraska. Although the alliance has the expertise through its staff and members to assist in establishing fair housing programs, it unfortunately lacks the financial resources necessary to meet the mounting requests.

Private Fair Housing Agencies and Enforcement

The 1988 amendments to the Fair Housing Act provided greater enforcement power and direction to both HUD and the Department of Justice to initiate, investigate, and litigate housing discrimination complaints. Even with the strength of these amendments, which for the first time give HUD and Justice the power to bring legal actions on behalf of aggrieved persons, it is the private fair housing movement that continues to bring the cutting-edge litigation that is challenging the institutionalized, systemic practices of housing discrimination in the United States.

It is the private fair housing movement that continues to challenge discriminatory sales, advertising, mortgage lending, and appraisal practices, private mortgage insurance, and home owners' insurance practices. It is the private fair housing movement that is securing nationwide relief by eliminating policies that are artificial barriers to equal access. It is the private fair housing movement that is developing mobility programs for low- and moderate-income families through programs like Gautreaux in Chicago and similar programs in Memphis and Cincinnati.

It is the forty-four alliance members who have recovered over $9 million in damages and attorney fees since March 1989, while HUD has recovered $4 million and Justice just over $1 million in damages for victims of housing discrimination. To its credit, the Justice Department has filed amicus curiae briefs or intervened in several cases brought through private fair housing agencies involving large rental management companies, sexual harassment complaints, and private mortgage insurance complaints.

Since the government has not engaged in complaint-based testing and has conducted only limited national education and outreach about fair housing, it falls to the private fair housing movement to uncover the practices employed to discourage and deny housing opportunities to home seekers and to educate home seekers and the housing industry about their rights and responsibilities under the fair housing laws. Both of these services must be available on a large national scale if the problems of housing discrimination are to be seriously addressed. Without the ingenuity of the private movement, housing discrimination would go virtually unchecked in the United States (U.S. Senate 1990).

FAIR HOUSING TESTING

Testing was developed and perfected by the private fair housing movement as one of the most effective tools in the arsenal of fair housing enforcement, yet it is a tool that is still evolving, in response to the subtle and sophisticated practices used to discourage and deny minorities housing opportunities. Although testing is extremely effective, there are situations when only a thorough review of the business records will uncover the sophisticated practices developed to deny housing and financing to minorities. Private fair housing agencies combine their resources with attorneys and researchers to review these records and document unequal treatment.

Rental Testing. In the early days of investigating discriminatory rental practices, it was enough to simply have African American and white testers inquire about the same apartment within a short time period and compare the information each tester team was given. This simple testing is still effective in communities where there has been little or no fair housing enforcement which, unfortunately, translates to a large portion of the United States.

"Full-Application" Testing. In the communities where private enforcement has been effective, we have had to develop different and more complex testing methodologies, such as full application testing. An apartment manager may provide truthful information about the availability of rental units to anyone who inquires, but once applications are completed, the minority application will be delayed until the unit is rented, or it will be rejected for reasons that are not applied to white applications.

A routine excuse given for rejecting minority rental applicants is that they have not been on the job long enough or do not have enough credit established. Yet, when white applicants with the same or shorter employment or credit history apply, they are accepted. Although managers provide applicants with what appear to be legitimate business reasons for a denial, "full application" testing often reveals that these same standards are not applied to white applicants.

Conducting full application testing requires a larger pool of testers who have the necessary credentials and are willing to submit applications. This methodology also requires a greater financial commitment from the fair housing agency to provide funds for the security deposits, application fees, and credit checks for all the testers.

Tester Identification. Some apartment managers are requiring applicants to show photo identification and are actually copying the driver's license of applicants and attaching it to the application. This requirement poses yet another obstacle for fair housing agencies and raises questions about how this information will be used by management companies. Managers can share this information in attempts to identify testers, once again forcing the private fair housing agency to have a large supply of testers and expend resources for continuous training and retraining of testers.

Caller Identification. Historically, managers have failed to return calls from people who have "racially identifiable" voices. Managers use answering machines and selectively place return calls to people who inquire about units. We are currently facing the challenge posed by caller-identification equipment, which provides the manager with the opportunity to record the telephone number of the caller and screen out the caller by identifying the telephone exchange.

Rental Investigation. Managers determined to exclude or limit access to housing by racial minorities have developed sophisticated practices that are difficult and sometimes impossible to test. Apartment complexes with very low vacancy rates and subsidized housing developments fall into this category. Therefore, fair housing agencies must rely on their nontesting skills to uncover the devices used to deny housing to minorities.

A challenging issue involves managers who illegally manipulate waiting lists for subsidized housing. It is difficult to test these complaints because most subsidized complexes do not have open waiting lists. Private agencies often contact the owner to discuss the problems. In the following instance, the owner cooperated with the private fair housing agency by allowing them to review the waiting list and application files. Undoubtedly the owner thought the fair housing staff would not be able to identify the method used to purge the list of minority applicants.

What the staff found was a practice in which the manager prepared an original and carbon copy of a letter requiring applicants to indicate their interest in remaining on the list within 10 days of receiving the letter or be removed from the waiting list. The original letter was destroyed and the copy placed in the file. After the 10 days passed, the manager made a notation to the file that an applicant never responded. The applicant was removed from the waiting list.

The staff found an interesting pattern developing that showed withdrawal of minority applicants at the end of 10 days, while white applicants remained on the list for up to 60 days. There were some instances where minority applicants were reinstated on the list after the manager received several telephone calls or letters inquiring about their status and challenging the manager about receiving a letter. Staff located past managers who confirmed that this practice was used to purge the waiting lists of African Americans.

Settlements in these types of cases include requiring the manager to send letters by certified mail to all applicants, with a follow-up telephone call, and to give the fair housing agency access to the waiting list records for monitoring purposes. In addition, all families who are illegally removed from the waiting list are reinstated in their proper chronological place.

Thorough record searches in private fair housing cases have uncovered practices in which managers charge minority residents higher monthly rents and larger security deposits, which the company retains when they move out. Fair housing agencies monitor these companies as conditions of settlement by requiring the company to supply monthly and quarterly reports that detail the name, address, telephone, race, and sex information on all applicants, the date they applied, whether they were accepted or reject for unit, the reasons for rejection, addresses of units rented, amount of rent and security deposit charged, and other information necessary to monitor compliance with the fair housing laws.

Sales Testing. The same level of sophistication found in discriminatory rental practices also permeates the sales market (Galster 1986, 1988; Leigh and Stewart 1992). Blatant racial steering still occurs; white testers are discouraged from seeking homes in integrated and minority neighborhoods while African American testers are steered to minority and integrated neighborhoods as their only housing options. This is fairly easy to test and document. However, what is more difficult to expose are the subtle practices by agents of failing to market certain neighborhoods because of their racial composition.

Agents will "technically" make homes in white neighborhoods available to minority buyers and even show whites homes in integrated communities, so they can say they provided a choice of housing to the buyer. However, these same agents fail to market these homes and neighborhoods actively. Therefore, testers must be trained to identify the marketing techniques used by the agent and document the amount of information provided. This kind of real estate testing requires several visits with the agent so that the test coordinator can compare the marketing practices and quality of information provided to the minority and white testers.

Another persistent problem that was recently and successfully challenged is the discrimination faced by minority real estate agents. Minority agents are reporting practices used to keep them from securing listings in white neighborhoods or appointments to show homes located in white neighborhoods. In the lawsuit, *Payne v. Coldwell Banker,* an African American agent received $125,000 in damages plus attorney fees in a court-supervised settlement agreement that calls for Coldwell Banker to adopt an agent-referral policy. The referral policy ensures that all sales associates in Washington, D.C., will be permitted to select areas of their own choosing to solicit listings, and they will not be denied the opportunity to hold an open house because of their race.

Minority agents have been reluctant to come forward with discrimination complaints. Yet, more agents are sharing with fair housing advocates information about the nature of the problems they face within their own companies and industry, as well as from lenders. Minority agents face a whole different set of discriminatory housing practices.

Minority real estate agents may find they are unable to schedule appointments for home showings in white neighborhoods because other agents believe they have a minority buyer. In addition, listings held by minority agents may not be marketed by white agents because they believe that whites will not buy homes from African American sellers. The alliance actually has instances where real estate agents asked minority sellers to remove the family pictures from houses during showings. It is difficult enough to make a living in real estate; minority agents find themselves faced with sellers who do not want a minority agent to list the property and discriminatory housing practices from people within their own industry.

A broker told me that he would hire "attractive black women" to work for him, but not a "black man because white women would be uncomfortable looking at homes with him." This type of racism permeates the thinking within the industry and must be addressed through education and litigation. It appears that behavior, practices, and policies change most quickly through legal challenges.

Testing must still be developed in this area. The cooperation of minority and white agents and real estate companies may be necessary to conduct such testing. Another difficult investigation involves the negotiation process once an offer to purchase a home is submitted. In some markets we are finding that African Americans are paying list price for properties, even though the investigation or testing shows that when whites made similar offers, they received more favorable treatment and lower purchase prices. Settlements in these cases usually include securing the home at the lower price, damages for the act of discrimination, and affirmative relief.

Sales Investigation. Because many real estate sales complaints cannot be tested before the complainant must submit a purchase offer, it is imperative that fair housing staff are skilled at interviewing agents, sellers, neighbors, lenders, and anyone else who might have information about the property. Reviewing previous purchase offers from white buyers is important, as well as interviewing the complainants and other buyers who worked with the agent to determine if race was discussed during their housing search. Once again contacting agents who previously represented the company can reveal unwritten policies and practices that violate the fair housing laws.

Advertising Issues. Advertising is used to attract people seeking to buy, rent, finance, and insure property. Advertising is designed to target certain populations, as well as specific income and educational levels. Advertising that uses one race to market its housing, financing, or insurance is sending a discriminatory message to its readers or viewers. When addressing a white audience about marketing issues and the impact this has directly and subliminally on people, I ask this question: "How many of you buy and read *Ebony, Essence,* or *Jet* magazines?" Invariably eyes are cast down and usually no one raises their hand. I quickly point out that they do not even pick up the magazines because they do not identify with the pictures on the cover. If they feel that these magazines are targeted to African Americans because they show them on the cover and throughout the magazine, they need to understand how African Americans may feel when they see apartment advertisements that only depict white people at pools or home builder ads that only show white families enjoying the new subdivision and white loan officers making loans to white couples, and insurance companies showing great coverage and protection to white home owners.

The people companies choose to show in an advertisement can influence who will come to see the property. Where they choose to run advertisements also directly impacts who will come to see the property. The failure of real estate companies to use the minority media to advertise apartments, homes, financing, and insurance products directly affects the market share they secure.

An additional caution given to housing providers is that they should not only use the minority media, but advertise homes from a variety of neighborhoods and price ranges in these media. Too often the housing providers only advertise the lowest-priced homes located in minority neighborhoods in the minority press. Fair advertising means making choice available and advertising racially inclusive.

Lending Testing. Lending testing is past its infancy but only entering the toddler stage of development. Complaint-based, full-application lending testing has been successfully conducted in Ohio. Pre-application testing, which involves contacting the loan officer about the lending process but stops short of completing an application, was conducted in Louisville, Kentucky; Chicago; Cincinnati and Toledo, Ohio; and Detroit. Although pre-application testing is very useful in identifying discriminatory practices in the initial phase of mortgage loan inquiries, it fails to uncover the full nature and extent of discrimination occurring throughout the loan application process.

Discrimination can and does occur at every stage in the mortgage lending process. Learning to identify discriminatory practices at each stage has been the objective of several fair housing agencies. These agencies are training other fair housing agencies how to identify discrimination during the following steps of the mortgage loan process:

Initial Interview
Credit and Employment Review
Appraisal Process
Private Mortgage Insurance Decision
Loan Committee Review
Home Owner Insurance
Closing
Sale to Secondary Mortgage Market
Retention in Portfolio

The lawsuits brought through the private fair housing agencies in Toledo, Ohio, and Gary, Indiana, set the prima facie or threshold case standards for mortgage lending discrimination as follows:

Applicant-Based Discrimination—*Thomas v. First Federal Savings Bank of Indiana,* 653 F. Supp. 1130, 1338 (N.D. Ind. 1987):
1.   The applicants are members of a protected class.

2. They applied and were qualified for a loan from the defendant.

3. The loan was rejected despite their qualifications.

4. The defendant continued to approve loans for applicants with qualifications similar to the applicants.

Neighborhood-Based Discrimination—*Old West End Association, et.al. v. Buckeye Federal Savings and Loan,* 675 F. Supp. 1100, 1103 (N.D. Ohio 1987):

1. The housing sought to be secured is in a minority neighborhood.

2. An application for a loan to purchase the housing located in a minority neighborhood was made.

3. An independent appraisal concluded that the value of the housing equaled the sale price.

4. The buyers were creditworthy.

5. The loan was rejected.

Lending Investigation. It is a violation of federal law to use false information when completing a mortgage loan application. With this serious problem facing lending testing, it becomes even more important for fair housing staff to be skilled at identifying discriminatory policies and practices in the application of the underwriting guidelines of the lender, private mortgage insurance company, and secondary market purchaser. Combining the investigative skills of fair housing staff with social science researchers with expertise in statistics and data analysis resulted in the successful settlements of all of the Toledo, Ohio, lending lawsuits. All of these lawsuits were settled shortly after discovery disclosed different treatment of loan applications based on the race of the applicant or racial composition of the neighborhood. These lawsuits were brought by African Americans, Hispanics, whites, interracial neighborhood associations, and the fair housing agency. They involved allegations of discriminatory treatment based on race, national origin, racial composition of the neighborhood, and discriminatory appraisal, credit, and underwriting practices.

THE RESULTS OF PRIVATE FAIR HOUSING ENFORCEMENT

Private fair housing agencies have obtained the most comprehensive conciliation, enforcement, and monitoring programs, including training, compliance reporting, inclusive advertising, affirmative employment practices, and unit availability. They have also secured the largest monetary damage awards in settled and adjudicated cases and continue to investigate and litigate the cutting-edge fair housing cases.

LANDMARK CASES:

~ An alliance member negotiated the first HUD conciliation to include set-aside of free units for homeless persons and families, Toledo, Ohio.

~ Alliance members in Ohio negotiated the first Community Reinvestment Act agreements that included affirmative employment requirements and access to appraisal reports for any loan applicant whose loan terms were changed or whose loan was denied. In addition, the Toledo and Gary members were the first to negotiate settlements of fair housing claims for monetary damages as part of the CRA agreements.

~ The largest race discrimination agreement ever reached in a rental complaint is $450,000 secured by Westside Fair Housing Council (California) on February 20, 1990. Previous settlements or adjudications included $375,000 (New York); $327,000 (Washington, D.C.); and $310,000 in (Chicago), all involving alliance members.

~ The first case to define sexual harassment in housing as a violation of the fair housing law, *Shellhammer v. Lewallen,* was investigated, tested and litigated by the alliance's Toledo member. Fair housing attorneys in Oakland, California, recently settled the largest fair housing case ever for $650,000 in damages plus more than $250,000 in attorney fees. Other cases were brought in state court in Wisconsin where the victims was awarded nearly $20,000, and other cases have settled in Chicago.

~ The right of testers and fair housing agencies to sue on their own behalf was won before the U.S. Supreme Court in 1982 in a lawsuit brought by HOME of Richmond, Virginia. This landmark case is known as *Havens Realty v. Coleman.* Standing to sue for municipalities was obtained in *Gladstone, Realtors v. Bellwood* by the alliance's Chicago member.

~ Discriminatory advertising cases have been won through settlements with major newspapers and advertisers. A case settled against an advertiser in New York resulted in $245,000 in damages plus the equivalent of $200,000 free advertising designed to include African Americans. A Washington, D.C., advertising case settled for more than $300,000 plus affirmative advertising.

~ Significant legal precedents have been obtained in lawsuits challenging discriminatory practices in lending, private mortgage insurance, and home owners' insurance brought by alliance members in Toledo, Cincinnati, and Dayton, Ohio *(Old West End Association v. Buckeye Federal Savings and Loan*

Association; Dunn v. Midwestern Indemnity; McDiarmid v. Economy Fire and Casualty Co.).

~ Alliance members in California, Georgia, Illinois, Indiana, Maryland, New York, Ohio, and Virginia have brought successful civil suits against persons who have engaged in acts of harassment, intimidation, and violence against minority families exercising their fair housing rights. The largest damage award in such cases was $625,000 in the *Rudolph v. Taberner* case in Toledo, Ohio.

From March 1989 (when the Fair Housing Act Amendments became effective) through September 1991, 44 alliance members reported securing nearly $8 million in damages and attorney fees for victims of housing discrimination. It is evident that when there are more private groups, there are more cases, and the cases result in larger damage awards.

GAPS IN THE CURRENT HUD PROCESS

Part of the role of the alliance includes addressing problems with HUD, Justice, and state agency enforcement procedures. A serious deficiency was identified when a HUD administrative law judge (ALJ) ruled against the complainants in a Buffalo, New York case. The complainants, HOME and an African American woman, both wanted to appeal the decision. HUD attorneys advised the complainants that although they represented them during the hearing, they could not appeal the ALJ decision. The decision would become a final order of then-HUD Secretary Jack Kemp thirty days after the ALJ ruling, and no one within HUD was willing to ask the secretary not to sign the final order.

The complainants were now without any representation for an appeal, and their right to file an appeal was in jeopardy because they had used HUD attorneys instead of engaging private legal counsel during the ALJ proceeding. The alliance secured representation for the complainants through the Washington Lawyers' Committee, but the first issue to be addressed was whether or not the ALJ would allow the complainants to intervene at this step in the process so they could appeal the decision. The ALJ granted a motion allowing the intervention. Now the complainants will be opposed by the Department of Justice representing the secretary's decision and the defendant's attorney on this appeal.

The same government which originally found cause in the case and issued a charge will stand against the complainants during the appeal. An obvious lesson to be learned from this experience is that complainants must intervene with their own legal counsel in every ALJ proceeding just to ensure their right to appeal when the decision goes against them.

It may also be appropriate for complainants to have their own legal counsel during either the HUD or Justice Department legal proceedings because the government attorneys are obliged to follow the current administration's civil rights agenda. As a result, legal points that would be routinely argued by private attorneys, such as intent versus effect issues, will not be brought by government attorneys.

On a positive note, the ALJ process is much faster than federal district court, and the ALJs have handled their cases in a timely fashion. The Justice Department has almost unlimited resources to conduct investigations of large apartment companies and interstate real estate firms, resources which most fair housing agencies lack.

Awards remain very low in the ALJ procedure. Neither HUD or Justice refers victims of housing discrimination for counseling to determine the nature and extent of any emotional distress caused by the act. Psychologists explain that symptoms of emotional distress from housing discrimination may not appear during the first few months, but they may be manifested later by symptoms of disturbed sleeping patterns, distrust of whites in general, irritability, and feeling of a loss of control over their environment.

Recognizing symptoms of emotional distress and helping victims articulate their feelings to the court are important factors in securing appropriate damages for victims of housing discrimination. Victims have described housing discrimination as an assault on their dignity, a challenge to their self-esteem. It is important for the government to do everything to make the victims whole again by communicating to the victims and the court that it understands the negative impact of housing discrimination.

Currently, government lawyers lack the experience that civil rights and personal injury lawyers have in identifying and articulating damages. As a result, government settlements and litigations will likely set a very low damage benchmark in housing discrimination cases.

FAIR HOUSING EDUCATION

Fair housing agencies in the nonprofit sector have led the decades-long battle against housing discrimination. The lack of federal regulatory enforcement power of fair housing laws resulted in private individuals and fair housing agencies investigating and litigating housing discrimination cases. Just a handful of these agencies with limited resources, cooperating with civil rights attorneys, worked against the odds to establish a legacy of powerful and impressive victories over real estate companies, rental firms, and lending institutions with unfair practices, procedures, and policies.

As a result, local fair housing agencies have identified and defined the spectrum of discriminatory rental, sales, lending, and insurance practices, as well as race and sexual harassment practices. These agencies have successfully litigated and conciliated thousands of housing discrimination complaints covering these areas. This successful enforcement experience logically led to the development of education and training programs designed to eliminate and prevent discriminatory practices in the housing market. The educational efforts were designed to promote awareness of the subtleties of discrimination, to teach members of the housing industry how to avoid discriminatory practices, and to help the general public understand the benefits of multicultural, multiracial, and economically inclusive neighborhoods .

Housing Consumer Outreach and Education. Education is essential in the plan to promote fair housing and eliminate discriminatory practices. The type of education provided to the housing consumer is threefold. First, since housing discrimination is so cleverly disguised, it is important to teach people how to recognize discriminatory practices. The methods of reaching people include television, radio, and print media, as well as direct contact through community education programs in churches/synagogues, neighborhood meetings, service organizations and through the social service networks in each community. Additionally, role playing sessions are employed to show consumers how very subtle discrimination is and how testing is used to substantiate or refute allegations.

These programs help the listeners/viewers identify the subtle tactics used to discourage or deny minorities housing. Discussions about the protections of the fair housing laws are presented, but more importantly, examples of discriminatory housing practices are shared. People are taught to be suspicious whenever there is a delay or denial of housing, financing, or insurance for a property. Educational programs are designed to address the specific fair housing needs of the audience. For example, people looking for their first home are told how racial steering occurs and how to identify and report it. Staff share examples of actual cases of housing discrimination and explain that the nicest rental manager may tell you with a smile and handshake, "I'm sorry, we have two other applications for that apartment, but I'll call you if they fall through," when in reality the apartment is available. We explain how testing is used to determine the truth so there will be evidence to support the claim and the complainant will not end up in a "it's your word against mine" situation. The credibility of the fair housing provider is critical in generating complaints of housing. It is also critical in curbing discriminatory practices by housing providers.

Housing Industry Education Strategies. Education to the industry is introduced as a two-edged sword. The fair housing agency teaches real estate agents, property managers, mortgage lenders, appraisers, and insurers how to avoid discriminatory situations and how to handle situations where sellers, renters, or other employees try to make them a silent partner in an act of housing discrimination. They also learn how to document their activities so that if a charge of discrimination is made against them, they can explain their policies and practices. During training, fair housing agencies explain why testing is used and how it benefits them; legal cases, and the mistakes their counterparts in the industry made that resulted in judgments against them, are reviewed.

Fair housing agencies throughout the country have been certified by state real estate commissions to conduct required fair housing training courses. Some fair housing groups even contract with real estate companies or lenders to test employees in order to identify problems and eliminate them before they violate a home seeker's right. All of this information is provided as a preventive measure and to affirmatively further fair housing in cooperation with the industry.

The other edge of the sword, however, will cut housing providers if they or their agents violate the law in spite of receiving this training. The fair housing agency will testify that this housing provider knew better; therefore, the acts of discrimination were willfully committed, and punitive damages and civil penalties are reasonable and indeed, necessary, to send a message throughout the industry that real estate agents must not only hear but practice fair housing to the letter of the law.

Training to minority housing providers is similar, but it focuses on helping them to identify other real estate companies and lenders who refuse or otherwise make unavailable housing services to them, their clients, or the neighborhoods they are serving.

Education also includes teaching all agents that it is a violation of the law to intimidate, coerce, or harass anyone promoting fair housing. So when agents encounter harassment from other agents or neighbors who object to their showing homes to minorities, agents are assured that the fair housing agencies will defend their fair housing rights with the full force of the law.

Fair Lending Education. The majority of lawsuits and administrative complaints filed against lenders, appraisers, private mortgage insurers, and the secondary mortgage market have come from Ohio and Indiana. Educational efforts are designed to reach potential buyers, neighborhood groups likely to be victims of disinvestment, and religious and community groups to discuss reinvestment efforts and greenlining strategies. Other efforts urge real estate agents to report redlining and mortgage lending discrimination.

This last issue is very important because real estate agents often hear appraisers, loan officers, or underwriters make negative comments about racially integrated neighborhoods. In fact, five of the lending discrimination lawsuits brought through the Toledo Fair Housing Center were referred by white real estate agents who recognized mortgage lending discrimination occurring and chose to be a part of the solution instead of a silent partner in the problem.

As a result of the lending lawsuits, the alliance is training members on how to identify discrimination in the mortgage lending process, how to conduct testing, and how to educate lenders and appraisers about their rights and responsibilities under the fair housing laws.

This education also extends to the federal regulators who are charged with examining lending practices for discriminatory conduct. The alliance staff has testified three times on mortgage lending, private mortgage insurance, and secondary mortgage market practices before the U.S. Senate Banking and Financing Committee, and members have trained the staff of the Federal Reserve Board and its member banks.

Methods/Materials Used for Education and Outreach. Methods used for training real estate agents involve pretests that measure their knowledge of what actions constitute violations of the law, knowledge about legal decisions, and general marketing skills for homes located in minority and integrated neighborhoods. Role playing is also effective. It may seem surprising to learn that there are agents who have not had real estate transactions with African Americans or other racial and ethnic minorities. Therefore, the role playing, using minority staff, is effective to help agents identify how and why they treat minority buyers differently.

Radio and television advertisements are the most effective media tools in generating complaints of housing discrimination. Materials developed by the alliance under a HUD grant have been quite successful in increasing the number and types of complaints being filed with HUD and private fair housing agencies. Alliance members using the material reported a 34 percent increase in complaints. Some cities, such as Chicago, Detroit, and Los Angeles, reported a 50 percent increase in the number of complaints reported. These advertisements were designed to demonstrate how subtle discrimination is and to encourage people to report all suspicious delays or denials in rental and sales transactions.

The products developed by the alliance and the follow-up promotion to four hundred television and fifteen hundred radio stations to use the materials resulted in an unprecedented response to the HUD Housing Discrimination Hotline. During 1990, for example, HUD reported just over 12,000 calls per year on the Hotline. During the six months that the alliance's campaign was operating, HUD received over 110,000 calls to the Hotline.

CONCLUSION AND RECOMMENDATIONS

Unless the public and private sector establish coordinated enforcement, educational, and outreach efforts, the nation will continue to address fair housing issues in a piecemeal, inefficient fashion. The failure of our government to have a major impact on segregated residential housing patterns is due, in part, to the failure to teach the general public why and how to recognize and challenge housing discrimination and the serious consequences on society of forced residential segregation.

Fair housing is the step-child of the Civil Rights Movement. Fair housing stands at the foundation for providing multiracial, multicultural, and economically inclusive living experiences, integrated educational opportunities, and access to employment opportunities. As a nation, however, we have not had the financial support necessary to make these goals a reality for all Americans.

Unlike civil rights groups that promote school desegregation, equal employment opportunities, and voting rights issues, fair housing organizations have not enjoyed the same sustained funding support from the federal, state, and local governments or the financial support from the philanthropic community. Yet, the forced segregated housing patterns—American apartheid—directly and adversely affect educational and employment opportunities in our country.

Enforcement. If housing discrimination is to be eliminated, the future must contain coordinated efforts between public and private enforcement agencies and between enforcement agencies and the housing industry. HUD can have a major and powerful impact in the creation of private fair housing agencies where none currently exist.

The Community Development Block Grant (CDBG) program provides millions of dollars to more than eight hundred U.S. cities. The regulations for this program require recipient cities to have programs that "affirmatively further fair housing," yet fewer than thirty cities use CDBG funds to promote fair housing enforcement within their jurisdictions.

A major reason for the lack of compliance is HUD's failure to define what are legitimate or acceptable activities to meet this requirement. What is needed? HUD should define minimum fair housing standards that include:

~ comprehensive education and outreach programs to increase the awareness of the minority community and low-and moderate-income persons of their fair housing rights;

~ education to housing providers about their rights and responsibilities under the fair housing laws;

~ investigation and enforcement tools to all victims of housing discrimination through testing, conciliation, and litigation services;

~ research components to investigate and measure the nature and extent of housing discrimination within the community;

~ ability to design education and enforcement programs necessary to challenge systemic housing discrimination practices.

Government needs help from other sectors. For example, the philanthropic and religious communities should financially support local, regional, and national fair housing programs designed to address the problems of housing discrimination. In addition, the religious community should assist fair housing agencies in recruiting testers who are an essential component in combating housing discrimination.

The problems surfacing within the HUD administrative process should be quickly remedied so that victims of housing discrimination can be afforded the free legal counsel promised under the amended Fair Housing Act.

The psychology community should be encouraged to work with victims of discrimination, especially housing discrimination, to assist in the healing process and to help juries and judges understand the serious emotional impact housing discrimination has on African Americans and other victims of discrimination. In this way, appropriate damage awards will be made, serving to make the victim whole and to act as a deterrent to other housing providers.

Education and outreach. To ensure an understanding of the intent of Congress to eliminate racially segregated housing patterns, there must be a coordinated national education campaign between federal, state, and local governmental agencies and the nonprofit fair housing movement and the housing industry. Fair housing agencies have developed model programs of training and cooperation with local industry groups. Coordination within certain HUD regional offices and cooperation with the Department of Justice have also been developed and proven, in most instances, to be beneficial in promoting the spirit and intent of the fair housing law. These successful models must be duplicated across the country and sustained financially by a combination of public and private funds.

The effectiveness of the grassroots advocacy cannot be replaced by federal or state government intervention, but can be dramatically enhanced by financial support and cooperation. The need for enforcement and education at the local level to ensure elimination of discriminatory practices will never diminish.

Certainly the idea of comprehensive, coordinated enforcement efforts between the federal government and private fair housing and civil rights advocates can raise fears in a housing and lending industry that has historically engaged in illegal practices to limit and deny housing opportunities to African Americans. Politicians who depend on donations from builders, developers, lenders, and others related to the housing industry may not have the courage to support credible fair housing education and enforcement programs. Trade associations representing the rental, sales, lending, and insurance industries assert that discrimination is not a problem and decisions are made based upon sound financial reasons.

All of these groups have a vested interest in making sure that fair housing enforcement and education continues as a piecemeal effort by underfunded and understaffed civil rights advocates. But report and after report indicates that race plays a major and discriminatory part in the denial of housing, lending, and insuring of property. It is time for the government, religious leaders, and foundations to make fair housing an important part of their agendas. Progress will be made when this happens. After all, look at what a handful of private fair housing agencies has accomplished with limited resources, by the strength of faith in their ability to successfully challenge housing discrimination every where they find it.

REFERENCES

Dane, Stephen M. 1991. Federal enforcement of the fair housing lending, equal opportunity, and community reinvestment laws: 1989-1990. In *Lost opportunities: The civil rights record of the Bush administration mid-term,* edited by Susan M. Liss and William L. Taylor. Washington, D.C.: Citizens Commission on Civil Rights.

Dedman, Bill. 1989. Blacks turned down for home loans from S&Ls twice as often as whites. *Atlanta Journal and Constitution,* 22 January.

Galster, George. 1988. Racial discrimination in housing markets during the 1980s: A review of the audit evidence. *Journal of Planning Education and Research* 9:165–75.

———. 1986. More than skin deep: The effect of housing discrimination on the extent and pattern of racial residential segregation in the United States. In *Housing desegregation and federal policy,* edited by John M. Goering. Chapel Hill: University of North Carolina Press.

Leigh, Wilhelmina A., and James B. Stewart, eds. 1992. *The housing status of black Americans.* New Brunswick, N.J.: Transaction.

Quint, Michael. 1991. Racial disparity in mortgages shown in U.S. data. *New York Times,* 14 November.

Rockefeller Foundation and The Urban Institute. 1991. Testing for discrimination in America: Results and policy implications, conference held 26 September in Washington, D.C.

U.S. Senate. 1990. Testimony of Shanna L. Smith, representative of the National Fair Housing Alliance, Inc., before the Subcommittee on Consumer and Regulatory Affairs of the Committee on Banking, Housing, and Urban Affairs of the U.S. Senate, *Hearing on Discrimination in Home Mortgage Lending.*

Wallace, J., W. L. Holshouser, T. S. Lane, and J. Williams. 1985. *The Fair Housing Assistance Program evaluation.* Washington, D.C.: Office of Policy Development and Research, U.S. Department of Housing and Urban Development.

CHAPTER 11

Community Reinvestment:
The Privatization of Fair Lending Law Enforcement

by Gregory D. Squires

"Jesus Christ himself could not get a loan in Brooklyn."
Savings and Loan President (Art 1987, 1097)

Despite an array of laws, regulations, and other administrative actions prohibiting racial discrimination in the provision of credit, racially discriminatory mortgage lending and disinvestment of older urban communities remain facts of city life. Yet these are facts around which there is significant struggle. Most lenders as well as their regulatory agencies have generally denied the existence of widespread redlining or discrimination, claiming that each loan application is evaluated strictly on the basis of objective financial criteria. Since financial institutions make their money by making loans, it is argued that they have a self-interest that assures the elimination of any subjective practices that would undermine profitability. Recent research, however, has demonstrated systematic racial and geographic bias in lending, and today even some within the industry are wavering in their denials.

Community organizations, civil rights lawyers, some sympathetic public officials, and others who have long suspected redlining and racial discrimination are fighting back with some success. In fact—although this was not the intent of proponents of civil rights legislation—enforcement of fair housing and equal credit laws has been dominated by private actors. Such deferral of public authority to private, generally nonprofit organizations is at best a mixed blessing. Clearly, barriers to opportunities for life, liberty, and the pursuit of happiness could be reduced more effectively with a more aggressive public posture. Given fast-developing changes in the structure of financial industries and the deregulatory thrust that continues among lawmakers, the significant achievements of private actors will need to be complemented by more effective public activity if reinvestment efforts are to continue and meaningful progress is to be made toward the goal of replacing the nation's ghettos with truly balanced and integrated living patterns.

When the federal Fair Housing Act was passed in 1968, the U.S. Department of Housing and Urban Development (HUD) was designated as the chief law enforcement agency. The U.S. Department of Justice and several federal financial regulatory agencies also have critical law enforcement authority for fair housing and fair lending under the Fair Housing Act and subsequent legislation. Yet the vast majority of fair housing cases have been brought by private litigants, and private litigation is responsible for the major decisions interpreting the 1968 Act. The significance of private action is demonstrated by the fact that cities with private fair housing organizations generate a higher incidence of cases than communities not served by a fair housing group. Perhaps more important is the substantive development of the law resulting from private action. Privately initiated lawsuits resulted in rulings that the Fair Housing Act prohibited racial steering and exclusionary zoning; that discriminatory effect as well as intent can violate the law; that substantial damages for humiliation and other intangible injuries can be inferred from the fact of being victimized by discrimination; that discrimination against mortgage loan applicants due to neighborhood racial composition—redlining—is unlawful; and other interpretations that have provided substantial relief for victims of discriminatory housing and related practices (Schwemm 1987, 1989; U.S. Commission on Civil Rights 1987; Kushner 1988).

If private fair housing groups and litigants have been the principal force for fair housing law enforcement, private community organizations have been the major force for compliance with the nation's fair lending and community reinvestment laws. The key statute is the Community Reinvestment Act enacted in 1977, which requires lenders to be responsive to the credit needs of their entire service area, including low- and moderate-income neighborhoods. Virtually all the formal rulings by the federal financial regulatory agencies charged with enforcing this law resulted from challenges brought by private community groups (Art 1987, 1095). Reinvestment agreements totaling over $30 billion have been negotiated with lenders by neighborhood organizations in over seventy cities (Bradford 1992; National Community Reinvestment Coalition 1993, 3). "The true 'watchdogs' of the lending community with respect to home finance discrimination matters have been private fair housing groups and private citizens" (Dane and Henderson 1990, 223).

This chapter reviews the history of uneven lending practices, focusing on the racial exclusion that has been a central dynamic of mortgage lending and related housing industry practices. If private groups are primarily responsible for recent enforcement activities, the public sector long sanctioned racially discriminatory housing and lending practices. Significant developments in fair lending law and law enforcement are traced, followed by examples of how community-based organizations have effectively used the leverage provided by recent legislative initiatives. But there are serious limitations to private action, particularly in light of current and proposed industry restructuring. In conclusion, recommendations are offered to ensure more effective public and private enforcement of fair lending laws and to nurture more comprehensive reinvestment in urban America.

RACE AND MORTGAGE LENDING

Throughout most of this century, intentional racial discrimination has been an explicit requirement of housing finance and related housing industry practices, with the full support of federal law. As indicated earlier, both private sector and public sector actors have used race as a criterion in making housing and housing-related services available in a manner that has segregated and destabilized neighborhoods in cities across the country.

A central actor in the housing market is the appraisal industry. Appraisers, upon whom lenders rely for determining property values, have long used racial composition of neighborhoods in their evaluations (Schwemm 1993). If Frederick Babcock's observation half a century ago that "race can result in very rapid decline" (Babcock 1932) appears somewhat dated, the more recent 1975 edition of *The Appraisal of Real Estate,* which states that "economic obsolescence is caused by changes external to the property such as neighborhood infiltration of inharmonious groups" delivers the same message (Greene 1980, 10). Appraisers are often considered to be the eyes and ears of lending institutions. To this day, subjective assessments of neighborhoods frequently bias appraisal reports, to the detriment of communities with large minority populations (Greene 1980, 7–10; Fair Lending Action Committee 1989, 5).

Similarly, real estate brokers have long practiced racial segregation, contending that to do so was consistent with the highest ethical and professional standards of their industry. Not until 1950 did the National Association of Realtors remove from its code of ethics the warning that real estate brokers should not bring into a community, "members of any race or nationality, or any individual whose presence will clearly be detrimental to property values in the neighborhood" (Judd 1984, 284). As the Federal Housing Administration (FHA) observed for many years, the two key groups in question were "Negroes and Mexicans" (Hoyt 1933, 315–16).

No innovation in housing policy has more effectively stimulated home ownership or suburbanization of metropolitan areas and the dual housing market associated with that decentralization than the federally insured mortgage. With the FHA insuring the majority of mortgages nationwide between the mid 1930s and early 1960s and less than 2 percent of these loans going to blacks, the agency directly subsidized suburban development and racial segregation of metropolitan areas. When the FHA shifted its policies in the 1960s and began doing most of its business in central cities, the principal effects were to line the pockets of unscrupulous lenders and real estate agents, destroy many central city neighborhoods, and deplete the savings of unwary first-time home buyers.

Racial fears were often exploited, further destabilizing many urban neighborhoods. Real estate agents fostered the belief among many residents in older communities that their property values would decline if blacks moved in. In turn, the agents used a variety of tactics to encourage such white residents to sell, frequently at inflated prices initially. Black families would be enticed to buy, encouraging other white families to sell, often at subsequently depressed prices as the race card was played by real estate agents. Black families were then sold these homes, at great profit for the real estate agents as neighborhoods "tipped" from white to black. This process played out in several major cities during the 1960s, leaving behind dual housing markets that continue to plague these communities (Bradford 1990a; Jackson 1985).

Toward the end of the 1960s, federal law shifted dramatically, and the private housing industry began what was at least a verbal about-face in its racial policies. With the Federal Fair Housing Act of 1968, the Equal Credit Opportunity Act of 1974, the Home Mortgage Disclosure Act (HMDA) of 1975, and most importantly the Community Reinvestment Act (CRA) of 1977, along with several other federal, state, and local statutes, government policy shifted from a posture requiring segregation to one prohibiting it, at least in terms of the letter of the law. Not only is racial discrimination in housing and housing finance prohibited (along with other forms of discrimination that frequently serve as a cover for racial discrimination, such as discrimination against families with young children), but affirmative marketing and other positive remedies are often required (G. Sloane 1983; M. Sloane 1983; Dane 1989; Schwemm 1989). During these years, real estate agents, appraisers, lenders, and other segments of the housing industry also officially expressed their support for the principles of fair housing and equal opportunity.

The Community Reinvestment Act of 1977 has been a particularly significant factor in shaping mortgage lending activity. By federal law, most depository institutions that originate mortgage loans (ie. banks and thrifts) have an affirmative duty to address the credit needs of low-income neighborhoods. More importantly, the law created organizing opportunities for community groups to influence mortgage lending policies of private financial institutions. The CRA was enacted two years after the federal HMDA, which required lenders to report the number and dollar volume of mortgage loans by census tract within metropolitan areas. As part of the savings and loan bailout plan, the Financial Institution Reform, Recovery, and Enforcement Act (FIRREA), HMDA also required disclosure of mortgage loan application and rejection rates by race, gender, and income, beginning in 1990. Despite limitations of HMDA, most notably the lack of information on credit rating, employment status, and condition of property (Wienk 1992; Galster 1991b), the information supplied by HMDA, coupled with the requirements of CRA, has altered the terms of the redlining debate.

Under the CRA, federally regulated lenders "have a continuing and affirmative obligation to help meet the credit needs of the local communities in which they are chartered . . . consistent with safe and sound operation of such institutions." A critical component of the law is a provision allowing third parties—including community-based neighborhood organizations, nonprofit housing developers, and community development corporations—to file challenges to such applications in light of poor CRA records. Challenges can delay regulators' consideration of applications and even result in denials of the applications. Those delays can prove quite costly to the lenders. The costs provide the leverage for community groups. In order to expedite the processing of their applications, lenders often seek negotiations with those filing the challenge so that they will withdraw the challenge. With the information supplied by HMDA, community groups have negotiated several lucrative reinvestment agreements in recent years. Specific examples are discussed below. The CRA has dramatically altered the economic and political context in which mortgage lending occurs. Perhaps most importantly, few lenders today claim that their only concern is with the safety and soundness of their investments to be achieved solely by maximizing profitability for stockholders and depositors. Most lenders today acknowledge a responsibility to better serve diverse community credit needs (Art 1987). And many see no contradiction between community reinvestment and traditional business interests. As the former CRA officer and now Vice President for Bank One in Milwaukee recently stated, "It's good business, you don't lose money doing CRA, it's the right thing to do" (Elverman 1990). Not all lenders, of course, are convinced. In expressing his strong faith in the free market, a suburban Milwaukee lender stated that getting an outstanding CRA rating was "like being given the iron cross for service from the National Socialists Party" (Banker 1993, 23).

FIRREA is also likely to make federal financial regulatory agencies more effective in encouraging reinvestment. As of July 1, 1990, regulators are required to publicly disclose the CRA ratings of all institutions reviewed after that date. Each institution is now placed in one of four rating categories; (1) outstanding record in meeting community credit needs, (2) satisfactory record, (3) needs to improve, and (4) substantial noncompliance in meeting community credit needs. Tighter regulatory oversight and publication of the overall CRA ratings should make the organizing efforts of community-based organizations even more effective.

Despite these favorable legal developments, the dual housing market and discriminatory effects of housing finance practices did not disappear in the sixties, seventies, or eighties. With black and Hispanic home seekers still experiencing discrimination in over half their encounters with real estate agents (Turner et al. 1991, vi, 37) and HUD reporting two million instances of unlawful discrimination annually, racial inequality and racial segregation persist in our nation's housing markets (Schwemm 1989, 272). Between 1970 and 1990 the extent of segregation between blacks and whites in major metropolitan areas remained virtually unchanged (Massey and Denton 1993). Despite the decentralization that has occurred in metropolitan populations in recent years, blacks are still more heavily concentrated near the city center than whites (Galster 1991a). Racial segmentation and stratification in housing remain defining traits of urban communities in the 1990s.

A persistent contributing factor is the nation's mortgage lending industry. Blacks continue to be rejected for mortgage loans twice as often as whites nationwide even among applicants within the same income groups (Dedman 1989; Canner and Smith 1991, 1992). Within metropolitan areas mortgage loans are more readily available in suburban and predominantly white neighborhoods than in central city and predominantly minority areas, even after the effects of such factors as family income, quality of housing, residential turnover, and other factors associated with the credit worthiness of residents and security of their property are taken into consideration (Schafer and Ladd 1981; Shlay 1989; Bradbury, Case, and Dunham 1989; Squires and Velez 1987). And as researchers with the Boston Federal Reserve Bank found in their examination of over three thousand applications with 131 lenders in that community, blacks are 60 percent more likely to be rejected than whites with identical credit records, debt histories, income, and other financial characteristics (Munnell et al. 1992). Intentional racial discrimination still exists, but in addition to instances of explicit discrimination and steering are the continuing effects of prior decades of mandated racial segregation and the adverse racial effects of contemporary institutional practices.

Several economic, social, and political factors account for continuing racial disparities in the mortgage market. Racial minorities do possess, on average, fewer economic resources than whites. And lending institutions enter into the home buying process after other discriminatory acts may already have taken place by real estate agents, appraisers, property insurers, and others (Wienk 1992). (Both historical and contemporary discrimination in employment and education, no doubt, contribute to a racial gap that even precedes entry into the housing market at any level. At the same time, housing discrimination, because of its effects on school choice and employment opportunities, makes the entire process a vicious circle.) Current policies and practices by financial institutions, nevertheless, contribute significantly to these racial disparities, and not simply by extending into the future the effects of historical discrimination within other institutions. Contemporary underwriting guidelines and the culture of many financial institutions, coupled with lax law enforcement by regulatory agencies, are major factors that perpetuate the adverse racial effects of home finance.

While explicit references to race may have disappeared from most underwriting manuals, underwriting guidelines still often adversely affect racial minorities. For example, many mortgage lenders will not make loans on low-valued properties, generally homes whose market value has been appraised at $25,000 to $35,000 or less. The reason is simply that since the cost of processing home mortgage loan applications varies little with the size of the loan, the profit margins on the smaller loans are frequently viewed as inadequate to justify the expenses. The solution for many lenders is to avoid the low end of the market. Such a policy, arguably, is predicated on no racial animosity. Yet it clearly has racial implications. Because racial minorities are more likely to live in lower-priced homes and in neighborhoods characterized by below-average home prices, this underwriting practice will disqualify a disproportionately high number of applications from racial minorities. To illustrate, in Milwaukee 21 percent of single-family dwellings were valued at $35,000 or less in 1988. Yet in those neighborhoods where racial minorities exceeded their citywide representation of approximately 25 percent, 78 percent of single-family units were valued at this level (Squires, Velez, and Taeuber 1991). Similarly, some lenders have tighter underwriting restrictions for older homes; refuse to offer loans with a greater than 80 percent loan-to-value ratio, thus requiring down payments of 20 percent or more; offer no fixed-rate loans with maturities over 15 years, or refuse to offer FHA loans (Kohn 1993; Lawton 1993). Racial minorities tend to own older homes and to live in communities where the housing stock is generally older than in the balance of the metropolitan area. Due to their relatively lower income, they are more likely to participate in mortgage programs that allow for greater flexibility in down payment requirements and longer amortization periods and in government-insured programs. Again, no racial discrimination may be intended, but one result of these practices is to exclude minorities more often than whites.

Subjective guidelines in many underwriting manuals can often be interpreted in ways that adversely affect racial minorities or any applicant who does not fit the norm for a given institution. For example, the Equitable Savings Bank in Milwaukee states that applicants should "have good character" and "a good reputation" and emphasizes that underwriters should use "GOOD JUDGMENT AND COMMON SENSE."

Underwriting guidelines of related institutions frequently discourage lenders from making particular loans. Requirements of private mortgage insurance companies and guidelines of secondary mortgage market institutions (for example, Federal National Mortgage Association, Government National Mortgage Association, Federal Home Loan Mortgage Corporation) where lenders frequently sell their mortgages are often more restrictive than those of the originating lenders. One consequence is fewer loans to minority neighborhoods.

Even when the underwriting rules themselves are objective, the traditional culture of many lending institutions can shape the review process in a manner that adversely affects racial minorities. Most lenders prominently post signs indicating that they are equal opportunity lenders. But old ways die hard. Mortgage loan applications contain a wealth of information. While the information may be objective, evaluating the total package and making a final decision often entail subjective dimensions. If the underwriting standards are objective, inconsistent use of those standards frequently has racial effects. Overt racial prejudice clearly has not disappeared. Anecdotes are still reported from mortgage-lending test audits where blacks are directed to a lender's mortgage corporation whereas whites are encouraged to apply at the bank that both testers initially contacted. In some cases blacks are steered to other lenders, which make FHA loans, while whites are encouraged to apply for conventional financing. In other instances blacks are told it would be a lengthy process to determine if they qualify for a loan, while whites are assured it will take only a few minutes (Center for Community Change 1989; Lawton 1993). Some lenders are more likely to require credit checks for minority applicants than for nonminorities. Where substantial cash is available to the applicant for the down payment, questions are more likely to be asked about how a minority family was able to accumulate the money, under the rarely stated but frequently suspected belief that in the case of minorities, the money may have been derived from an unlawful source. In other cases, nonminority applications may be more closely scrutinized in order to determine if there are factors that may compensate for specific problems that might arise. For example, if the debt-to-income ratio is slightly higher than a lender's standards normally require, the lender might decide that a stable employment record, excellent credit record, or high down payment might compensate for potential problems posed by the ratio. Lenders are more likely to look for such factors and to work with the applicant to secure a favorable outcome in the case of nonminorities (Peterson 1990). The small number of minorities employed in lending institutions exacerbates these problems. In 1989 approximately 10 percent of officials and managers employed by banks and savings and loans were minority (U.S. Equal Employment Opportunity Commission 1989). And even when one out of ten loan officers is nonwhite, applications brought in by that person are frequently scrutinized more carefully than others, often adversely affecting minority home seekers (Peterson 1990).

Unflattering racial stereotypes may have faded from the nation's financial institutions, but they have not disappeared. In a recent series of focus group interviews in twelve cities lenders were asked what distinguished black and white neighborhoods. Several pointed to "pride of ownership" and "home owner mentality," which they believed were more pervasive in white communities (ICF Incorporated 1991).

Lax law enforcement by federal fair housing and financial regulatory agencies is another critical factor in the perpetuation of racially discriminatory housing finance, leading one legal expert to conclude that "'federal fair housing enforcement effort,' like such terms as 'military justice' and 'honest lawyer,' is an oxymoron" (Kushner 1988, 348). HUD's limited enforcement activity, described earlier, applies to its oversight activity related to financial institutions as well as real estate agents, property insurers, and other providers of housing-related services. The major federal financial regulatory agencies (that is, Office of the Comptroller of the Currency, Federal Deposit Insurance Corporation, Federal Reserve System, Office of Thrift Supervision, formerly the Federal Home Loan Bank Board) have been similarly inactive in their enforcement responsibilities under the CRA, Equal Credit Opportunity Act, Federal Fair Housing Act, and other rules.

One reason is their tendency to minimize prevailing fair lending problems while emphasizing "safety and soundness" matters in their regulatory activities.

In 1989 a member of the Board of Governors of the Federal Reserve System told a subcommittee of the House Banking, Housing, and Urban Affairs Subcommittee, "Personally, I find it difficult to reconcile the notion that there is widespread racial discrimination in mortgage lending with the fact that bankers want to make loans . . . I find the industry strongly committed as a matter of self-interest to make every sound loan possible." (LaWare 1990, 6). One year earlier the Comptroller of the Currency stated "banks historically have helped to meet local community credit needs, consistent with safety and soundness requirements, and they continue to do so" (Dane 1991, 262).

At least in part because of these attitudes, the regulatory agencies have not used enforcement tools that have proven so effective in private litigation. Minimal use of statistical analysis, testing, and the effects test (defined by the FDIC as "conduct which has a disproportionate adverse impact on a protected group or which has the effect of perpetuating segregated housing . . . regardless of intent" [Seidman 1990, 69]) are some of those tools that have not been adequately employed by HUD, Justice, and financial regulatory agencies (Dane 1991, 1989; Schwemm 1989). In fact, it was only following a lawsuit (*Urban League et al. v. Comptroller of the Currency et al.*; U.S. District Court for the District of Columbia, C.A. No. 76.0718) by a coalition of civil rights groups that the financial regulatory agencies even promulgated regulations to enforce the CRA, the Fair Housing Act, the Equal Credit Opportunity Act, and other federal fair lending rules (Dane 1991, 261).

There is evidence that some federal agencies may become more aggressive in the future. At a 1992 conference on housing discrimination research sponsored by the Federal National Mortgage Association (Fannie Mae), the chairman and chief executive officer of the association concluded, "The papers presented today make clear that discrimination continues to limit access to housing and mortgage credit for many citizens. The challenge now facing the housing community is to fashion solutions that remedy these disturbing findings" (Federal National Mortgage Association 1992). HUD recently sponsored a nationwide testing program in mortgage lending, and the U.S. Department of Justice settled the first pattern and practice lawsuit brought by the federal government against a mortgage lender, resulting in $1 million for forty-eight black applicants rejected by the bank and several changes in the lender's underwriting, marketing, and employment practices (U.S. Department of Justice 1992). And the Office of the Comptroller of the Currency, which regulates national banks, announced in May 1993 that by the end of the year it would develop a pilot program to use testers as part of its efforts to explore two related issues: (1) whether loan applicants with the same qualifications achieve the same results regardless of race or national origin and (2) whether banks provide the same levels of assistance to minority and nonminority applicants during the loan process (Comptroller of the Currency 1993).

Yet enforcement of fair housing and fair lending rules has been spotty at best. The financial regulatory agencies responsible for compliance with the CRA have been the least sympathetic to equal opportunity matters among those with fair lending enforcement authority. The CRA has proven to be a valuable resource. However, as one observer noted, "the driving force behind the successful implementation of the CRA's purposes has been activist community organizations" (Dane 1990, 262).

The focus of most activity has been on mortgage lending. But there is also evidence that racial minorities have encountered discrimination in efforts to secure commercial and other types of business loans, that black-owned businesses receive smaller loans than white-owned businesses with comparable financial characteristics, and that central cities have experienced redlining in these credit areas as well (Updegrave 1989; Bates 1989, 1991). No data set comparable to HMDA is publicly available to allow for analysis of business lending similar to the research that has been conducted on mortgage loans. Yet it is evident that successful community reinvestment requires access to business as well as home loans. If HMDA, CRA, and related laws pertaining to fair lending were motivated primarily by concerns over discrimination in mortgage lending, they have also been used to stimulate commercial and business loans in distressed communities.

THE REALITY OF REINVESTMENT

The existence of laws alone, of course, is rarely sufficient to significantly alter behavior. But as part of a diversified tool kit, CRA has proven critical in successful efforts to secure new dollars for home financing and community reinvestment generally for residents of low- and moderate-income areas, many of which have large minority populations, in cities throughout the country. Working with knowledgeable reporters in local print and electronic media, supportive academic researchers, aggressive labor and church groups, and sympathetic local and state officials, many community-based organizations have used the information available through HMDA and leverage provided by CRA to stimulate reinvestment activities in dozens of cities. The following stories are illustrative.

CHICAGO

The city of Chicago has perhaps the longest history of effective grassroots community organizing. Prior to HMDA and CRA, community groups used a variety of Alinsky-style direct-action tactics to bring banks to the negotiating table. These included picket lines, disruption of normal business by dropping hundreds of pennies on the floors of bank lobbies at peak hours, and flooding bank offices with people who opened and closed accounts for one dollar. One Chicago community group, the Organization of the NorthEast, negotiated a written reinvestment agreement with the Bank of Chicago in 1974, three years before the CRA was enacted, following a citizen-organized direct-action campaign against the bank.

Community-based organizations in that city led the political fights to secure passage of HMDA and CRA, and Chicago-area community organizations were among the first to use these laws subsequent to their passage. In 1984 the Community Reinvestment Alliance, a coalition of more than thirty community organizations, negotiated agreements totaling $173 million over five years with three major banks in that city; First Chicago, Harris Bank, and Northern Trust. In 1988 and 1989 all three announced extensions of these agreements for an additional five-year commitment of $200 million. (Agreements were also subsequently signed with several smaller community banks and community groups throughout the city.) The agreements, known as the Neighborhood Lending Program, called for specific types of loans and for particular dollar amounts in designated areas. This program created new dollars for mortgages, home improvement loans, home equity loans, business and commercial loans, mixed-use real estate financing, and other types of housing and commercial lending. Community groups play central roles in designing the loan programs, packaging the loans, and monitoring the agreements. Review boards consisting of community and banking members have been established to provide accountability and oversee implementation of the agreements. To strengthen the capacity of the community members of these partnerships, the three banks have committed up to $3 million in direct grants from their foundations for those involved in housing and business development. Many of the elements of the Chicago programs have served as role models nationwide and have been incorporated in agreements signed in many other cities (Bradford 1990b; National Council for Urban Economic Development undated; Pogge 1992).

BOSTON

A study for the Federal Reserve Bank of Boston triggered a major reinvestment commitment by that city's ten largest banks (Bradbury, Case, and Dunham 1989). In their research for the Federal Reserve, three economists analyzed mortgage lending patterns between 1982 and 1987 and found a substantial disparity in lending activity between predominantly black and predominantly white neighborhoods. This gap persisted after various nonracial characteristics that could account for differences in lending across neighborhoods were taken into consideration. The key finding was that the ratio of mortgage loans to potentially mortgageable housing was 24 percent higher in white areas, after controlling such factors as family income and wealth, housing value and age, vacancy rates, new housing construction, and other economic and demographic factors. Shortly after the press releases were issued announcing the findings of this study, six community organizations formed the Community Investment Coalition. After months of public pressure and private negotiations, and with the aggressive support of Mayor Raymond Flynn, Boston's ten largest banks and the community coalition announced a $400 million five-year lending program. The program includes increased dollars for mortgage loans (some at below-market rates) in inner-city communities, funds for new construction of affordable housing, new branch banks, and improved services for inner-city residents, including cashing of welfare and social security checks, additional automatic teller machines, expanded services, and others (Campen 1990a).

ATLANTA

A Pulitzer Prize-winning series of newspaper articles, "The Color of Money" (Dedman 1988), stimulated a $65 million lending agreement among several banks in Atlanta. With the assistance of Calvin Bradford of Community Reinvestment Associates and Charles Finn of the Hubert Humphrey Institute at the University of Minnesota, reporter Bill Dedman found that whites received five times as many home loans as blacks with similar incomes. The *Atlanta Journal/Constitution* series stimulated widespread debate in that city. State banking regulators called for more stringent rules governing lending. The Fulton County Commission unanimously approved a fair housing ordinance. And a coalition of neighborhood groups, the Atlanta Community Reinvestment Alliance, filed a series of CRA challenges. While refuting accusations of racism, the city's major lenders agreed to a reinvestment program that included the creation of a $20 million loan pool by nine lenders targeted to working-class neighborhoods, a $25 million commitment for low-interest loans for home purchase and home improvement for families with incomes below $35,000 in any community by Citizens and Southern Bank, a similar $10 million commitment from First Atlanta Bank, and a $10 million program with low-interest loans in targeted areas from Trust Company Bank.

DETROIT

In Detroit a 1988 newspaper series, "The Race for Money," also played a major role in launching a $2.9 billion lending program in that city. *Detroit Free Press* reporter David Everett led an investigation, again with the help of Bradford and Finn, which found that local lenders were not as heavily involved in major local development projects as were other lenders in major cities nationwide, Detroit lenders had low participation in government loan programs designed to help individuals and businesses experiencing difficulty securing conventional loans, and mortgage loan patterns were racially biased favoring white home owners. The Ad Hoc Coalition for Fair Banking practices, including an array of housing groups, the United Auto Workers, the NAACP, churches, New Detroit Inc. (a powerful civic organization including leaders with Detroit's business, political, and cultural institutions), and others, was formed to negotiate more support from local lenders. Aggressive implementation of a state community reinvestment act by Eugene Kuthy, commissioner of the Michigan Financial Institutions Bureau from 1983 to 1990, also served as a critical catalyst. When Kuthy denied an application by Comerica Inc., the second-largest banking company in Michigan, to purchase a Texas bank because of a poor CRA record, the negotiations began. Altogether seven institutions—Comerica, First America Bank of Southeast Michigan, Manufacturers National Bank, Michigan National Bank, First Federal of Michigan, Standard Federal Bank, and National Bank of Detroit—agreed to a total of $2.9 billion over three years in a combination of housing, business, and consumer loans. It is estimated that this will amount to an increase of $350 million in new loans that otherwise would not have been made, with at least $70 million for new home mortgage loans. Perhaps more importantly, what began as a most contentious adversarial process has evolved into a collaborative effort to reinvest in Detroit (Everett 1992).

PITTSBURGH

In Pittsburgh a coalition of twenty-three community development corporations used leverage provided by the CRA to negotiate a $109 million five-year neighborhood reinvestment agreement with Union National Bank (UNB). The Pittsburgh Community Reinvestment Group (PCRG) secured financing for conventional home mortgages, commercial real estate, and minority business development. In addition the bank agreed to implement CRA training for its personnel, improved branch banking services, and affirmative action hiring. Direct grants are also provided to fund operating costs of community development corporations in Pittsburgh. Implementation of the UNB agreement was followed by successful negotiations with several additional banks and savings and loans in that community (Metzger 1990).

MILWAUKEE

A coalition of community-based organizations in Milwaukee negotiated $50 million in lending agreements with that city's third-largest bank in 1986 (Marine Corporation later changed to Bank One when Marine was taken over by Banc One Corporation) and its largest savings and loan (First Financial) in 1989. In addition to a variety of loan and banking service commitments, the bank agreed to open a new inner-city branch and the thrift agreed to an affirmative action hiring plan.

The 1989 *Atlanta Journal/Constitution* (Dedman 1989) news story generated additional interest when it reported that Milwaukee had the highest racial disparity in mortgage loan rejection rates of any city nationwide. (Blacks were rejected four times as often as whites in Milwaukee compared to a 2-to-1 ratio nationwide.) Milwaukee's Democratic mayor and the state's Republican governor created a Fair Lending Action Committee (FLAC) consisting of lenders, regulators, civil rights groups, city officials, and other community organizations to formulate a plan to increase lending to racial minorities. A set of twenty-eight recommendations was developed, including specific numerical goals for residential and commercial real estate, as well as business loans for racial minorities in the Milwaukee metropolitan area.

While implementation of these recommendations has proceeded slowly, FLAC has helped spur related reinvestment efforts. In part because of disappointment in the efficacy of FLAC, a Fair Lending Coalition (initially called the Fair Lending Project) was formed in 1990 under which a variety of neighborhood associations, civil rights organizations, churches, labor unions, faculty and graduate students at a local university, and others began meeting with individual lenders to negotiate lending programs. With the assistance of the Fair Lending Coalition, Norwest Bank launched a $25 million program including residential and commercial lending objectives, a feasibility study for a new inner-city branch, and outreach efforts to increase minority employment. Equitable Savings Bank agreed to a $7 million program in addition to several new marketing tactics. For example, brochures describing bank products will be distributed in several languages including Spanish, Laotian, and Hmong. And the bank will work with five central city employers to assist their employees in purchasing homes near their place of work (Glabere 1992). Five other formal agreements have been negotiated totaling over $40 million in commitments for central city mortgage and business loans, an additional branch bank, and additional changes in marketing and employment practices (Norman 1992, 1993; *The Business Journal* 1993; copies of the original agreements are available in author's files). Other lenders, on their own initiative, have contacted the coalition to develop similar reinvestment programs. While some lenders expressed concern with some tactics of the Fair Lending Coalition, clearly its aggressive approach has been critical to its success. As the headline of an editorial by the local business newspaper read, "'Confrontational' style is lending project's strength" (*The Business Journal* 1992, 4).

OTHER COMMUNITIES

There are many other examples where community groups have used similar tactics to achieve similar results. In Cincinnati, Communities United for Action secured a $113 million five-year agreement with the four major banks in that city (Braykovich 1990). In Dallas, ACORN negotiated an agreement with Texas Commerce Bank for $2.5 million in mortgage and home improvement loans. ACORN and the Innercity Development Corporation then negotiated a $25 million five-year agreement with RepublicBank, subsequently taken over by North Carolina National Bank, which has agreed to honor the commitment. In Dayton, Ohio, the city government and seven participating banks announced a Neighborhood Lending Program with a goal of investing $10 million in housing in selected city neighborhoods. In Denver ACORN negotiated a three-year $5.4 million program with United Bank of Denver for residential lending. Two CRA agreements in Washington, D.C., culminated in five-year lending commitments: $10 million by United Virginia Bankshares (which subsequently changed its name to Crestar) and $40 million by Riggs National Bank. Both programs focus on business and economic development (National Council for Urban Economic Development undated).

Two statewide reinvestment campaigns, one on the East Coast and one on the West Coast, have resulted in major reinvestment commitments. In Florida the state's five largest bank holding companies responded to a request from Legal Services with a statewide lending agreement. Though no dollar amounts were specified, Legal Services estimates that the five-year programs combined will generate $100 million per year in credit, investments, and contributions to affordable housing initiatives and minority businesses.

In California, organizing on reinvestment issues goes back at least to the 1970s. By the late 1980s a statewide coalition of community-based advocacy groups, local public officials, and consultant organizations negotiated agreements with California lenders totaling over $350 million. Continued efforts by neighborhood groups, regulators, local officials, and industry groups have resulted in more sophisticated monitoring by reinvestment advocates, a range of city programs, and a ten-year $8 billion commitment by three major banks; Bank of America, Security Pacific, and Wells Fargo (National Council for Urban Economic Development undated; Rosen 1992). Reinvestment is occurring, albeit in varying degrees, in communities throughout the United States.

PUBLIC ENTREPRENEURSHIP

Sympathetic public officials have assisted many CRA initiatives. In Boston, for example, Mayor Raymond Flynn took an active leadership role that led directly to that city's $400 -million agreement. In Milwaukee, Mayor John Norquist took the lead in forming the Fair Lending Action Committee, and the city has provided financial support for the Fair Lending Coalition. More entrepreneurial initiatives to stimulate reinvestment have been launched by these and many other local officials.

Boston and Milwaukee are two of at least twelve cities, and Massachusetts is one of at least fourteen states, which have recently implemented linked deposit programs under which depositories of public funds are required to have a good community reinvestment record. At the end of 1989, state and local government deposits totaled $73 billion, over 2 percent of all deposits held by depository institutions (Campen 1990b). The criteria vary among the different linked deposit programs. They include a commitment to mortgage lending in low- and moderate-income areas, loans to minority- and female-owned businesses, affirmative action and equal opportunity in employment, ongoing communication with community groups to assess credit needs, participation in publicly sponsored low- and moderate-income lending programs, and contributions to community philanthropic activities. Given lenders' concerns with public relations (and their desires to achieve a good CRA rating) simply publicizing relative reinvestment performances of local lenders can be beneficial.

A related and potentially more effective dimension of linked deposit programs occurs when other institutions, such as union pension funds, religious organizations, nonprofit agencies, and individual savers, follow their city's lead (or sometimes precede city action) by depositing their funds with more responsive lenders. These institutions, in fact, control far more deposits than do state and local governments. Accurate and widely publicized reporting of lender reinvestment records by the public sector can significantly strengthen these activities. While no systematic evidence has been compiled on the extent of these efforts, such greenlining campaigns have substantially expanded the pool of capital for reinvestment.

Various approaches have been used in recent years to increase the availability of housing and community development finance, with CRA organizing campaigns being perhaps the most notable. Most are too recent to permit systematic evaluation. One conclusion that can be drawn, however, is that these local community-based efforts would be strengthened considerably by a more aggressive approach on the part of federal regulatory agencies.

THE FUTURE OF FAIR LENDING AND COMMUNITY REINVESTMENT

Successful local reinvestment efforts offer promise for the future. But that future is clouded by recent trends toward centralization, globalization, and homogenization of the nation's financial industries and the push for deregulation, justified by many within these institutions as essential for meeting foreign competition and maximizing the efficiency with which capital is invested. With a strong federal CRA enforcement effort, however, such restructuring may offer even greater opportunities for reinvestment.

Financial institutions have responded to increasing foreign competition and declining profitability in recent years in part with increasing merger activity, acquisitions, and concentration generally, nurtured by deregulation. One concrete result of these developments has been a declining number of lenders—from 20,000 in the early 1970s to 16,000 in 1990 (Bradford and Cincotta 1992)—and increasing concentration among those remaining competitors. Lenders claim they need more flexibility if they are going to be able to compete in the new world market. Deregulation, permitting thrifts and commercial banks to enter financial services (for example, commercial real estate development for thrifts and insurance for commercial banks) and geographic locations (via expansion of interstate and international banking) previously closed to them under the post-Depression financial industry regulatory structure that was established and held firm through the early 1980s, has been demanded and, in large part, granted though large commercial banks are seeking even greater regulatory relief (Meyerson 1986; Labaton 1991). The recent merger of two of the nation's ten largest banks, Chemical Bank and Manufacturers Hanover Trust, is both a symbolic and substantive indication of recent developments within financial institutions. Prior to the merger, Chemical Bank, with $72.5 billion in assets, was the nation's seventh-largest bank. Manufacturer's Hanover Trust, with $64.8 billion, was the eighth largest. After the merger, with $137.3 billion, the newly formed bank was the nation's second largest (Quint 1991).

Deregulation, concentration, and globalization of financial institutions raises serious questions about the availability of funds to finance home ownership, particularly for low-income families, as the ties between particular institutions and communities are weakened. When lenders who previously devoted substantial resources for home mortgages offer new products and enter new markets, housing investment becomes one of several options that must compete with virtually all other types of investment. If suburban shopping malls in San Diego or steel production in Seoul become more attractive investments for financial institutions than housing, then that is where capital will flow. The movement of capital through various circuits is expedited, along with the instability it breeds at the neighborhood level, particularly in already depressed urban communities. In recent years savings and loans have indeed diversified out of housing as the percentage of thrift investments in residential real estate declined from 80 percent in 1978 to 54 percent in 1988 (U.S. League of Savings Institutions 1990, 30). And, as many savings and loans in the United States have demonstrated, deregulation can result in lenders entering markets unwisely, leading to the bankruptcy of their institutions (Pizzo, Fricker, and Muolo 1989). In general, concentration of financial institutions tends to result in increasing costs for customers (U.S. House 1991). One direct consequence is the increasing unaffordability of housing, rising homelessness, and related problems discussed earlier.

At least at the present time, however, applications for mergers, acquisitions, and other changes in business operations must be approved by federal financial regulatory agencies that are charged by law to consider CRA performance in each application. Restructuring of U.S. financial institutions can present opportunities to enhance fair lending and reinvestment, if key regulatory agencies take a more aggressive approach to their CRA responsibilities.

Several specific steps could be taken to immediately improve the effectiveness of fair lending law enforcement. Other more ambitious steps could be taken over a longer period of time, but would assure the permanence of the incremental gains that are being made.

First, pre-purchase counseling could be expanded, particularly for the benefit of first-time buyers, to help more renters become home owners and to assure that they purchase homes they can afford to maintain. Congress could authorize increased funding for community-based nonprofit organizations currently providing these services, and counseling could be included as an activity that would be considered by financial regulatory agencies in determining CRA ratings of lenders and evaluating challenges to their performance (Bradford 1990a, 5).

Law enforcement agencies could more aggressively monitor current lending policies and practices by conducting their own analyses of HMDA and other data that they collect. Rather than simply responding to complaints, applications, or CRA challenges, the agencies could identify potential problem areas through statistical analyses. Only within the past two or three years have financial regulatory agencies begun to make use of such tools and to complement their complaint investigations with agency-initiated investigations into these issues (Dane 1991, 120-21; Chud and Bonnette 1993; Goldstein 1993). While the use of statistics alone may not prove unlawful discrimination, such studies can help agencies target scarce law enforcement resources.

Far more comprehensive and effective use could be made of testing for mortgage lending bias by law enforcement agencies. Statistical analyses of mortgage lending patterns can be particularly useful in determining where testing would be most productively used. Agencies themselves could perform the tests, and increased funds could be made available to those private agencies that have demonstrated the capacity to use this tool (Smith 1990, 268–70; Smith and Cloud 1993; Fishbein 1990, 176–77; Lawton 1993; Leeds 1993; Wallace et al. 1985). Over the past two years HUD has provided increasing funding for private fair housing groups to conduct testing programs, including tests of mortgage lenders. (The U.S. Equal Employment Opportunity Commission now accepts charges based on testing evidence and has issued guidelines on their use, testifying to the utility of testing as an enforcement tool in the area of equal employment opportunity [U.S. Equal Employment Opportunity Commission 1990]). Again, however, federal financial regulatory agencies have been slow to follow this lead (Relman 1991, 111–12; Dane 1991, 123–24). Testing could be an effective instrument for public officials in monitoring lending patterns, assessing individual complaints, documenting unlawful lending practices, and assuring compliance with court orders, regulatory agency rulings, and court decrees (The Rockefeller Foundation and The Urban Institute 1991).

Coupled with the use of statistics and testing would be greater use of the effects test in law enforcement activities. Underwriting rules that adversely affect minority or low-income mortgage loan applicants, such as minimum loan amounts, closing costs, interest rates tied to size of loan, or use of age alone as a criterion, could be prohibited (Dane 1989; Relman 1991, 117).

One extremely simple step would be to provide routine mandatory disclosure of appraisal reports for buyers and their brokers. Given the central role of the appraisal in underwriting decisions and the fact that mortgage applicants pay for this service, public disclosure would be a logical step. Knowing that these reports would be disclosed, lenders would take greater care in assuring the accuracy of reports on which they base adverse decisions, and appraisers would likely provide more objective and reliable information (Fishbein 1990).

A valuable additional area of disclosure would be commercial loans. Availability of mortgage loans, in the absence of adequate credit for commercial businesses, would only temporarily delay disinvestment in both business and home lending. Disclosure of business loans, and use of that data in enforcement activities, would facilitate many current reinvestment efforts.

CRA requirements could be applied to other types of financial institutions, including insurers, finance companies, mutual funds, mortgage banks, brokerage firms, and others (Campen 1993). In June 1993 the Treasury Department announced that it would launch a study to assess whether or not money market funds, consumer financing companies, and automobile finance companies should be required to comply with the CRA. Frank N. Newman, Undersecretary for Domestic Finance, observed that as nonbanking institutions like these grow, in part by attracting funds that previously would have been deposited with commercial banks or thrifts, they become increasingly significant actors in the larger economy and, therefore, it is appropriate to determine what their community reinvestment responsibilities ought to be (Greenhouse 1993). Such financial institutions could bring additional resources to the reinvestment effort, and appropriate regulatory action would encourage movement in that direction.

Employment practices by mortgage lenders and other financial institutions could be brought under the auspices of CRA. Existence (or nonexistence) of effective affirmative action plans could be incorporated as one of the criteria on which CRA ratings and reviews of CRA challenges would be considered. Lenders participating in federal insurance programs could be viewed and treated like federal contractors and, therefore, required to meet the affirmative action and equal employment opportunity responsibilities that contractors must meet under Executive Order 11246.

Penalties for violation of fair lending laws could be strengthened. One sanction regulatory agencies could invoke would be to cancel or increase the cost of federal depository insurance for any lender who violated fair lending or community reinvestment laws (Bradford 1990a, 3–4). Such a tool could be used flexibly to assure that the punishment was commensurate with the violation. Criminal laws could be enacted that would result in forfeiture of property sold or financed in violation of fair housing or fair lending laws and revocation of licenses of real estate brokers, lenders, and others who facilitate such transactions (Zarembka 1990, 117–18).

Other longer-term policies should be considered. Greater effectiveness and efficiencies would be obtained by combining all fair lending and community reinvestment rules into one statute administered by one agency (Dane and Henderson 1990, 224–28). While lending expertise would obviously be required, the focus of the agency's work should be civil rights law enforcement. Among those who currently have civil rights compliance responsibilities in these areas, HUD might be the appropriate department to house such a consolidated law enforcement effort.

To dramatically increase the supply of credit for low-income and other depressed neighborhoods, a simple, yet comprehensive, and probably politically unfeasible approach in the current climate would be the creation of publicly funded nonprofit housing banks. Without the pressure to generate profits, interest rates sufficient to cover the costs of administration and the risk of bad loans could be reduced, to as low as 2 or 3 percent according to some experts (Zarembka 1991). Savings over the life of a loan would be significant. For example, a twenty-five-year $40,000 loan at 12 percent would cost $86,300 over the life of the loan compared with $10,860 at 2 percent. Capitalization for such banks could come from the elimination of mortgage interest and real estate tax deductions for wealthy home owners, deposits from some tax exempt organizations in return for their exemption, and high capital gains taxes on short-term speculative real estate transactions. Political resistance would be expected from several quarters. But as the costs of the savings and loan bailout increase, while increasing numbers of families are priced out of home ownership, that resistance might quickly fade. If such a proposal is not feasible today, debate over President Clinton's call for a series of development banks may lead to a discussion along these lines within a few years.

These federal initiatives would complement the many local and state efforts, both public and private, that have grown in recent years. And expansion of these experiments would feed back into further recommendations for federal initiatives, thus strengthening fair lending and reinvestment activities at all levels nationwide.

It is doubtful that current dependence on private initiatives can lead to adequate law enforcement, or that such privatization is good for the economy, except perhaps for a few special interests in the very short run. The limits on private civil rights law enforcement generally or fair lending in particular are severe. Many victims do not even know that they in fact are being victimized. Many who are aware of the injustice they suffer do not have the funds to take legal action, nor do they have access to a fair housing center that can act for them. Among those with the means, many simply do not have the time or energy to invest in a lawsuit (Schwemm 1987, 379–81). Private action will always be a vital part of fair lending and reinvestment law enforcement.

Many of these recommendations would meet with at least initial resistance, particularly from representatives of the lending industry. CRA and related fair lending activities have often been initiated amid great conflict, frequently generating even more personal and institutional antagonism in the early stages. Yet those animosities have often been overcome by community organizers and lenders, who came to perceive common interests. Many lenders who have worked with community organizations and fair housing groups have found those relationships quite productive, eventually recognizing no conflict between their business interests and the community needs. Fair lending, community reinvestment, and balanced development of metropolitan areas are in the long-term interests of most if not all parties to these debates. The health of the nation's cities depends on achieving these goals.

REFERENCES

Art, Robert C. 1987. Social responsibility in bank credit decisions: The Community Reinvestment Act one decade later. *Pacific Law Journal* 18:1071–1139.

Babcock, Frederick. 1932. *The valuation of real estate.* New York: McGraw-Hill.

Banker, John. 1993. Let free market, not the CRA, be the regulator. *The Business Journal,* 16 January.

Bates, Timothy. 1991. Commercial bank financing of white- and black-owned small business start ups. *Quarterly Review of Business and Economics* 31 (Spring): 64–80.

———. 1989. The changing nature of minority business: A comparative analysis of asian, nonminority, and black-owned businesses. *The Review of Black Political Economy* 18 (2): 25–42.

Bradbury, Katherine L., Karl E. Case, and Constance R. Dunham. 1989. Geographic patterns of mortgage lending in Boston, 1982-1987. *New England Economic Review* (September/October): 3–30.

Bradford, Calvin. 1992. *Community reinvestment agreement library.* Des Plaines, Ill.: Community Reinvestment Associates.

———. 1990a. Housing finance and race: A time to end the dual market. Unpublished manuscript.

———. 1990b. *Partnership for reinvestment: An evaluation of the Chicago neighborhood lending programs.* Chicago: National Training and Information Center.

Bradford, Calvin, and Gale Cincotta. 1992. The legacy, the promise, and the unfinished agenda. In *From redlining to reinvestment: Community responses to urban disinvestment,* edited by Gregory D. Squires. Philadelphia: Temple University Press.

Braykovich, Mark. 1990. Cincy group inks major reinvestment agreements. *Disclosure* 119 (November-December): 4–5.

The Business Journal. 1993. Guaranty Bank makes $15 million pledge. *The Business Journal,* 5 June.

———. 1992. "Confrontational" style is lending project's strength. *The Business Journal,* 9 March.

Campen, James T. 1993. Banks, communities, and public policy. Working Paper Series, Department of Economics, University of Massachusetts at Boston.

———. 1990a. Payment due. *Dollars & Sense,* April.

———. 1990b. The political economy of linked deposit banking programs. Paper presented at the meetings of the Union for Radical Political Economics/Allied Social Sciences Associations, 28 December, Washington, D.C.

Canner, Glenn B., and Dolores Smith. 1992. Expanded HMDA data: One year later. *Federal Reserve Bulletin,* November.

———. 1991. Home Mortgage Disclosure Act: Expanded data on residential lending. *Federal Bulletin,* November.

Center for Community Change. 1989. *Mortgage lending discrimination testing project.* Washington, D.C.: Center for Community Change and U.S. Department of Housing and Urban Development.

Chud, Ann, and Hal Bonnette. 1993. Targeting a lending discrimination investigation. Paper presented at the Home Mortgage Lending and Discrimination Conference, U.S. Department of Housing and Urban Development and the Office of the Comptroller of the Currency, 18–19 May, Washington, D.C.

Comptroller of the Currency. 1993. OCC to use new examinations to identify loan discrimination. News release, 5 May. Washington, D.C.

Dane, Stephen M. 1991. Federal enforcement of the Fair Lending, Equal Credit Opportunity, and Community Reinvestment laws: 1989-1990. In *Lost opportunities: The civil rights record of the Bush administration mid-term,* edited by Susan M. Liss and William L. Taylor. Washington, D.C.: Citizens Commission on Civil Rights.

———. 1989. Federal enforcement of the Fair Lending, Equal Credit Opportunity, and Community Reinvestment laws in the 1980s. In *One nation, indivisible: The civil rights challenges of the 1990s,* edited by Reginald C. Govan and William L. Taylor. Washington, D.C.: Citizens Commission on Civil Rights.

Dane, Stephen M., and Wade J. Henderson. 1990. Statement of the Leadership Conference on Civil Rights concerning mortgage discrimination. *Discrimination in Mortgage Lending,* hearing before the Subcommittee on Consumer and Regulatory Affairs of the Committee on Banking, Housing and Urban Affairs of the U.S. Senate. Washington, D.C.: U.S. Government Printing Office.

Dedman, Bill. 1989. Blacks turned down for home loans from S&Ls twice as often as whites. *Atlanta Journal/Constitution,* 22 January.

———. 1988. The color of money. *Atlanta Journal/Constitution,* 1–16 May.

Elverman, Tim. 1990. Interview by Sally O'Connor. 14 September.

Everett, David. 1992. Confrontation, negotiation, and collaboration: Detroit's multi billion dollar agreement. In *From redlining to reinvestment,* edited by Gregory D. Squires. Philadelphia: Temple University Press.

Fair Lending Action Committee. 1989. *Equal access to mortgage lending: The Milwaukee plan.* Report of the Fair Lending Action Committee to Mayor John Norquist of Milwaukee and Governor Tommy G. Thompson.

Federal National Mortgage Association. 1992. Fannie Mae's Fourth Annual Housing Conference Presents Leading Research on Housing Discrimination. News release, May 19. Washington, D.C.

Fishbein, Allen. 1990. Mortgage lending discrimination and fair lending enforcement. *Discrimination in Home Mortgage Lending,* hearing before the Subcommittee on Consumer and Regulatory Affairs of the Committee on Banking, Housing, and Urban Affairs of the U.S. Senate, 16 May. Washington, D.C.: U.S. Government Printing Office.

Galster, George C. 1991a. Black suburbanization: Has it changed the relative location of races? *Urban Affairs Quarterly* 26 (4): 621–28.

———. 1991b. Statistical proof of discrimination in home mortgage lending. *Banking Financial Services* 7 (20): 187–97.

Glabere, Michael L. 1992. Milwaukee: A tale of three cities. In *From redlining to reinvestment: Community responses to urban disinvestment,* edited by Gregory D. Squires. Philadelphia: Temple University Press.

Goldstein, Ira J. 1993. Methods for identifying lenders for investigation under the Fair Housing Act. Home Mortgage Lending and Discrimination Conference, U.S. Department of Housing and Urban Development and Office of the Comptroller of the Currency, 18-19 May, Washington, D.C.

Greene, Zina G. 1980. *Lender's guide to fair mortgage policies.* Washington, D.C.: The Potomac Institute.

Greenhouse, Steven. 1993. Nonbanks' community role will be target of U.S. study. *New York Times,* 9 June.

Hoyt, Homer. 1933. *One hundred years of land values in Chicago.* Chicago: University of Chicago Press.

ICF Incorporated. 1991. *The secondary mortgage market and community lending through lenders' eyes.* Report prepared for the Federal Home Loan Mortgage Corporation. Fairfax, Va.: ICF Incorporated.

Jackson, Kenneth T. 1985. *Crabgrass frontier: The suburbanization of the United States.* New York: Oxford University Press.

Judd, Dennis R. 1984. *Politics of American cities: Private power and public policy.* Boston: Little, Brown.

Kohn, Ernest. 1993. The New York State banking study: Research on mortgage discrimination. Home Mortgage Lending and Discrimination Conference, U.S. Department of Housing and Urban Development and the Office of the Comptroller of the Currency, 18–19 May, Washington, D.C.

Kushner, James A. 1988. An unfinished agenda: The federal fair housing enforcement effort. *Yale Law and Policy Review* 6 (2): 38–60.

Labaton, Stephen. 1991. Administration presents its plan for broad overhaul of banking. *New York Times,* 6 February.

LaWare, John P. 1990. Statement before the Subcommittee on Consumer and Regulatory Affairs of the Committee on Banking, Housing, and Urban Affairs of the United States Senate, hearing on *Discrimination in Home Mortgage Lending.* Washington, D.C.: U.S. Government Printing Office.

Lawton, Rachel. 1993. Pre-application mortgage lending testing program: Lender testing by a local agency. Home Mortgage Lending and Discrimination Conference, U.S. Department of Housing and Urban Development and Office of the Comptroller of the Currency, 18-19 May, Washington D.C.

Leeds, Barry. 1993. Testing for discrimination during the pre-application and post-application phases of mortgage lending. Home Mortgage Lending and Discrimination Conference, U.S. Department of Housing and Urban Development and Office of the Comptroller of the Currency, 18-19 May, Washington, D.C.

Massey, Douglas S., and Nancy A. Denton. 1993. *American apartheid: Segregation and the making of the underclass.* Cambridge, Mass.: Harvard University Press.

Metzger, John T. 1990. The Community Reinvestment Act in the 1990s: Lessons From Pittsburgh. Paper presented to the National Congress for Community Economic Development, 11 November, Boston.

Meyerson, Ann. 1986. Deregulation and the restructuring of the housing finance system. In *Critical perspectives on housing,* edited by Rachel C. Bratt, Chester Hartman, and Ann Meyerson. Philadelphia: Temple University Press.

Munnell, Alicia H., Lynn E. Browne, James McEneaney, and Geoffrey M.B. Tootell. 1992. Mortgage lending in Boston: Interpreting HMDA data. Working Paper Series, Federal Reserve Bank of Boston.

National Community Reinvestment Coalition. 1993. *Community Reinvestment Act fact sheet.* Washington, D.C.: National Community Reinvestment Coalition, n.d.

National Council for Urban Economic Development. *The Community Reinvestment Act and economic development: A profile of community lending in eight cities.* Washington, D.C.

Norman, Jack. 1993. St. Francis, coalition sign deal. *The Milwaukee Journal,* 25 May.

———. 1992. Deal to boost lending reached. *The Milwaukee Journal,* 12 February.

Peterson, Margaret. 1990. Interview by author with Loan Officer for Republic Capital Mortgage Corporation, 12 November.

Pizzo, Stephen, Mary Fricker, and Paul Muolo. 1989. *Inside job: The looting of America's savings and loans.* New York: McGraw Hill.

Pogge, Jean. 1992. Reinvestment in Chicago neighborhoods: A twenty-year struggle. In *From redlining to reinvestment: Community responses to urban disinvestment,* edited by Gregory D. Squires. Philadelphia: Temple University Press.

Quint, Michael. 1991. Big bank merger to join Chemical, Manufacturers. *New York Times,* 16 July.

Relman, John P. 1991. Federal fair housing enforcement under President Bush: An assessment at mid-term and recommendations for the future. In *Lost opportunities: The civil rights record of the Bush administration mid-term,* edited by Susan M. Liss and William L. Taylor. Washington D.C.: Citizens Commission on Civil Rights.

The Rockefeller Foundation and The Urban Institute. 1991. Testing for discrimination in America: Results and policy implications, conference 26 September in Washington, D.C.

Rosen, David. 1992. California: Lessons from statewide advocacy, local govrnment, local government, and private industry initiatives. In *Redlining and reinvestment,* edited by Gregory D. Squires. Philadelphia: Temple University Press.

Schafer, Robert, and Helen F. Ladd 1981. *Discrimination in mortgage lending.* Cambridge: MIT Press.

Schwemm, Robert G. 1993. Housing discrimination and the appraisal industry. Home Mortgage Lending and Discrimination Conference, U.S. Department of Housing and Urban Development and Office of the Comptroller of the Currency, 18-19 May, Washington, D.C.

———. 1989. Federal fair housing enforcement: A critique of the Reagan administration's record and recommendations for the future. In *One nation, indivisible: The civil rights challenge for the 1990s,* edited by Reginald C. Govan and William L. Taylor. Washington, D.C.: Citizens Commission on Civil Rights.

———. 1987. Private enforcement and the Fair Housing Act. *Yale Law & Policy Review* 6 (2): 375–84.

Seidman, L. William. 1990. Testimony prepared for the Subcommittee on Consumer and Regulatory Affairs of the Committee on Banking, Housing, and Urban Affairs, United States Senate, *Discrimination in Home Mortgage Lending.* Washington, D.C.: U.S. Government Printing Office.

Shlay, Anne B. 1989. Financing community: Methods for assessing residential credit disparities, market barriers, and institutional reinvestment performance in the metropolis. *Journal of Urban Affairs* 11 (3): 201–23.

Sloane, Glenda. 1983. Discrimination in home mortgage financing. In *A sheltered crisis: The state of fair housing in the eighties.* Washington, D.C.: U.S. Commission on Civil Rights.

Sloane, Martin E. 1983. Federal housing policy and equal opportunity. In *A sheltered crisis: The state of fair housing in the eighties.* Washington, D.C.: U.S. Commission on Civil Rights.

Smith, Shanna. 1990. Testimony of Shanna L. Smith, representative of the National Fair Housing Alliance, Inc., hearing before the Subcommittee on Consumer and Regulatory Affairs of the Committee on Banking, Housing, and Urban Affairs of the U.S. Senate, *Discrimination in Home Mortgage Lending.* Washington, D.C.: U.S. Government Printing Office.

Smith, Shanna, and Cathy Cloud. 1993. The role of private, non-profit fair housing enforcement organizations in lending testing. Home Mortgage Lending and Discrimination Conference, U.S. Department of Housing and Urban Development and Office of the Comptroller of the Currency, 18-19 May, Washington D.C.

Squires, Gregory D., and William Velez. 1987. Neighborhood racial composition and mortgage lending: City and suburban differences. *Journal of Urban Affairs* 23 (1): 217–32.

Squires, Gregory D., William Velez, and Karl E. Taeuber. 1991. Insurance redlining, agency location, and the process of urban disinvestment. *Urban Affairs Quarterly* 26 (4): 567–88.

Turner, Margery Austin, Raymond J. Struyk, and John Yinger. 1991. *Housing discrimination study.* Washington, D.C.: The Urban Institute.

Updegrade, Walter L. 1989. Race and money. *Money* 18 (12): 152–72.

U.S. Commission on Civil Rights. 1987. Testimony of John J. Knapp before the U.S. Commission on Civil Rights, *Issues in Housing Discrimination,* Vol. 2.

U.S. Department of Justice. 1992. Department of Justice settles first race discrimination lawsuit against major home mortgage lender. News release, 17 September. Washington, D.C.

U.S. Equal Employment Opportunity Commission. 1990. EEOC Notice No. N.915.062, (Nov. 20).

————. 1989. Unpublished data.

U.S. Federal Housing Administration. 1938. *Underwriting manual.* Washington, D.C.: U.S. Government Printing Office.

U. S. House. 1991. Statement of Jonathan Brown before the Committee on Banking, Finance, and Urban Affairs of the U.S. House of Representatives.

U.S. League of Savings Institutions. 1990. *Savings institutions sourcebook.* New York: U.S. League of Savings Institutions.

Wallace, J., W. L. Holshouser, T. S. Lane, and J. Williams. 1985. *The Fair Housing Assistance Program evaluation.* Washington, D.C.: Office of Policy Development and Research, U.S. Department of Housing and Urban Development.

Wienk, Ronald E. 1992. Discrimination in urban credit markets: What we don't know and why we don't know it. *Housing Policy Debate* 3 (2): 217–40.

Zarembka, Arlene. 1991. Housing banks. *The Nation* 252(24): 837.

————. 1990. *The urban housing crisis: Social, economic, and legal issues and proposals.* New York: Greenwood Press.

CHAPTER 12

Residential Apartheid:
Removing the Barriers

by J. Eugene Grigsby, III

Previous chapters in this book leave little doubt that residential separation, particularly between African Americans and whites, persists. Ample documentation has also been presented showing that racial separation is not only harmful to the nation as a whole, but also particularly debilitating to many minorities, who, because they have been relegated to certain neighborhoods, find their life chances severely compromised.

The question before us now is: Can anything be done about this intolerable situation? The skeptics among us are probably dubious. But keep in mind that ten years ago there were not many who would have bet that by 1994 racial apartheid in South Africa would be abolished and that Nelson Mandela would be elected president. Surely, if barriers to that country's separatist system could be removed, then there ought to be hope for us. What will it take? There is no simple solution to this extremely complex issue. But there are a series of steps which, if taken, will retard and perhaps ultimately reduce the degree of racial separation that we now encounter.

LEADERSHIP FROM THE TOP

A major contributing factor to the ultimate downfall of the apartheid scheme in South Africa was the fact that key political and corporate leaders took up the gauntlet and publicly proclaimed that the existence of racial separation—be it official policy or "general practice"—is simply wrong and should not be tolerated. This is precisely what is called for here, starting with the president of the United States and echoed by key corporate leaders.

The reasoning is quite simple. Separate societies are inherently unequal and counterproductive to the well-being of a strong healthy America. As if the riots during the 1960s and the rebellions that started anew in Los

Angeles in 1992 were not sufficient wake-up calls, chilling accounts from Ireland, Bosnia, Rwanda, and the Gaza Strip should serve to remind us that sanctioned separation that disenfranchises people ultimately sows the seeds of destruction.

It has been estimated that the negative effects of racial separation reduces our gross national product by as much as 2 percent per year (Updegrade 1989). It has also been argued that the increased concentration of ethnic minorities, particularly the poor, is the single greatest crisis facing the United States today (Byrum 1992). The crisis in our educational system, mounting crime, and increased violence can all be linked to racial and economic isolation.

Meaningful steps to reduce this isolation will only be sought if those in elected office and/or leaders of our most successful enterprises make it their priority that solutions be forthcoming. This enlightened leadership, of course, will be enhanced by scholars and by civic and civil rights advocates who continue to press the case that racial isolation is not only still with us but is also taking a disastrous toll on our neighborhoods and communities.

Leadership is certainly a prerequisite for action designed to reduce racial isolation. But leadership without institutional action will be virtually meaningless. There are several different areas where institutional action needs to be focused. The first involves information collection and dissemination. A second area for action focuses on removal of barriers inhibiting ethnic minorities from obtaining residential units in locations that they desire. A third action area entails more vigorous enforcement of current laws that prohibit discriminatory practices. A fourth area includes increasing the supply of and accessibility to affordable housing for minorities, particularly those with limited incomes. The fifth area focuses on new forms of incentives that the federal government could initiate in order to forge collaborations between local jurisdictions in seeking ways to reduce racial isolation.

DATA COLLECTION AND INFORMATION DISSEMINATION

Knowledge that a problem exists is a key factor in designing a set of actions to remedy the situation. The following suggestions are some specific activities that could be undertaken to bring to the attention of decision makers in the public and private sectors the magnitude of the problem and some of its consequences for the well-being of neighborhoods and communities across the United States.

Annual Report on the State of Racial Isolation in America: The U.S. Bureau of the Census should produce an annual report that provides data on the progress being made to reduce racial isolation within metropolitan areas throughout the United States.

Urban League State of Black America Report: The National Urban League already produces an annual State of Black America Report. This report, which is released to coincide with the president's State of the Union Address, should periodically take up the issue of racial isolation and its consequences.

Selected Media Stories: Without question, media coverage of the situation in South Africa helped to stimulate debate in this country as to what should be done to improve conditions there. Similarly, well-written stories in prestigious print media such as the *New York Times, The Washington Post, Wall Street Journal, Los Angeles Times, Time Magazine, Newsweek, The Christian Science Monitor,* and so on, could produce similar results. Special in-depth stories by television journals such as *60 Minutes, Date Line,* and *Prime Time Live* would also be beneficial in focusing the nation's attention on this serious problem.

Foundation-Sponsored Research and Demonstration Projects: Foundations, such as Ford and Rockefeller, have the potential to be significant players by sponsoring good research that would document the amount of drag on our economy that occurs when we allow racial isolation to persist. These same foundations could also sponsor demonstration projects and develop case materials, which could in turn serve as models for successfully reducing racial isolation. These case studies would focus on successful examples promoted by the private sector, community-based groups, and government partnerships.

REMOVAL OF INSTITUTIONAL BARRIERS

Throughout this book we have learned of a number of barriers erected by financial institutions, real estate brokers, appraisers, and landlords, barriers that have inhibited minorities from acquiring or renting dwelling units in locations of their choice. Potential solutions to remove some of these barriers have also been presented. Here are some additional thoughts on ways to reduce discriminatory barriers perpetuating racial isolation.

Expansion of HUD/University-Sponsored Consortium: The U.S. Department of Housing and Urban Development (HUD) could expand its efforts to fund universities that work with local governments, private developers, real estate brokers, financial institutions, home owners, and rental associations on techniques for reducing racial isolation. HUD has recently expanded its university initiative program. Future efforts should challenge universities to come up with unique solutions to the problem of racial isolation.

HUD-Sponsored Seminars: HUD could expand its seminar and sponsored-research program to document empirically the benefits of reducing racial isolation. Findings from these endeavors could be presented at various regional forums around the country.

HUD-Sponsored Monitoring Programs: Results from the HUD-sponsored Housing Markets Practices Survey (HMPS) and Housing Discrimination Study (HDS) have been instrumental in documenting the extent of racial isolation. Continued efforts along these lines should help to identify where future intervention could be useful in reducing or eliminating barriers encountered by minorities in the housing market.

Community Reinvestment Accountability: Perhaps one of the most significant legislative initiatives passed in the past two decades was the Community Reinvestment Act (CRA). Armed with this vehicle, community-based groups and legal aid advocates have been able to obtain commitments from major financial institutions to make needed financing available to minority communities. Federal regulatory agencies must continue to be diligent in upholding this act. An opportune time to do this is when these institutions apply for mergers or acquisitions or seek authority to reorganize. Furthermore, appraisal reports, made widely available to buyers and their brokers, could be required to disclose not only CRA performance of the lending institution, but also a range of other relevant data. For example, the employment practices by the mortgage lender could be brought under the umbrella of the CRA, with affirmative action records incorporated as a part of the agency's rating.

Community Partnerships with Financial Institutions: Begrudgingly, many financial institutions are finally taking their CRA commitments seriously. But most are unfamiliar with the rapidly growing number of community-based organizations that have been created in order to address the housing needs of their constituents. These financial institutions should seek out the numerous community development corporations, which exist in most major metropolitan areas, and enlist their aid in developing effective programs to direct lending resources and counseling services to appropriate parties. In many instances, working through existing community-based organizations can be more cost effective than setting up independent offices.

Change Underwriting Criteria: Current underwriting criteria have been identified as a major barrier in identifying eligible minorities who need loans. Some financial institutions have initiated their own seminars for individuals who would not normally qualify under current underwriting criteria. All individuals who complete these seminars automatically are eligible for loans. Other institutions have established loan committees consisting of small-business owners in low-income minority areas. Often these individuals can better judge the credit worthiness of applicants than can bank loan officers, who too frequently do not reside in the area. These specialized committees also serve as technical-assistance advisers to successful loan applicants.

VIGOROUS ENFORCEMENT OF ANTIDISCRIMINATION LAWS

During the Bush and Reagan administrations, a concerted effort was made to deemphasize the role of the federal government in enforcing housing discrimination suits. Under the Clinton administration, HUD has increased its efforts to ferret out bias cases and to get them prosecuted as quickly as possible.

Increase the Capacity of the Justice Department to Prosecute Discrimination Cases: Racial discrimination in housing is against the law and should be vigorously prosecuted. In order to do this more effectively, the Justice Department should have the staffing and budget to assure that cases presented to it are vigorously prosecuted. In addition, the Justice Department should be proactive and not simply reactive in identifying wrongdoers. The Justice Department should encourage other local law enforcement agencies to also be more proactive in identifying potential problem areas in their jurisdictions by utilizing in-house statistical analysis of HMDA and other data sets they choose to collect or monitor. These agencies could use statistical analysis of mortgage lending patterns to determine where testing might be employed to more effectively catch those who flagrantly break the law.

Develop Stiff Penalties for Offenders: Catching and convicting guilty parties have proven to be difficult. But publicity about the size of fines imposed on those who have been convicted might serve as a deterrent to others. As in the case of "three strikes and you're out" legislation, guidelines should be established that make penalties for repeat offenders automatic and stiff. Regulatory agencies could be granted authority to cancel or increase the cost of federal depository insurance for any lender who violates fair lending or community reinvestment laws.

Increasing the Supply of and Access to Affordable Housing

Anyone who has seriously studied issues of housing knows that, in addition to discrimination, having a sufficient supply of affordable housing and gaining access to housing one can afford are also critically important. Differences in local politics and housing markets often play important roles in whether or not there is sufficient access to or supply of affordable housing, particularly for minority groups. Furthermore, the robustness of the national economy significantly influences the types of financing mechanisms, as well as the amount and form of assistance that can be made available to address this issue. Three factors seem to be involved in increasing the supply of affordable housing. The first involves providing greater incentives to developers to produce affordable units, the second is making financing available for those individuals interested in purchasing homes, and the third involves providing rental assistance to those most in need.

Reinstitute Tax Credits for Passive Investment in Rental Housing Units: The 1986 Tax Reform Act drastically reduced the benefits individuals could derive from investing in the construction of new apartment buildings. As a consequence, the supply of new units was drastically curtailed. A slowdown in the supply of new multiple units has put pressure on the existing housing supply, which has not only kept rental prices relatively high, but has also served to constrain minorities, particularly low income minorities, to the least desirable residential areas. Steps should be taken to increase tax benefits to individual investors as one means of increasing the supply of affordable housing. If previous experience holds true, these newly constructed units would be distributed throughout metropolitan areas and not concentrated in low-income residential neighborhoods.

Increasing the Funding Pools Available to Community-Based Housing Developers: Nationwide, community-based organizations have taken up the slack created when the private sector reduced its commitment to the production of apartment buildings. In some areas these neighborhood groups are amassing quite enviable track records as housing producers. But the rate of production in most instances has hardly kept pace with the growing demand. One of the reasons the private sector is able to move faster in producing new units is its access to capital. Larger funding pools should also enable community-based organizations to increase their production output.

Increase the Supply of Housing Vouchers: As demonstrated by the Gautreaux experiment, individuals who are provided with housing vouchers can expand their access to the housing market. And when they avail themselves of this opportunity, quality of life is improved. In many municipalities, the housing market is tight at the low-income end of the spectrum, but much higher vacancy rates exist at the middle- and upper-income range. This means that while the supply of available units is quite low in traditional low-income minority neighborhoods, numerous opportunities exist through the greater metropolitan area. Racial isolation would be reduced if individuals had access to and/or knowledge about these vacant units. But in order for an expanded voucher system to work, it will also be necessary to convince resistant landlords to accept vouchers. Here is where aggressive marketing by both local municipalities and private sector corporate leaders could produce meaningful results.

CREATING INCENTIVES

No one is naive enough to believe that without the full weight of the federal government, the prospect of reducing racial isolation is very good. Activities listed above, if implemented, will certainly be big steps in the right direction. But there are also be some other steps that the federal government and others might take to provide greater incentives for local municipalities to work together in addressing questions of affordable housing and reducing racial isolation.

Link Future Federal Funding to Cooperative Housing Agreements: One of the by-products of the changing nature of cities is that people's housing arrangements are not necessarily determined by strict municipal boundaries. Similarly, local governments in and of themselves can have very little impact on increasing the supply of affordable housing or actually reducing racial isolation. A part of the problem stems from the fact that there is little incentive for local governments to develop corporative housing agreements. The federal government could play a significant role in forging such agreements by letting municipalities within metropolitan regions know that their priority for receiving federal funding for infrastructure projects, such as regional rail systems, sewage treatment plants, power facilities, ports, or dams, would be tied to whether local governments in the region agreed to a cooperative housing plan designed to increase the supply of affordable units and at the same time to reduce racial isolation.

Critically Examine Potential Adverse Impacts of Federal Program Initiatives: Some well-intentioned federal programs may do more to foster racial isolation than contribute to its solution. Take regional rail systems, for example. Most proponents argue that these systems hold out the potential to give inner-city residents greater access to employment opportunities. There is little in the way of research findings to support this contention. Most systems are designed to bring suburban commuters into downtown areas. They are not designed to take inner-city residents to rapidly expanding suburban job opportunities. Opportunities to directly link suburban station locations to employment or affordable housing opportunities for low-income minority residents could potentially help to reduce racial as well as income isolation. The newly unfolding empowerment zones may also adversely contribute to isolating inner-city residents if ways are not found to link job-seeking residents within these zones to rapidly growing job markets outside of the zones. If linkage strategies do not include incentives to firms outside of the zones to provide employment or housing opportunities to zone residents, then the potential of the zones to reduce racial isolation will be seriously compromised.

National League of Cities Initiative: The National League of Cities could also play an instrumental role in addressing this problem. One of its national conferences, for example, could focus on this issue, with a particular emphasis on workable solutions. The League could also initiate an award, similar to its All-American Cities Award, which would provide recognition to the location that had accomplished the most to reduce incidences of racial isolation.

CONCLUSION

Racial isolation may be the most serious problem to face this nation as we move into the 21st century. Problems associated with the national deficit, unemployment, declining educational achievement, or environmental warming may pale beside the destructiveness that could ensue if civil disturbances flare up periodically across the nation.

It seems inconceivable that with our technological capabilities to send space launches into other galaxies, or our ability to develop the most destructive weaponry known to man, it is impossible for the nation to set the reduction of racial isolation as a priority goal.

Leadership, economic sanctions, and strategic initiatives helped to end racial apartheid in South Africa. Ethnic tensions and strife have wreaked misery and destruction in Bosnia, Ireland, Rwanda, and Somalia. We may not be at the brink of societal breakdown yet—but there are a number of indicators that suggest that we are moving in that direction. Perhaps it is time to apply some lessons learned from these far-away lands to our own ever-growing nation states.

REFERENCES

Byrum, Oliver E. 1992. *Old problems in new times: Urban strategies for the 1990s.* Chicago: American Planning Association.

Updegrade, Walter L. 1989. Race and money. *Money* 18(12):152–72.

INDEX